The **Adventures**
of
Disco Dave

David Picton

To Richard
    Merry Xmas
       DS

Pen Press Publishers Ltd

Published in Great Britain by

Pen Press Publishers Ltd
25 Eastern Place
Brighton
BN2 1GJ

ISBN 978-1-906206-46-8

PREFACE

The book contains twenty years of my fun-packed life from when I left school to when I spent four years as a holiday representative moving around the ever-changing world. It tells the story of my adventures, some good, some bad. As you can see by the chapters I have been a jack-of-all-trades, master of none, coming into contact with many people from many backgrounds and origins.

The book is aimed at a cross section of people, in particular at holiday representatives all over the world. It was they who encouraged to me to write a book because I had so many stories to tell about me enjoying life to the full. They even said that they would buy a book and persuade their friends to buy it. I can see pound signs in my eyes!

When working on cruise ships again I was encouraged to write a book. All this encouragement is the reason for my first book. If nothing else it will be a record of my life for my kids to read when I am gone to the skies above. Only one problem, I have no kids.

I believe that this book will make people laugh, as it is light humour and not difficult reading. Also people can relate happenings to situations of their own, because you never know what is around the corner or when and how something will happen. Everybody has been on holiday, seen bad weather, had special moments that will never be forgotten and played sport during their lifetime. I hope that my book will give readers plenty of relaxing and enjoyable reading.

Contents

Introduction

INTRODUCTION

I am just a normal human being with no superstar image but very kind and considerate in the eyes of most people. I have seen many countries and had many encounters with people from different walks of life. I would like to share some of these experiences with you. I'm sure there are many stories you can relate to in different ways, you may have experienced some of the events yourself.

When you pick up magazines or books or watch television you hear of people who are rich and famous, fictional characters, girls who are too thin and in need of a good square meal or people who have suffered through no fault of their own. Within the book I will draw pictures of down-to-earth people who only want one thing in life and that is to enjoy themselves wherever they may be, on holiday or just enjoying the company of their mates. Like a good old-fashioned night out with no cameras around. If you don't enjoy your own life nobody else will.

I believe that the best education in life is travel and meeting people. Everybody is different and travelling gives you an insight into how people live and what obstacles they need to overcome to survive, sometimes to their peril. In your own comfort zone everything is manageable but put yourself in an unfamiliar position and that's when you learn about life and fending for yourself.

There are different customs, religions, points of view and climate changes in different countries around the world. Many factors come into living, the biggest one being your own life. I think it helps to be knowledgeable and to have experience of many things. Then you can understand and relate to what people around the world are going through and give yourself something to talk about when you meet them, a topic of conversation that you have in common with the other person instead of digging yourself a hole. You never know when this experience might be called upon. The simple things in life are appreciated such as health and a sense of well being, which in turn means less stress and a longer, better quality of life that you would not change.

Chapter 1

NAVY DAYS

When I left school in the summer of 1981 I did not know what I wanted to do. School to me was a place that you had to attend but gained little experience of the outside world. The school was mixed for the first time the year that I started so we were the experiment. Before that the school was boys only with very good standards of grades so had a high esteem in parents' minds. The discipline was also good and students were punished if they stepped out of line. The school was very much an old boys' school with teachers wearing gowns on certain occasions and the main sport being rugby for the boys. When the girls came it was joined by lacrosse. There was also a sixth form if you wished to carry on studying. The thought of studying for another second had me coming out in a cold sweat, like a fever. One good thing that came out of all this is the friends that I made during that time are still around now and have come to my assistance from time to time.

At school we had careers lessons and all that jazz but it was far too early to make a decision given that no one, apart from my parents, gave me any guidance or encouragement to develop my career. Most of the career options were academic involving studying for long periods of time going to college or university. That was against my religion. I was heavily into sport and, if good enough, wanted to become a professional sportsman. Having this vision I knew that I had to be exceptional at a given sport but was prepared to give it a go. Obviously having a dream like this depended on many things, one of the biggest being money. My parents could not afford to sponsor me or give me any financial backing so if I was going to succeed and make my dream come true changes had to be made. I had a free spirit about me and liked the outdoors; I hated to be in the same place for a long time. I was very impatient and impulsive; the only way to express myself was at sport where I could feel part of a team with restrictions taken off me, which meant that I could do whatever I wanted whenever I wanted. At school it was always about results and the school academic tables, which was not my strong point. My ability at sport was mainly golf and football having achieved a high standard at a young age but needed further improvement to keep on climbing that ladder.

So when leaving school in the June I went for various jobs. At the time I was not bothered what the job was, as this was going to provide my first pay packet at the end of the month. The thought of how to spend it was a million miles away. My parents were not aware that I had gone for this particular job at the Naval careers office in Reading. It was only when a letter came through the door to say that I had been selected for an entrance exam that my parents knew about it. Depending on the results of this they would give me a job in Her Majesty's Service.

I had to go through an interview that was loads of questions about my school life, hobbies, family life, any convictions and a few more thrown in for good measure. The maths test was next, which consisted of 100 easy calculations done in a short space of time; calculations being adding, subtracting, percentages but with difficult numbers and lots of them. The pass mark was around 75%. The English test was again basic education such as spelling, punctuation and letter writing. Again all had to be completed in a short space of time and correctly with the pass mark being 75%. Sounds easy but when you are under pressure it can all go Pete Tong (WRONG). The last part was the medical, which I was confident in passing. I played sport or did exercise most days so was not too unfit. When I walked in for the medical I thought that it would all be physical, such as press-ups and sit-ups, more like a gym test. I had a shock when the doctor said drop your trousers, I was waiting but not with a smile on my face for the next command, bend over. Fortunately this did not come but I had another shock when he started walking towards me. My parents had always said never talk to strangers especially in white coats. Here was a man walking towards me in a white coat, I had my trousers and underpants (apple catchers in some parts of the world) around my ankles, meat and two veg exposed to the elements. As the white-coated man approached rubbing his hands together I did not know where to turn my head (innuendo). I gave him a quick wink and his hand went below the horizon. I felt this tickle and a booming voice saying, COUGH. I coughed but it came out more like a squeak from a strangled chicken. Once he had finished the examination and said those well-chosen words, "pull up your pants and trousers," I could hardly bend. I had got so stiff (bad choice of word but you get the picture) due to the fact that I was holding my body rigid and tense. Another moment of amusement was when he said give me a sample. I had been to the toilet before I went in because I was apprehensive, so I was not the least bit in need of relief. It took me one hour to give a sample and I nearly missed my train. The doctor was giving me water and exercise to make me go. At least when my medical finished I was fit and healthy.

The following week I had a letter through the door, the Navy wanted me. I had no other job offers so decided on the Navy as a career. The Navy seemed to be all that I had wished for – travel, sport and some glitz and glamour. The films portrayed the Royal Navy as something special and admired by everybody throughout the world, it also had a reputation as being the best in the world; I was hooked on the ocean waves. I did not have to wait long before a letter came through the door telling me when and where to report. So there I was, 17 years 2 months old, about to embark on a career that was to last 8 years. My parents had mixed emotions, they were happy because I had a job where I would be safe and looked after. At the same time sad because their little boy was moving away from home having to look after himself for the first time in his short life so far.

August came and I was told to report to HMS Raleigh at 0800hrs with various pieces of clothing. The clothing was a list sent by the RN for trainees about to embark on an adventure without parallel and with no knowledge of its content. The clothing issued would hopefully be useful for every occasion we would find ourselves in. This was not only on dry land but at sea as well, as bad weather conditions were not to be taken lightly. Before I left with my dad we had to pack the case, mother was up to 90 degrees and stressed, father was trying to keep the peace. Items were being put in and taken out of the case, do we need this? Is it necessary? And so it went on. After we had finally finished packing it was time for the tears. Floods of teary mixed emotions from everyone in the household. Phone calls from family and friends. You would have thought I was going to an execution. Eventually Dad and I left the house and started on our way. The journey to Raleigh was very quiet and time for thought and to ponder about the future. After all, this was all new to me.

When I arrived, pulling up outside the large black gates for the first time, it was daunting. Guards with guns and people in uniform, I felt a sense of alone and afraid. I knew that once my dad had gone I was in a strange new world. Time to put on a brave face and be a man. Time to say goodbye to my only link with the outside world, my dad. As the car dove away it was too late to change my mind. Crossing the road and getting ever nearer to my fate I noticed no one seemed happy, everyone was busy working with a stern, hard face. I felt as though I was walking into a den of wolves. The walk seemed like entering eternity wearing blinkers. When I eventually got to the main gate and the wolves I handed over my papers in a very unsure manner, certainly not with confidence. The words of the sailor seemed to be lost in a wilderness of no one else but me. I think he told me where to go but could not be sure. I was walking around the barracks asking everybody every step of the way where was my bed for the night. Getting to my dormitory or communal room for the night was an achievement in itself; I cannot even remember anyone being there. I was so glad to be in what seemed a normal kind of place; at least it had a bed. As I gradually got used to the surroundings the other chaps and I started to mix and mingle. We were talking with fear and confused sentences, our mouths getting dry. Military life to us all was new so we had to stick together. Unpacking before lights out was another event, not enough space for all your clothes, all these little things would be sorted out tomorrow.

Waking up in the morning I found myself lying awake in a dormitory with forty other cadets around me, some I had met last night and none of us sleeping that well. I must have heard every sound, including flatulence (farting to relieve built-up gases). We all gradually started to talk to each other and we met our instructor for the first time. This was very early in the morning about 6.30; he came in and shouted WAKEY WAKEY, no good morning or pleasant gesture. He was an old Petty Officer who had been in the Navy all of his life, part of the furniture. His appearance was very thin with dark hair but well presented. He had a few visible small tattoos and had a large gob (mouth) although we did not say this to his face. His first words were, "You are going to hate me by the time you leave here," and he was correct. He was our worst enemy. He was quite ruthless and had no regard for people's well being or so it seemed. This was bearable as we had leave after a short period of time. Time enough to realise what was coming up and to prepare for battle. After two weeks I was sent home for 4 weeks' leave, what a fantastic job, I was even paid cash in my hand, £120 to be exact. What job would pay you cash in hand for two weeks' work? We had to wear our uniform when going on leave. That certainly got us noticed on our journey home. When I was being tortured at boot camp I never thought that I would ever get homesick but I did shed a tear when I saw my parents and uncle. I had so many stories to tell and people to see, the four weeks went past in a flash. My parents where trying to talk me out of going back but I was determined to complete the course.

When returning to HMS Raleigh I knew a little of what to expect but it was a learning curve with no end. I was lucky in a way because my parents were disciplined so I always did as I was told and never answered back. I had seen a few recruits answer back to their superiors with only one result, they lost big time. To get on the wrong side of the training instructors was your biggest nightmare. They would single you out, so any mistakes on the parade ground or any volunteers required for extra duties would end with you being that man. This was normally cleaning, the finished product gleaming, if this was not the case then you would do it again and again until correct. Our basic training was BULLSHIT (This is where you are constantly being worn down and any weakness in personality being exploited, your confidence in tatters. In the end you become a number serving in Her Majesty's Forces). The good from this barrage of abuse is that it builds your character into a disciplined person who can adapt, improvise and overcome any situation and can work under stressful conditions. These attributes go a long way in life. During your first week you signed a contract for a number of years, I had signed on for a straight nine years, the other option being three years. During training, for the first six weeks, if you hated the life and wanted to go home you had permission. During our basic training we lost a couple of volunteers. The ones who stayed knew that this was going to be tough but get through this and the rewards would be beyond our highest expectations. During training the idea is to break your spirit, for some people this will take longer than others. The key is to have backbone and a determination to succeed, setting your mind on something and striving for that light at the end of the tunnel.

One time, when polishing our marching boots for parade in the boot room, a funny thing happened. Your boots had to be of a very high standard, so much so that you had to see the reflection of your face on the toecaps and on the heels. There were many ways to achieve this by cheating. One was to use Brasso or clear varnish to put over the polish. This formed a clear protective layer over the polish giving a fantastic shine. This was good until someone stood on your toe and the varnish cracked, which meant taking the whole lot off and starting again. Another way was to melt the polish until it became a liquid, which was then poured over the boot. The only trouble was that whilst the polish was melting a small flame was apparent, this was quite safe but smelly. The boot room itself is very small with not much ventilation so any odour coming from anywhere tends to stay. Whilst we were doing this one of the young sailors knocked over a tin of black polish, we had a major flow of molten hot flaming polish go across the room. The guys calmly put out the fire and used the molten polish for their boots; the guys thanked me for being generous even though they were coughing and spluttering.

Before I tell you the next story about a kit muster let me describe the Petty Officer. He was our instructor sent to guide us through basic training, he was sent by the Devil. He gave us orders to be obeyed. He had been in the Navy longer than Nelson, had dark hair and was thin like a racing snake. He also had silly tattoos. We hated him but that was only natural. He was mentally taking us to the abyss. Pushing us to see if we would break under conditions of torture. There is a naval term used to describe such a man – a HAIRY ARSED 3 BADGE STOKER. This is a person who has been in the navy a long time, losing the plot.

The scene is set, now time for the story. We had a kit muster and one of the guys put his kit out on his bed the night before, all neatly folded to a certain size and in neat rows like a grid, it took him hours of time and effort for the kit to look the bees knees for the morning. We had been told not to do this but never expected the hairy one to give us a visit at 4am. When he saw kit lying on beds ready for the morning he went daft; the look on peoples' faces was of disbelief and anger as he turned over the beds sending kit flying all around the room. Once our kit was thoroughly messed up and the room looking like a rubbish tip the stick insect left, our morale was in tatters. He made things worse for us when our entire dormitory was ordered outside into the courtyard with our underwear on and nothing else, with a mattress over our heads looking silly walking around in a circle in our bare feet. There was only one small problem, it was December and snowing so we were freezing by the time we went back to lie on our cold and damp mattresses. We seemed to be walking around in the snow for ages but probably not that long, at least he had some kindness in his heart and let us back in when one of the guys started turning blue. This is what training is all about, trying to break you first and making sure you do not disobey orders from your commanding officers. In a war situation taking orders could save your life. Taking the bullshit is part of military training.

Another time we had to get up early and I was tired, so I slept until the very last minute, not a good idea because the hairy arsed Petty Officer came in to see if everyone was up, everyone was – apart from me. I was having a quality dream and just getting to the juicy bit so was not aware of my surroundings. He came to my bedside and for a split second was surprisingly polite. Then he asked me to get up. He spoke in a very gentle voice so I did not take any notice, answering with a girlie whimper. Then came the shock of my life, without any warning he grabbed the bed with a firm grip using both hands, I could see in his eyes he was up to no good, he then proceeded to turn the bed over with me in it. Everything was upside down, back to front and inside out. I felt like I had been picked up by the eye of a hurricane getting thrown around inside. As my senses came back to my body and my eyes by now open wide, I saw his friendly face, in a matter of seconds a nice man had turned into a crazed nutter. He was eyeballing me from about two inches; I thought to myself how could anyone with one head be so ugly, his face was like the Somme in WW1. I had to get up as he gave me no option and five minutes exactly to get ready; I was his best friend for the rest of the day during training. Nothing escaped his watchdog eyes. If I sneezed or coughed he would appear like a rash.

Part of the training is to do an assault course. The assault course is pretty much how people imagine it to be. There are lots of things to climb and go through with everything being made of rope, concrete or metal. These courses are designed to stand the test of time and all weathers. Good for certain things but not for humans. Not much fun in winter when it's cold and wet and all you have on is overalls and boots, nothing to keep you warm apart from your dwindling fat reserves. It was your typical course full of ropes and obstacles that physical instructors loved to see you break a leg on. I had never done an assault course before and it looked daunting. One of the targets was not to be last crossing the finishing line, as then you would be in for some extra exercise. So I was trying really hard to conquer the obstacles. Going along on the monkey rope near the end, I could see the finishing line, I did not have much further to go until I lost my concentration and fell off, I knew that from here on in it was not funny. The Physical Training Instructor (P.T.I.) called me across and led me to a lovely cold puddle. I had to do twenty press-ups and thirty sit-ups in a freezing cold pool of water and then start the assault course all over again, nice man! Needless to say I was last to finish, which meant no rest, as it was a quick march back to the barracks for a shower in double quick time followed by physical training. For physical training we had to be in our whites, we were off to the gym. Luckily enough all my clothes were waiting just to be put on so time for a very quick wash.

Part of our training was parade and rifle drill. The rifle range is miles from anywhere and protected by a security fence and system. You have the targets one end and yourselves the other. The targets are set at various distances with a large grass bank behind stopping any stray bullets which missed the target. On the rifle range we were all going along smoothly, shooting away at our targets, when we heard the order 'stop firing'; this usually meant that something was wrong. We could not believe our eyes when from nowhere a truck came across the range with a man standing on the back, not a clever thing to do as we had him in our sights about to pull the trigger. At the time we were using self-loading rifles (SLRs), which were being used in Ireland by our soldiers so they were accurate. How he and the vehicle managed to get that far into the range was a mystery. None of the instructors could work that one out.

"I will finish this course."

During rifle drill on a bleak and windswept parade ground out in the open we were practising various manoeuvres and I dropped my rifle, not on purpose, a complete accident. I was told from an early age that you don't have accidents in military barracks. I quickly picked up my rifle hoping that the drill sergeant did not see me or hear anything, I moved swiftly back into line acting as though nothing had happened, fearing the worst. He had seen me and he came over and gave me a BOLLOCKING (a telling off with feeling). Being young and not used to being bollocked, I was shaking in my shoes literally and was terrified. I did not know what the punishment was going to be but something that I would not enjoy. He then proceeded in making me run around the parade ground holding the rifle at arm's length until he was satisfied that I had learnt my lesson. When I got back to the squad he was waiting and my arms were slowly dropping off, he gave me no sympathy and told me to fall back in with the others. For the remainder of the drill my arms were like dead weights and I could not wait for the final whistle. The drill instructors did have a fearsome reputation and I could see why.

Part of our programme was Physical Training – things like climbing ropes, vaulting and things that I was not very good at. Being supple was never one of my assets. They called this a gym test; to me more like a medieval torture chamber. I had never accomplished gymnastic feats of skill of any level. The biggest problem for me was that before we went to our next base we had to pass out (at which stage you have become a disciplined naval rating) of HMS Raleigh. To do this our P.T.I. made us pass various gym tests. I could never ever climb a rope but when you are told that you will do it or be back-classed (where you get your training time extended by a number of weeks and you move back to a different entry number, having to start some of your training again) there is no such thing as can't. You have no option. That is the only time in my life that I have ever climbed a rope. I was nearly at the top and the P.T.I. was not going to let me down until I had climbed all the way to the top. He gave me one option, up! So for the last few feet I gritted my teeth and somehow made it. Part of the learning curve, there is no such thing as "I can't do this". My biggest drive to complete this challenge was the fact that I wanted to leave Raleigh as soon as possible and not endure any more suffering. Since that day I have never ever climbed a rope or vaulted anything. Vaulting the horse, what a silly idea anyway.

During practice sessions for this difficult apparatus I was useless, I spent more time on the horse itself instead of going over it. I had no confidence in my ability, only nightmares. The time came for me to do the impossible. I stood at the top of the runway waiting for my turn; it was my last chance to overcome my fear. With sweat and funny sounds coming from every hole I was in motion, the vault horse getting ever closer until I was upon it. I rose into the air and all my training came into an upsurge of talent through my body, I had made it over the horse even though the landing was not the prettiest. I was so glad that my injury did not matter until the pain became unbearable. I looked at my hand to see where the pain was coming from. I could see one finger different from the rest; the finger was sticking up at an odd angle and getting more painful by the second. When vaulting the horse I had forgotten to take my hands off the box and dislocated my finger. I had no option but to do first aid on myself. I grabbed my finger pulled it backwards until it clicked back into place. This had to be done as our next task involved using our hands. After this piece of surgery I came to the conclusion, the only horse that I want to see is the one that wins at 50–1 on Saturday and you've backed it.

Dartmoor played a part in my character building. Think of the films you see where there is a mist across a vast area of open ground, spooky sounds. The weather is closing in as dampening rain falls making everything wet and cold. You have nowhere to dry your clothes having to stay in the ones you have on. Every sound is treated with caution and alarm. Above all that I had very limited experience with camping, especially Forces style. The Division (group of men) were on expedition. The group consisted of twenty raw recruits marching for miles in a cold, wet, misty, gloomy middle-of-nowhere bleak place carrying a backpack which was not full of Mum's home made pies. Have you got the picture? We were there for two to three days, not for long but seemed like forever. Again the exercise served its purpose in that the need for team building and working together had to be accomplished if we were to maintain our high standards of survival, which is necessary to get back to camp and essential in any military operation. As tiredness crept in during the later stages it became apparent we needed to look after each other, at the same time looking forward to a hot shower or bath when arriving back at the barracks.

The only time I had been camping before was in a caravan with the parents where everything was done for me. Putting up a tent and cooking your own food was going to be a challenge as living with parents all the cooking is done for you, Mum's cooking is always the best because she cooks what you want. When we got to our camp site, or should I say by a river out in the open with a howling wind, wet and damp, our enthusiasm vanished (looking on the bright side to cheer us up) the site was free and very cost affective. Once we had decided on our piece of land we got the tent up as best we could after some wrestling with the equipment. Next was to get the fire going as soon as possible. We had little stoves and by this time were famished. There was only one way forward, to cook all our tinned rations in a pot (pot mess), when you're hungry it tastes fantastic. We had baked beans, corned beef, dried biscuits, hydrated milk; it was like being on *Can't Cook Won't Cook*. In the morning, again not a nice day, wet and miserable, our Sergeant Major was on our case, not being a father figure to us raw recruits. We were up as soon as brightness appeared on the horizon looking out to the way ahead, all you could see was sparkling dew across the rain soaked land.

Life must go on and the early morning ritual of having a shower, shit and shave has no bearing on where you are. In a cold river with no mirror, we shaved wincing with every stroke hoping for a smooth finish. We washed rather than showered in a cold river cleaning our hands and face. This certainly woke you up in the morning. To have a shit was no problem as there were lots of places around where no one could see you, and you would probably have some-one to keep you company anyway. So after the rituals had finished and our scent left for the worms it was time to pack away our tents and camping equip-ment, which was easier said than done. In our group there were three in the tent so to put the gear away should not have taken long? We were in all sorts of bother with the gear, which did not seem to fit back into its rightful place. The more we tried to hurry the worse it got knowing that the last tent down would be catastrophic. Needless to say our tent was last to be packed away so the Ser-geant called us over and I could not believe my eyes when he pointed at this hill with the mist hiding the summit. We guessed what was coming next and surely enough as eggs is eggs we ran up to the top and down again in double time before joining the other recruits, when the instructor said 'hill' he had not seen the mountain above the clouds, the mountain of Muhammad. What a good start to the day – that was if you enjoyed pain and suffering in God's garden.

As part of our main gate duty at HMS Raleigh we checked people's identification cards and made sure that cars going in and out of camp had passes. This was to make sure that no terrorists or unwanted people came into the base. We were told of car markings that indicated High Ranking Officers, such as flags or registration numbers identifying an important person. I was on the main gate standing outside in my tin hat and raincoat with not much to do. I had been standing there for some time, so by now getting fed up waiting for my break. A black car rolls up and stops yards from where I was standing on its way into camp. Beforehand we were briefed that FOSM (Flag Officer Submarines) was arriving in an unmarked car. I stopped this car and did not realize that inside was FOSM as it had tinted windows and a small flag flying on the bonnet. Another clue as to the person inside was that it was chauffeur-driven and a well looked after black body shining in the sun. So I went to the window of the car and asked for the identification cards of the passengers as I had been told to do. I then turned to look at the guardhouse and they were making signs to say wave the car on. Then the penny dropped. I said thank you and nervously waved the car on. I had to wait until my shift finished before going back into the guardhouse, which I was not looking forward to. I went in and was glared upon by an officer and told how stupid I was and not to do that again, but not as nicely as that. After the initial telling off once the officer had gone and I was with the lads we had a laugh about the situation.

To give us some training at sea on a sea-going vessel we took a little trip across the water which was supposed to be a bit of fun and to give us a break from our barracks. After all we were in the Navy. We went on a small vessel, a minesweeper going from Plymouth to Torquay. The minesweeper was old but still part of the RN's flotilla, the crew were experienced and looked old, giving the impression of menacing pirates, some of them even had long straggly beards and a patch over one eye. These were modern times, so there was no walking the plank if you were out of line. The distance we were sailing was not very far but gave us a chance to feel like a sailor. All the guys were going to be part of the ship's company, which meant helping the crew above and below decks. The ship below decks was small; everything was small including the living quarters. A communal mess where everything happened was the focal point. In the mess you socialised, ate and slept. To some of us it had the distinct impression of a prison ship; at least a prison ship had windows. Despite first impressions we were all looking forward to this, the biggest bonus was to miss out on drill and a change of scenery.

On the day we set sail it was a bit windy but not too bad. The sun was out and a rainbow curled across the multi-coloured sky. The sky was bright with many colours, not just from the rainbow's glow but also from the sun beaming through the broken cloud. The noise of birds in the sky swooping down trying to catch breakfast, not caring where it came from just glad of food in their stomachs. The noise was a crescendo of squawks as the conversations increased. As the day went on the weather got worse, much worse and none of us were able to stand up. We did not find our sea legs; instead we were all huddled in a group sitting down feeling unwell. The sea by now was not the place to be, every horizon was of wavy lines. The sky and sea blended into one colour, a grey wall with no sign of breaking. The fine spray from the ocean starting to cover our faces with salt water, the sea was taking control. To try and make us feel better we were taken in small groups by the crew of experienced sailors to do various jobs, no one volunteered to help the cook. I wonder why? None of us were feeling better after many hours of the ship taking a battering. We had all turned a funny colour, too weak to move because we could not eat or drink anything that the crew gave us. The crew loved it tempting us with food and drink, making us feel more like captives on a slave ship. When the recruits were no longer able to communicate a decision was made to pull into harbour earlier than planned. Not only were the young sailors taking a lesson in violence from the sea but the ship was also taking a real body blow from the persistent attack of the weather conditions.

When we got to our destination, and so we thought safe haven, the sailors berthed the ship on their own as we were too ill to even stand up and we all exuded a sigh of relief. We had made it back to port. The idea now would be to still carry on the training but not at sea; this could be a blessing in disguise. The weather was still not any better and the tiny minesweeper was being battered against the side of the harbour wall. The battering carried on for hours leaving the ship to fend for itself. The weather was not improving, the question was asked, how much can a ship take? The answer came soon enough as a few holes were appearing in the side of the ship, we had to try and stop the water from coming in. Part of our training had been to prepare for such an incident – we used mattresses, bedding and tables, anything that was at hand to try and plug the holes. This was no game but a real live "abandon ship". A couple of weeks before we had been on a damage control course for such an event so we were all familiar with the drill. We did as best as we could until there was no point in continuing as the ship was not going to sink. The pirates took over the ship, a ship that by now had a nickname, *The Black Pig*. We all sat on the quayside in the midday sun, the weather by now the same as when we started our voyage, waiting for our dry and much needed transport. We all made our homeward journey back to barracks by coach; we were all so disappointed that our outing had been spoilt. At least we were safe, but what happened to the tiny minesweeper? I do not know.

When our training was finally over the Division had a passing out parade. A passing out parade is a very proud moment in the life of a young rating. You are watched by top commanding officers not just from the Navy who have come down to pay tribute to you becoming part of Britain's defence. Parents come and watch as well, sometimes overcome with emotion. During training we had this event once a week and your Division of raw recruits starts at the back because you are new and only just joined the ANDREW (navy). As training progresses you gradually move to the front so when week 14 or 15 approaches it is a special moment in your life. When on Divisions the marker is usually the tallest person in your entry, which happened to be me. This can be and is a nervous ordeal as you are the first person to be seen by everybody, if you make a mistake by messing up the orders given it will be spotted. You are on your own until the rest of the parade joins you, time seems to stand still. On the ground is a little white spot where you must stand. I marched out with the other markers to my spot with my parents and other families watching my every move. I was feeling proud at facing Admirals, army officers, lots of gold and brass – a splendid sight. Once the parade has formed, orders are given leading up to an inspection, we open order marched ending up with spaces in between each line. Now the inspection.

You cannot move an inch, just stay perfectly still. An officer comes behind you; you can feel his presence, if there is anything out of place beware. He then walks around in front of you, all the time watching and listening. He starts to walk away and you move slightly, a millimetre one way or the other. Then comes a familiar voice in your ear, "Stand still and face front." Where has this voice come from? Is it your drill sergeant or Petty Officer? Either way you freeze on the spot and quake in your boots. The worst thing is if the day is cold. You are standing still for quite a while before given an order, so when you move your body takes a jolt and there is a rush of blood to the area concerned. Once the inspection has finished back into normal formation, some more drill orders and the end is not far away now. When on parade the best squad to be is Guard. This is where you wear white gloves, white gaiters (ankle straps) carrying a gun with a white strap; you look the bee's knees. The real bonus being that you are the last ones on parade and the first ones off, a shorter time than the rest.

At the end of Divisions there is a march past, where a salute is taken by the Admiral and Officers. This is where the whole division of men walk past the stand, the markers look ahead so as to keep the formation correct whilst the others look right to take the salute. The march past is in respect of your achievement being able to handle all the bullshit and late nights in becoming a Naval Rating, the salute is in respect of the Officers' commissions as well. Afterwards a party is held for all the guests with a bit of a knees-up in the evening. During this party it gives the parents a chance to meet and greet as well as exchanging stories about their wonderful son. This can be potentially dangerous and could ruin your new image so you tend to blend into the background. This is in the barracks normally taking the form of a disco with everyone present, including your Petty Officer who has in his own way turned you into someone different.

The next step is to decide the path of your career, from this moment on you decide your own fate. Some of the options you had were Ships, Submarines, Clearance Diver and so on. I chose submarines because I knew nothing at all about them. Everyone knows what ships do and where they go because you can see them floating on the water. I had only seen submarines on TV in war films. When I told the folks back home they were stunned into silence. The thought of being miles under the water never fazed me and I did not suffer from claustrophobia. I had confidence in water and loved watching underwater programmes. One of the questions I was asked was, "Have they got windows?" That was a good question, one that I could not answer for the time being. I had a few questions myself which I could not get my head around such as what do you breathe and how. All of the questions and doubts would be answered soon enough. Every chance I had I would be looking at pictures and reading as much information as I could get my hands on. The more knowledge collected the more eager I became to join one of Her Majesty's elite fighting forces.

Now that I had chosen my career I had to specialise in a particular field of expertise. Again I had a choice, all of which were specialist fields of knowledge designed for submarine warfare. I chose analysing underwater sound (SONAR). For this I had to go to HMS Dolphin located in Fareham, Gosport. My first day's training in the classroom was a blur with no information sinking into my confused brain. My first look at a sonar set and so many buttons to press, I was shitting bricks. It got worse as the bricks turned into rocks as I was told to press a button. My imagination was running riot; I was half expecting to be beamed up by the Star Ship Enterprise or see Flash Gordon coming out of retirement. Besides buttons there was a wheel to turn, and I had the shock of my life when turning this wheel I heard a sharp whistling sound, this was the first time I had heard another sonar transmitting. The trainer laughed as I had a dumb blank expression on my face and a yelp coming out of my mouth. Before the sonar course started I was not equipped in any way for the amount of high intensity studying. We had to learn about and operate all the sonar sets used by British subs still in commission at that time. Bombarded with information, which you hoped would sink in because at the end of the course an exam was getting ever nearer. I must stop there as I am not able to go into too much depth (excuse the pun) the rest is top-secret information that only I know. What made the training course harder was the fact that I was part of the ship's company during my stay; this meant that I had to do watch-keeping duties in the small hours of the morning.

At HMS Dolphin there is a tank, the SETT (Submarine Escape Training Tank) that holds 100ft of water, which every submariner has to conquer if he wishes to be part of an elite fighting force, a fact that I might have mentioned before! This test must be passed, if you fail this you cannot become a submariner (member of Her Majesty's elite fighting force), it is that important. This was the only obstacle left to prevent me sailing under the high seas. When you get into the tank for the first time you have a lecture all about what you will experience and the effects of pressure. For example, the deeper you go your lungs fill up with twice as much oxygen as normal. The term used for water pressure is PSI (pounds per square inch), too much pressure and the bends become a reality. This is caused by air pockets trapped in your blood stream. If you get the bends you need to go into a decompression chamber to equalise with the pressure in the atmosphere. This process is where the blood vessels in your body expand and relax allowing the transfusion of air pockets in your blood to escape under normal conditions getting rid of the trapped oxygen. This whole process could take hours with no guarantee of success.

After the lecture you put on swimwear and a dressing gown and make your way to the top of the tank where the instructors give a demonstration. Watching this demonstration is fascinating; the instructors are only naval ratings but can hold their breath for ages, a bit like the man from Atlantis. All of us are gathered around the top looking into the water, what to see we were not sure. Then suddenly a large air bubble appears making its way to the top. At the bottom of the tank is an orange glow with divers around this thing. It took a while to realise that this orange thing had been released by the divers and was coming towards us at great speed. Taking one step back for safety an orange figure comes from beneath the waves with a mighty force, bursting up from the depths breaking the surface at a mighty speed giving you palpitations. We all made sounds never heard before as a man got out of the suit. The sound of astonishment turned into a gentle chuckle before falling silent. The instructor said with a cheesy grin on his face, "Tomorrow it's your turn." The silence now turned into a deadly hush as our dry mouths opened wide.

Tomorrow arrives and you march down to the tank with your bathers and a towel, your only protection. You have a talk on the day's proceedings so you know what to expect. So far it sounds a piece of cake. Your first ascent is from 30ft wearing goggles and a lifejacket; this will be done in small groups. As you wait in your dressing gown for this to happen your body temperature fluctuates and the sphincter fluctuates, hot and cold flushes enter your clammy skin. Now it's your turn and into the compression chamber you go before you get pressurized to the various depths. There is no way out now as the hatch BOOMS! shut and water rises as pressure starts building. Whilst the pressure is building you must clear your ears in case they burst, this is to equalise the pressure inside your ear. Once the pressure is reached and the water level is slightly below your chest you then stand by the hatch to be pulled out by your lifejacket into the tank. On the count of 3 bend over, over you go and a sharp tug takes you by surprise, you are now in the tank being stared at by two divers. Once in the tank you must continuously breathe out to release the oxygen. The two divers hold you down to make sure that you are exhaling air, if you are not they punch you in the stomach so that you do breathe out. Even at 30ft the pressure, the PSI (pounds per square inch) inside your lungs doubles which could cause them to burst.

Next ascent is from 60ft, same routine as before. The difference being you know what to expect so the feeling of sheer panic turns to slight concern. During this ascent one person when pulled into the tank did hold his breath. To make him breathe out one of the divers did the only thing that was tried and trusted, he punched him in the stomach. This worked to some extent but at the same time all the air inside his body was gone in one blow. When he appeared at the surface he was gasping for air, certainly not relaxed. We did not see him again until the evening due to the fact that he was in the decompression chamber for three hours recovering.

The third and final ascent is from 100ft. This is slightly different from the others in that you climb into a small space. You are in a one-man escape chamber wearing a bright orange suit. The orange suit is made of a material that does not leak and is waterproof and warm. It is also very distinctive, being seen for miles around at sea or in the air. The reason for this is that if you are bobbing around on the ocean waves you stand a good chance of staying alive in time to be rescued. There is an air valve inside the chamber which is the female end, the male end being attached to the suit; marry these two ends together and the suit fills with air, this feeling makes you jump but not in the air as you would bang your head and rip the suit. This is probably the worst bit of the whole experience. You have to keep on pressing the air supply in as the water rises. At any time you cannot clear your ears you must signal this discomfort by tapping on your leg and the pressure will drop so you can equalize. Sometimes if you are close to reaching 100ft they will carry on pressurising because for your ears to heal once they have burst does not take long. Time passes very slowly at this point waiting for something to happen. When the pressure equalises between the escape chamber and the depth of the water the hatch will open. This forces you too shoot, and I mean shoot at a great rate of knots, like a torpedo out of the escape hatch. Two divers will catch you and hold you down and attach you to a wire running through the middle of the tank. At the same time making sure you are fully in control of your senses. On the way up the divers are making rude gestures to you putting your mind at ease as it takes thirteen seconds to reach the top. Once again reaching the top at speed having to be caught by the divers you are dragged to the side. Getting onto the ladder and climbing out of the tank so many feelings come over you. After relief, a big radiant smile and a glowing facial colour, comes a sense of enjoyment and actual pleasure. The best feeling is knowing that nothing can stop you becoming a submariner. This has to be repeated every three years to qualify for the ELITE submarine service.

Now was the time to learn all about sound waves in the water. For this I had to sign the Official Secrets Act because I would be dealing with Top Secret, UK/US Eyes Only material. I was also not allowed to visit any Eastern Block countries; if I did I had to have permission from the Queen, as she was my boss and a very busy lady, I'm sure that if she knew Disco Dave wanted to go there would be no problem. If I did go to these countries I would be followed by the secret police because I knew secrets that the Eastern Block did not know. This made me feel quite important and a bit of a 007.

The work itself was very interesting, learning all about the Cold War and being part of it. We had lectures about Russian submarines and ships, this would be to identify them through the periscope so we could gather information and collect valuable data. When you have a contact it is very important to know what you are dealing with. As in a war it is a fight to the death. A sonar operator must know all the various sonars and frequencies, characteristics on an enemy military target. Once all the information has been collected and studied the next task is to analyse and classify the contact. The contacts can range from a fishing vessel trawling its nets, to a rattle against the pressure hull or hull of a ship omitting a sound into the water. The technical side of the equipment is amazing with the slightest noise being detected. For example from a series of lines you could discover various characteristics of a contact, such as how many shafts and blades, speed, whether contact was approaching or going away, on the surface or under the water. Also you could hear various sounds in the water so you could determine between biological noise (fish) and submarines. The more experienced you became the more familiar the sounds. The sea is not quiet, for example one of the smallest sea creatures – a shrimp – makes a clicking noise. The various sonar sets are all designed for a specific purpose such as long range detection, short range detection, intercepting transmissions and so on. All of these facilities are vital if we are to remain undetected and stay alive in a war situation. All the sets operate differently so a good working knowledge is essential as these sets might one day save the life of you and your crew in the Cold War despite it being peacetime.

Once this is complete you move on to nuclear or diesel powered submarines. The difference between nuclear and diesel is immense. For one thing the space available below decks, diesel subs have limited head room so if you are six feet tall every inch counts, although hard hats could be an option. Does the submarine need to surface? Nuclear subs don't need to surface as the power comes from a reactor. With a reactor onboard all we have to worry about are the food supplies. Don't forget it is easier to detect a submarine on the surface than under the water. So after weighing up the pros and cons I was going to go on nuclear subs. Diesel subs were out for two main reasons, I did not fancy the cramped spaces and smelling like a grease ball. At this point in time you are taking in so much information it all seems confusing but all worthwhile coming apparent as your career moves on. You will be the eyes and ears of the submarine because without your expert knowledge there is danger lurking in the dark deep oceans.

My next base was in Faslane, on the west coast of Scotland. When approaching the base it looked very cold and uninspiring and well hidden from view. This is when I joined my first sea-going submarine, HMS *Valiant,* then the oldest submarine still in commission. I did not join straight away; I spent some time in the base itself working for the Coxswain. The work was clerical but gave me a chance to settle down and look forward to going to sea. During the time of the

Falklands war I was still in the Coxswain's office sending out family grams, sending and receiving mail to and from our lads at sea, keeping up morale.

Whilst at Faslane I was on watch-keeping duties and we had to go to the quayside. This was not in our normal daily routine. Someone important was arriving by Polaris submarine, we were not told who. From this limited information we were all guessing as to who it might be. We were also told to look smart and be on our best behaviour. So we turned up at the quayside as though we were on parade. A Polaris sub moved closer to the shore and a lady appeared on the top of the fin (conning tower). We were puzzled as there are no females on submarines as that would be a fate worse than death. It was Margaret Thatcher, our Prime Minister. She is one lady whom I have always admired and respected. She takes no prisoners and appreciates the Forces as defenders of the country. I was quite taken aback; she was the last person I expected to see. This was unusual and a bit of a secret because reading the papers this particular event was not mentioned nor were there any pictures on the television.

My chance to go to sea finally came when HMS *Valiant* returned from active duty after we had defeated the Argentineans. The crew were very upbeat and glad to be back at base to enjoy what spare time they had as the sub was going down to the Falklands again in a couple of weeks. A quick turnaround. I arrived on board and was shown to my bunk and met the crew and some of the officers. Because I was wet behind the ears (inexperienced) I had a 'sea dad' who would look after me and help me at sea with any problems that might arise. I was his shadow until I could be let loose on my own without supervision. One of the biggest and most important steps is to gel with your crew.

HMS *Valiant*, my first submarine.

The first time he took me ashore was in Helensborough. Helensborough is a small town with a beachfront attracting people for a day out in the summer. The landscape around the town is very picturesque, especially good for hill walking and providing solitude – a superb relaxation spot to take away the effects of a hard day's work. As with any naval town there is a flip side. The local lads can get jealous of us sailors as when we go out the women come out too. After spending months at sea, when the boys go ashore they tend to let their hair down and try to impress the girls. This starts off being funny and amusing but usually ends up in trouble, trouble with the locals. Sailors do have a reputation with the female kind wanting mainly one thing, sex and more sex. If you were without female company for months on end that frustration just builds up inside. So when you do eventually get your end away (sex) the female is in orbit circling the ceiling before re-entry begins. So a group of us, probably round about fifteen blokes went ashore. I went out stone cold sober going from pub to pub having a pint in each one. The boys also introduced me to some lovely looking females who all looked good after ten pints. To be fair the boys did look after me, I did not get into any trouble but came back a drunken sailor having drunk beer, beer and more beer. I was not a well man the following day, a hangover from hell itself, but it was a good way to bond with the crew.

I was part of the Scratchers party (casing party, casing being top of the submarine). Our job was to make sure that every part of the casing functioned correctly, things like checking that all nuts and bolts did not rattle. If this happened we could be detected whilst in enemy waters. All bollards (when entering or leaving harbour these were used to secure the ropes, to secure the submarine alongside the harbour wall) had to fit into their correct stowages. It was an endless task but a good way to learn about the location of fittings on the outside of the submarine. The worst activity was painting. The whole submarine had to be painted by four blokes in not that many weeks. We were about to go on a secret mission near to Argentina, so work had to be done in preparation for the long journey ahead. The paint was very thick so we had to avoid getting any on ourselves, as it would take a good scrub to remove it. This was easier said than done. To protect ourselves we wore overalls and waterproof gear, not leaving any skin or hair exposed. We went through plenty of rollers and tins of paint. The rollers did not last more than a day but they were in plentiful supply. We were using cranes to get ourselves lowered up and down the sides of the sub. At the end of the crane was a box; this is where we stood with long handles attached to the rollers so we could reach those awkward places. By the time we finished we were covered in black paint from head to foot. The easiest bit to paint is the casing (flat top bit) but this can be tricky. More often than not when you finish the casing late at night giving it time to dry you arrive in the morning to start work and something awful has happened. A few footprints appear, the yeti is back. The casing is easy but the paint is not. The paint contains sand from the beach to make it non-slip. It works on your boots but not on your skin. You have to scrub hard to get all traces removed leaving red marks. So if you get any on your hands, do not start scratching any sensitive areas.

HMS *Valiant* set sail and we left UK waters, our mission top secret, a bit like James Bond with a licence to kill if provoked. During the Falklands campaign we did not have much information on the Argentineans' one and only aircraft carrier, so we had to try and find it. We had intelligence reports on where it was likely to be so we headed for that destination. To get down to Argentina took roughly three weeks so on the way we practised our tactics and emergency drills for fire, flood and torpedo attacks. Argentina had some old German submarines, which were hardly in evidence during the war.

Our task was to gather as much information as possible but not engage the enemy. After all the guesswork we were now in position to gather information when or if our target appeared. We had to wait and keep very quiet, the wait was worth it because out of a cove came the aircraft carrier. The boat's crew sprang into action. We recorded the underwater sounds, took photographs, gathering as much information as possible in a short space of time. The Captain allowed the control room to look through the periscope at the carrier; I will never forget that picture. The carrier was dark and small, not modern in any way, moving very slowly, it had also been bought from another navy more as a deterrent, so had not seen much active service. This was my first taste of being a professional at war. The carrier was only out for a maximum of twenty minutes, all it did was go round the cove and back in again. Our intelligence was correct that the carrier was not seaworthy which was why it was never seen during the conflict. It would have been a sitting target for the Royal Navy. If it was seaworthy a longer and bloodier war could have taken place, Britain could have been licking its wounds and many more lives lost. After we had gathered our information we headed home back to safe waters.

On the way home we surfaced once we reached NATO waters and relaxed on the casing soaking up the sun and going for a swim in a very large pool, the sea. But I could not relax, I had a part 3 (exam) to do, this is the last part of becoming a fully qualified submariner. I had a task book full of tasks to do, funnily enough. We get paid more than personnel on ships because we have to learn about every job on board the submarine, from the skipper down. This is for safety reasons, should we have a major accident and people die, the remainder must be able to operate the submarine. To do this a working knowledge of every system on board must be gained. There are many systems involving hydraulics, high-pressure air and the reactor. Then there are all the different locations of valves that need to be opened and shut. All the valves have numbers making them easier to identify.

I had a few jokes played on me whilst completing part 3. One time I was sent back to the aft section and the engineer's panel to get some ink for the pens on the sonar sets. The sonar sets run on electrical voltage so they do not require ink. The engineers gave me some ink and sent me back to the sound room

(room where most of the sonar sets are located) and I gave the ink to the sonar controller who just looked then burst out laughing. It was only then that I realised what I had done, but don't forget I was still training and inexperienced.

When in the mess during meal times, especially breakfast, the cooks made me laugh. If you tried to steal a roll or an extra sausage a large spoon would come from behind the counter, as if by magic, and whack you on the hand. If you wanted any extra food you would have to wait till meal time had finished or chat up the cooks, the chatting-up being very hard as they had heard all the lines before.

Another time we were at the counter getting our food, we had just woken up from a deep sleep so not awake yet. We did not immediately realise it but the cook was bouncing an egg on the floor. So we looked, looked and looked again, saying nothing. By now the curiosity was building and people were looking at each other with a vacant lost expression. One of the lads could not take it any more and had to know how he did it. Was he in the magic circle or was it an actual bouncing egg? There was another cook lying on the floor throwing the egg back up to him; the effect had us all in a trance.

Some of the other guys on board were just as funny; we had English, Scots, Irish and Welsh. One lad from up North was about 6 feet 6 inches tall, speaking with an unmistakable deep Geordie voice. Everything about him was big, his hands were like shovels and he worked on the machinery back aft in small spaces. For this person to fit into a bunk space was almost criminal. The bunks were not that long so he slept with his size 15 feet outside the bunk. I am slightly over 6 foot and I found the bunks were a snug fit with little room to turn or change your position whilst getting comfortable, this person's build was also bigger than mine. Every time we walked past his feet in the dark we lost count of the number of times people bumped into them not causing any serious damage. The saving grace was that the feet did not smell because if they did the enemy would have been chasing us.

When having a shower we had to use the water sparingly. We would turn the water on to get ourselves wet, turn the water off, add the soap, then turn the water back on to wash the soap off. Sometimes when in a relaxed state the water supply to the shower would be turned off on purpose to leave the victim covered in soap. The victim would moan for a while because if you opened your eyes soap would get into them causing total blindness. This meant that you were totally incapable of doing anything. The lads turned the water back on and out it came with a force that would rock you from side to side. As the water rushed out you could not control the temperature so the water by this time was cold and the reaction of the victim was so funny to watch, a confused state of shock with arms and legs flailing uncontrollably in different directions, a good impression of a mad octopus.

On our way back to the UK after completing our mission, I saw a fantastic sight of nature. We were on the surface and I was lookout, I was there to assist

26

the Officer of the watch in spotting other targets so as not collide with them, avoiding any potential hazardous situations. I have been a keen follower of what creatures live in the sea and to see them perform in the wild would be a dream come true. On the surface the sub creates a bow wave and from where the lookout is situated he has a good vantage point of this. Looking down into the water I could see this torpedo-shaped grey thing going as fast as the sub or in some cases faster. We were being accompanied by wild dolphins leaping over the bow wave; this was the first time I had seen dolphins in the wild, it was a magnificent sight. The grace and power with which they leapt from the water over the bow wave had me staring with admiration. There must have been a whole school of them following the sub. One after the other, over and over for quite a long period of time, it seemed to be playtime. What wonderful creatures expressing a sense of happiness. Apparently this is a normal occurrence when a submarine is on the surface. The submarine is warm bodied so it does attract other warm-blooded sea creatures, a dolphin being one.

We arrived at base in Faslane and had to go back down to the Falklands to monitor an Argentinean exercise, same situation as before, to gather information but with specific orders not to get involved because we would be in hostile waters. So down we went again and everything was going well. We had not been detected but we did not anticipate what was to happen next. The submarine got itself involved in the exercise and we became part of it, at the time this was not apparent. Most of the Argentinean navy was participating in this exercise, submarines, ships but thankfully no aircraft carrier. We had various masts and periscopes up monitoring events. We found ourselves on a collision course with an Argentinean submarine with the same masts and periscopes showing. At that moment both submarines realised the immediate danger and to avoid collision turned and ran. We kept on running and went deep. We did not turn around or change course but ran for our lives. To this day I don't know if we were being chased and how close they were to firing a torpedo at us. This was not a situation to be in, there was nothing to stop the Argentinean navy torpedo-ing us and trying to sink us; after all we should not have been there. We had found ourselves right in the middle of the exercise and were about to become part of it. Luckily enough they must have thought that we were one of theirs and part of the exercise, maybe? At the time you didn't register the danger because you were a trained professional in Her Majesties Submarine service. Then it was back to Faslane and time off. We had been to sea for nine months out of twelve and I had almost completed my part 3. Getting back again knowing that you had months off was great, most of us were due leave so it was time now to relax and catch up on the news back home but not tell anyone of our adventures until now.

Leave over, and on return a firefighting course. I had heard about this from the lads and prepared myself, but for what I did not know. The Royal Navy has its own firefighting school that has been going for years. We had a lecture in a classroom about firefighting equipment and how to operate each piece of kit, this sounded very dangerous as to what was laying ahead, certainly no holiday camp. Before the fun and frantic action started we had to get dressed in our wet, cold and filthy overalls stinking of fire, also special rubbery fireproof boots had to be worn so that we could play with fire and freezing cold water. To protect our bodies we wore boiler suits, woollen gloves, hoods and not much more. This was when the fun started.

We were put into teams and told to put out a wood fire in a metal room using extinguishers. The unit itself was designed with three separate metal boxes called rooms. Our fire was in the bottom room. The reality of putting out real fires was daunting, no bullshit this time. As you stood on the top of the metal roof you could feel the heat through your boots, your number was called and down you went into hell. As you got closer to the fire everything was hotter than normal and when you reached the glowing radiant fire you were glad of the protective clothing. We had to kneel behind our extinguishers, which was the only thing protecting us from the heat of the fire, which was about 10 feet away and contained large pieces of burning wood. The command was given to fight the fire. We pressed the plungers on our extinguishers and jets of water hit the fire causing a fireball to go up the ladder we had come down. This was scary enough without black smoke filling the room. We had to keep low, as there was no oxygen higher up in the room and we had no breathing equipment to save us. We then advanced towards the fire until it was extinguished and the doors opened allowing us out of the room covered in thick black smoke.

Next stage was again in our teams to put out an oil fire in a compartment. This time we wore breathing apparatus and a full fire protection suit as the heat was going to be intense. Not words that conjure up relaxation and calmness. The only saving grace was that in some ways it was the same situation as before, going down a ladder into a room full of fire. You could feel the heat before you even started the exercise and that was from your own body perspiring. As you went down the ladder visibility was getting poorer and poorer until it became zero. Once we had accomplished this task another was set involving everyone.

With this particular exercise I can remember going down into the compartments fighting my way through fires. Whilst doing this, one thing you don't want to hear is a whistle because if a whistle sounds that means your air supply in your breathing bottles is low and you have minutes to get back to safety. The rule is that if the whistle sounds the whole team make their way back to the controller at the top of the unit because you could not see whose air was running out as visibility is down to zero. You can also tell if you have no air by the fact that you cannot breathe, which is not a good idea. That is all well and good but getting back is just as hazardous as moving forward. In fact worse, by now you are scared, frightened and at anytime you could be in serious trouble.

The final fire is a large compartment filled with hot burning material, which you have to go down into via a hatch. But this is not real enough for the Royal Navy so to make it like the inside of a volcano they let the oil burn for a while. By the time you get to the fire it is raging. By now the temperature is rising, the heat is surprising and it gets worse. There are now three of you around the hatch, two to open it, next one to put the hose in. Once the hatch is opened a great fireball comes out and you can feel the heat going over your head so you must stay low. The most important person is the guy with the hose as this stops some of the fireball and heat coming at you. This is jammed into the hatch as soon as it is cracked open. The jet of water is set on a wall-to-wall, which means that it forms a wall of water. The hose is then lowered into the room to dampen the elements of fire. Next step is for one person to then go down into the fire carrying a hose over his shoulder spraying water to protect him. By this stage you are knackered and running on fear and adrenaline. During the ascent down the ladder your mask gets a load of water on the visor from the wall-to-wall hose, as the hatches are not very big, enough for just one person. At the same time cold water gushes into your suit which is actually a cooling feeling, so by now you are cold and hot at the same time, blind, scared, disorientated – apart from that, fine. Once at the bottom you then turn around and manoeuvre yourself so the hose is in your grasp. You then move forward so that the next person down can join you. When all the team, three of you are down the ladder you are told to fight the fire. All you can see is a glow in the murky distance. You walk forward aiming for the glow until it has gone; the fire is out, the doors open and water off.

Once the fire is out you have mixed emotions but the adrenalin is still pumping, as the fear factor has not yet passed. You do feel tired, as everything seems to weigh a ton. Then you find out that the civilian fire brigade won't do this course, as it is too dangerous, it is too real. They always say the first is the worst as in this situation you are surrounded by danger. This course has to be done every three years. The thing is on a submarine you need to be fast and work as a team especially in a confined space and get used to fire. Reading a book is no good, you need to get stuck in there under supervision and have a go, not forgetting to write out your will first, just in case you don't come back.

Now it was back to *Valiant* and to sea, this time exercising with NATO and the Americans, a friendly enemy. We were going to play cat and mouse; we would be given a task to carry out and sneak up on the enemy, hopefully without them knowing. The exercise was to be up in the Norwegian waters, but first rendezvousing with an American submarine and ship called an AFA (American Fleet Auxiliary) for supplies, at a secret location in the fiords. As you can see from the picture there is a difference between American and British subs. The British sub being on the right of the picture, the American sub being next to the ship. On the AFA it was strange to see girls at sea but the ship was big enough to cater for both sexes. When we have any supplies at sea we usually get them delivered by helicopter, as we have no real support vessels like the Americans.

I bet the seamen on the American ship had fun with the females on board before the rendezvous took place. Reminds me of a cartoon called Captain Pugwash with seaman stains, master bates and the cabin boy, Rojer. Use your imagination and create that picture and keep it while tossing and turning in bed. At that time no women were allowed on British Naval ships, as it would have damaged the fighting potential of the crew! You can imagine all that bickering going on and not much work done. The only work completed in the bunks during lights out. Since the British navy was formed women have always been on land. One thing is for certain there will never ever be women on subs, for a start the bunks are not big enough for two people side by side.

This awesome sight of seeing two subs together is enough to deter anybody, including the enemy.

We also had some runs ashore (going out with the lads and getting drunk) planned in different countries. One of our stops was Bermuda; on the way there we went over the equator and had a barbecue on the casing (top deck). We always have someone with a gun on the top of the fin (conning tower, the middle part of the casing that stops the sub from spinning around in the water) as shark look-out. The lookout is really only there to shout "shark" if one appears, if he were to shoot at the shark the crew would be safe providing that the shark was scared of a bullets. We had hands to bathe (naval terminology for a swim); it was strange to think that the bottom of the sea was miles below your feet and no land in sight. There are no *Baywatch* lifeguards present so you do not want to be splashing around too much in case you attract the sharks. While we were swimming and the barbecue was nearly finished the cook was throwing the excess meat into the water attracting sharks. What are friends for? After that it was back to playing games with the "enemy". We had to see if we could take photographs of a ship's hull, an underwater look, without the ship knowing. This was so easy. An underwater look comes from the Second World War where our subs sneaked up onto the enemy target planting a bomb under the hull which would explode putting the ship out of action hopefully for good.

There is always a rift between the crews of skimmers (ships) and submariners. We call them targets, because they are just that, target practice for us. For a ship to detect a submarine is virtually impossible, but of course they disagree and think they are unsinkable. Their biggest weapon is the helicopter because they can detect us by dropping a buoy into the sea sending out a signal, which they monitor back on the ship. A helicopter is also fast and can get to the target within minutes dropping torpedoes or depth charges. Just to prove a point we took photographs of their hull twice, going all the way along and back again. It was only when our Captain told the target the news of our findings that he believed us; that's why we call them targets and the proof is in the pudding.

During a similar exercise we went onboard a ship for twenty-four hours. I went to see their detection sonars. On subs the extra money the crew get paid is for extra knowledge. The officer in charge was well impressed with my knowledge, the difference being that on targets the operations team does not have the specialized sonar that submarines have. Submarines, especially in a war situation, always accompany ships in a convoy for their protection. In fact submarines are more at risk from the sky. As mentioned before planes or helicopters can drop sonar buoys, which give off an electrical sound into the water. If this sound hits anything it will send an echo back to the detection set, if a submarine is within the detection range its position can be given away.

Another good point about subs is that if the weather gets rough you can always go under it and come up again, there's nothing worse than honking up at sea whilst doing your duty. On one occasion when on the surface the sea was particularly rough and the sub was being thrown around like a tin can, I was on the fin as lookout with an officer. We were both wearing harnesses for safety, just as well because the sub was not coping with the rough sea. At the top of the fin are two holes for people to stand in, the officer of the watch and lookouts. There is also a small window to see out of should you wish, this is hardly used because your range of vision is cut down considerably. The officer of the watch has communications at his disposal to the control room. He was thinking of diving as visibility was poor and communications getting soaked, the communications being of an electrical nature so getting wet was not a good idea. Just then a voice shouted, "duck" and we were under the water under a large wave. So we ducked, finding ourselves surrounded by water, looking through the small window all I could see was water. When we surfaced again the reality dawned of the precarious situation we were in. We had submerged and surfaced, nearly drowning two people. If it wasn't for the officer shouting "duck" I might not be here today telling you this story. I think that incident persuaded the Captain to dive the submarine.

Part of the lookout's job is to clear the bridge before the sub dives, taking down below all the equipment and to make sure that everything is securely stowed away on the bridge itself. Doing this when it is rough is almost impossible, as you have to go up and down ladders carrying awkward and heavy objects. If at any time you lose your grip or balance, and fall, a serious injury could occur. Everything on a sub is metal, so when you hit something it hurts and takes no prisoners. A situation that had me quaking was when I had to open the hatch to get down into the control room. The hatches are solid steel with a very sharp outer rim. The hatches are shut during rough weather to stop water getting into the sub's lower decks. To open the hatches takes strength and can be held open by a metal clip. This metal clip is normally good enough to hold but the severity of the storm had me wondering. If this clip did not hold and I was in the way I would certainly have lost parts of my body. The speed, sharpness and weight of that hatch would cut through skin and bone like a hot knife through butter. This was a moment of my career when I was seriously concerned for my life.

Talking of Captains, I actually had a recommendation to FOSM (Flag Officer Submarines) by our Captain for outstanding professionalism. It was strange because about half an hour before he had given me a good bollocking (telling off) because I had made an error. I was not his flavour of the month. The submarine had a fault with its electrical systems, this does not sound too much trouble but this system controls the surfacing and diving of the sub and the sonar systems. We had to come up to periscope depth staying just under the surface of the water before surfacing. The only sonar working correctly at the time was a short range passive (listening) device which is manned all the time when making this manoeuvre, but this time we had to rely solely on this detection set as the other sonars used were not operational. I had control of the sub and the lives of the crew on my shoulders. The only trouble was we were in the middle of a fishing fleet; this was not an ideal situation because if we happened to be caught in the nets we could cause serious damage to the sub and drag the fishing boat down with us. People might lose their lives. This incident has happened before and lives have been lost. I was aware of the risk so I had to be professional and use my experience and expertise. A mistake could not be made. During the ascent you could hear lots of sounds – chain noise (chains are put at the bottom of the nets to hold them down, chains also rattle which can be heard under the water), winch noise (nets being raised and lowered), engine noise (engines will suddenly stop and start) which can be most disconcerting if you happen to be beneath the ship when the engines start to turn, and biological sounds (fish). These noises you tend to be familiar with when gaining experience at sea. To give you some idea of how sensitive the detection equipment is, small shrimps can be heard in the water (as mentioned before, they make a clicking sound). As we were coming up I was constantly talking, giving bearings and ranges of the contacts, if any of them changed in noise level, any sudden changes in bearings and so on. When we eventually reached the surface the Captain, after looking through the periscope, was satisfied that the sub, crew and ships were not in any danger from the fishing fleet. He called me over. After my bollocking I did not know what to expect. The Captain said, "WELL DONE, PICTON"; I almost fainted.

Whenever a submarine comes up to periscope depth that is the most dangerous time. On one occasion an incident occurred during this manoeuvre when we lost all hydraulic power and the sub started to go backwards. The hydraulic system controls important things such as hull valves (valves that are external to the hull) and steering, with this system gone it meant that the hull valves would not open but remain shut, we needed them to be open to blow air into the large main ballast tanks (used to dive and surface the sub) filling them quickly with air. A rating (crew member) was on the echo sounder (records depth under the hull) and he was calling out the depth, which was getting less and less. We suddenly had power; hydraulics back on line (working) but the depth was still getting less. I can recall 3.3 fathoms being shouted before we started moving towards the surface. If the sub had hit the seabed our propeller would have dug into the sand, which might have caused a leak in the pressure hull. Around the propeller shaft is a watertight seal which when broken cannot be fixed so a continuous flow of water will appear, we do not have any spare parts for this item of kit as it is big and very specialised, only fitted in dry dock for obvious reasons. Also the sub could have ended up in any given position on the seabed making it impossible for a rescue mission to take place. Recently there was a submarine disaster onboard the *Kursk* (Russian). Every submariner knows that once a sub loses power it will sink to the bottom of the sea. Once at the bottom it will go over on its side and when this happens the chances of being rescued are minimal. At the front and back of the sub there are two escape chambers that if all were well would be used when abandoning the sub in an emergency. Remember the SETT or tank mentioned in an earlier paragraph. The tank is simulated to prepare you for what would happen under normal conditions in the escape chamber itself. This sounds straight forward until the sub rolls over onto its side, getting into the chamber could cause the suit to rip, as there are sharp pieces of metal around the hatch. When inside the escape chamber your body would be at an angle. It would be pitch black, cold and you would soon become disorientated, the worst is yet to come. When the pressure equalises you would be pinned against the side of the chamber due to the extortionate pressure, unable to be rescued. This would also block the chamber for any more attempts to escape. A sub must always have forward momentum to remain safe, otherwise it will sink to the bottom of the sea. Not only that, the depth is a major factor – too deep and the crew when escaping will get the bends.

On another occasion I had a real scare when coming up to periscope depth. I was on the short-range detection set again with not many contacts around. The contacts were merchant ships so not much danger there. One particular ship had been sailing away from us and then altered course to steer directly up our stern (back). This is the worst place possible; all our own engine noise comes from the back so it is hard to tell if a ship is there, both noises blend into one. Sometimes the noise increases, as more power is needed to surface the sub. The noise at the stern was getting louder but not enough to be of any threat. A normal occurrence is to raise the periscope at this point. We had the periscope up and just about to surface when the Captain looked at our stern and shouted dive. Just then on the sonar I heard a loud increase of noise and a ship was very, very close. The ship actually passed above our heads and missed by inches. In the control room (nerve centre) everyone was silent; all you could hear was loud propeller and engine noise. That's when you realise the importance of years of training and professionalism. When we did eventually surface we saw the merchant ship that nearly bumped into us. Not a particularly big one but big enough to cause damage. The next story is not as life threatening.

In rough weather we were coming into Nova Scotia, situated on the tip of Canada. An oil town where much of the population worked on rigs or in that line of business. It was freezing cold when we arrived. We were on the casing about to come alongside the wall (berth) and our approach was not correct, so we had to go around and try again. The casing party were told to hold on and grab the ropes in case they disappeared into the water. I have never felt so cold; being battered by freezing cold water, which might be good for polar bears, definitely not for humans. But you take the rough with the smooth. The second time round was much better but by now our hands were blue and could hardly feel the rope running through our fingers. I have never enjoyed a hot drink so much.

When in Gibraltar we were due to arrive one week after a British soldier had killed an IRA member outside a nightclub. This meant we had to have small arms (small machine gun) practice at sea before we berthed, just in case. We made targets out of black rubbish bags and tried to blow them out of the water. They always say give a sailor a gun and you have your worst nightmare, but we enjoyed it and made mincemeat out of the targets due to rapid fire. We were now prepared for terrorists. The submarine was going to be berthed in a dock, not a particularly secure place as it was not a military base. We had to be vigilant whilst on upper deck trot duties (guard on top of the casing) guarding the sub. For the first and only time in my naval career I had a gun loaded with live ammunition which had to be signed for in case any shots were fired. As if we would do that? Just give us half a chance. Fire first and answer questions later,

34

that was our motto between the lads but don't tell the Queen, our boss. To our disappointment nothing happened because we were ready to take on the world. The IRA would have stood no chance; submariners do have a reputation of being thorough when it comes to military matters being a disciplined fighting force. Submariners like playing with the enemy at close quarters taking a few prisoners. I was looking forward to the interrogation room.

Usually when we guard the submarine we have no weapons on our person, just ourselves. This is because they don't trust submariners with weapons unless it is essential. I don't know what they mean! However the Americans have loads of items hanging from their uniforms, from firearms to tin hats. They look like a DIY salesman or someone from YMCA. After a NATO exercise a few American and British subs pulled into Gibraltar, the contrast between our equipment and theirs was amazing. We got talking to the guys and we both got shown around each other's sub. The biggest contrast was their sub was new and ours old. They lived in luxury. By now we wanted some of their gear, their gear looking far superior to ours. We wanted to swap items taking them as souvenirs, items like caps, badges and flags. We were swapping all sorts of things trying to get a real bargain. Some of the guys tried to swap anything to get a hand-held gun, not in a million years. We had a good time with the Yanks and one of the things they found hard to understand was that we had no weapons on our person when guarding a multi million pound submarine, good job really as just think what you could swap for a gun.

It was around Christmas time so spirits were high and when we were being shown around the American sub we noticed that they had a bigger and better tree than us, but not for long. Our tree was pathetic with only a few branches to hang empty beer cans on, probably cost £5 from Argos. The lads got together and had a secret plan; this was to be a daring mission where every detail had to be executed to perfection. The plan was now set, everyone had their part to play. At 04.00 the plan began, distracting the guards was a piece of cake but had to be done in such a way that the alarm would not be raised. A few lads then crept on board, if challenged use their charm and cunning to confuse the sailors. We knew where the tree was located so we could go straight to it. We knew that this was a good time as most of the watch keepers were asleep. We needed a bit of luck and this was on our side, hardly anyone around. We pinched the tree and smuggled it up through an unguarded hatch. The boys had managed to move the guards away, distracting them totally from their duties. Later on that morning when the Yanks noticed no tree, they wanted the tree back. It was not going to be that easy, we held it for ransom and had demands. Both Captains were not happy and we were told to give the tree back to the Americans, so we did. Even though the Americans had batons, bulletproof jackets, machine guns, pistols and looked like Rambo, this facade did not put us off. We had achieved our well-planned attack.

Another experience with the Americans was again after an exercise. We were both in the same motel by the pool and had a few beers, just to relax of course. The motel was basic but had everything that you required, a pool and bar. Also had a few young females and guests soaking up the sun around the pool. The Americans started to get drunk and show off, typical American sailors, so not to be outdone we bettered them with whatever they tried. It got to the stage where they were not winning so the tricks became more daring and dangerous. Our final trick was to build a human pyramid, which nearly ended up in a nasty injury. The Americans made the pyramid with one person on top so we tried it with two people. We did it but when getting down one of the guys on top slipped and was lucky not to break his shoulder, but we gave ourselves a triumphant win during that encounter. The Americans again never finished what they started as they were licking their wounds. But saying that, the Americans are fantastic people and have hearts of gold. All the Americans that I have had the pleasure to be associated with have been welcoming to me and well mannered.

I have also had the privilege to work with one of the most feared regiments in the world, the SBS (Special Boat Service). They appear to be normal guys, but once given an order they change into a professional, well organised, disciplined fighting force, as the Argentineans and more recently the Afghanistans have found out to their cost. Anyway back to the sub. The SBS were on board for a training exercise to see if it was feasible to sneak along enemy coastlines and drop them behind positions for reconnaissance. Usually they use diesel subs because they are smaller and quieter. On a diesel sub the time it takes to drop them off and sneak away is minutes so we were seeing if the same time could be achieved on a nuclear powered sub. The biggest advantage with a diesel sub is that the Geminis (fast dinghies) could already be assembled along the torpedo rails so that when the submarine surfaced the Geminis were pulled out onto the casing, engines attached, SBS in, the submarine dives and makes like invisible. Nuclear subs pass everything up the escape hatch. This could cause the rubber Geminis to tear if caught on a sharp piece of metal when all the equipment is being assembled on the casing. This procedure took time before the sub could dive and hide. The quickest time we achieved was just over nine minutes.

The SBS are also very strong. I was struggling with an outboard engine on the casing. I was determined to carry this engine but could not get a good grip so it kept on slipping, I must have looked really awkward as one of the elite gave me a hand. He picked the engine up showing no sign of effort, put the engine on his shoulders and walked down the casing as if it weighed nothing. Believe me it was heavy but I was not a trained athlete, he was also used to doing things in the dark and had a gun.

After a submarine went into refit (repairing and fitting of equipment) or dry dock and the alterations that were made completed, the sub and crew was put through their paces with work up (working the crew to a high state of readiness for sea). If anyone says they enjoy this, don't believe them. No sleep, always having to get gear out, especially firefighting hoses, put gear away, loud bangs, not for people with a nervous disposition. On board for this period we would have sea riders (passengers) who were part of the work up team, when they came on board extra bags would appear full of things that go bang in the night. During this time you would try and avoid them as much as possible trying not to get caught in their web of destruction. This was impossible as they would even wake you up and say fire or hydraulic burst which would involve all the sub's crew. These events usually lasted one or two weeks as sleep deprivation was a big factor, we were having a maximum of four hours kip a day. By the time the sea riders had gone the whole crew was living on coffee hoping that the caffeine would keep them awake.

Part of the work up is to test the sub itself in a hostile situation. As an exercise we were being attacked by enemy ships, one of them dropping a rather large depth charge, the depth charge was real. A large explosion was heard and a 500lb bomb went off next to the sub. I heard nothing; I was dead to the world. I had to be woken up by one of the sailors telling me of this happening. At first I did not believe him, after all I was still in zombie mode. It was only when I walked through the control room and the Captain said, "Tired are we?" that the penny dropped. I was absolutely knackered, everybody was at his position apart from me and the lads gave me a clap when I appeared. The lads were not surprised as I never got out of bed straight away, always being just on time for my duty.

When you fight fires you have to wear a breathing mask with a hose attached, the hose is used to supply the air. The air is supplied by couplings (attachments for your hose), which are on a ring main (a ring of metal pipes carrying the air around the sub's decks). These are situated all over the sub; the reason for this is so you can move around. To move around you must hold your breath before disconnecting the hose moving to the next coupling. We used to have a laugh with these. Imagine you are standing around and you suddenly cannot breathe. You don't know what is happening or whether someone is playing a practical joke. You don't want to panic or look a fool but you start to get agitated. Then you realise that one of your oppos (friends) has the air lead squashed in his hand with a grin on his face. Who needs enemies when you have friends like that? So to get your own back you used to accidentally on purpose when walking past disconnect his. Or when he was trying to find an unused coupling having already disconnected, pretend that they were all occupied.

Another not enjoyable experience is to test respirators (gas masks). This is done when in barracks. You are in a secure room with no windows, just four brick walls. To test the mask properly the room is filled with tear gas to see if the masks leaked. All our masks worked, so no danger to us. I had never even dreamt of doing anything as silly as what happened next. The instructor made us take our masks off just as we made it out the door, so we could experience tear gas, they should save this for the enemy. It makes your eyes burn, water and sting, you cannot see, your throat burns, you can't stop coughing, very unpleasant gas. This gas is so bad that it could be used on badly behaved people as a deterrent.

There are many good things about being on submarines. One of these is the run ashore or the jolly (when you spend time in a country drinking the local beer and acting a fool). After you have been to sea for months on end a welcome break is visiting countries such as Gibraltar, Canada, America, Bermuda, Norway and the Scottish Isles. This gives us a chance to let our hair down and party. This is our treat for being tucked away in a tin can for months on end and protecting our country from hostile invaders.

When we went to a small town called Rothesay in Scotland, a very quiet place but that was soon to change as we had an overnight stay. The sub was anchored off so a boat had to take us ashore and collect us in the morning. We could not be late, we were under sailing orders which means that if you are late you get into double trouble, because the submarine needs all of its crew to sail on time. All the lads let their hair down, the only way possible to relieve all that tension after weeks at sea. We went on a pub-crawl visiting the only five pubs in the town. The locals were hospitable giving us ale and a warm welcome, making us feel at home. A few of the lads found a willing female to spend the night with, we all felt sorry for the girl as she was going to get weeks of built-up frustration lasting no more than seconds. In the early hours of the morning when all the nightlife had ceased and the daughters safely home in bed hopefully alone, we went to bed after a good session on the lemonade. I was sharing with three other lads so we were bound not to be late so set the only alarm clock to give us plenty of time to catch the boat. The alarm went off in the morning as planned and was very noisy as one of us awoke with a sore head. He switched the button to snooze; the alarm went off again minutes later. Again it was turned off quickly, back to sleep. The alarm went off for a third and last time as it was launched across the room. By now we had come to and were awake. One of us said, "What is the time?" We had time for another ten minutes. Our body, soul and mind were not as one so ten minutes turned into twenty-five minutes so by the time we actually got our paralysed bodies in working mode we had to rush down to the jetty.

Running down we must have looked so funny. Still uncoordinated with brain not engaged to arms or legs looking like drunken centipedes only to see the boat disappearing in the distance. We were in the kak (shit) and what do we do now. We could not phone the sub, as it was not in the directory, we could not send the postman around; we had no idea of the postcode. Only one thing left to do, have a non-alcoholic drink. After waiting a while and wondering what to do next the boat came back for us, they had obviously missed our presence. As we approached the sub we were bricking it (very scared). When we arrived at the sub everybody was waiting for us so the sub could leave. The Captain had a sense of humour failure as the three of us had important positions to man when the sub was arriving or leaving any destination. The skipper shouted something down to us but we did not dare look at him just shouting yes sir, no sir three bags full sir. I was casing party so a quick change and down the locker compartment ready to secure the ropes for sea. The only saving grace was that if I was sick I could produce diced carrots without anyone knowing and the evidence would be washed away at sea, fish like carrots. By the time we had finished I was sweating for Europe, or was it alcohol!

All three of us who were late had to go in front of the Captain one by one to receive our punishment. This is called Captain's table and is never pleasant. Waiting outside the room with your divisional officer who has a serious expression on his face, no hint of a smile. Your name is called and in you go at a brisk marching pace. Cap off standing at attention. In front of you is the Skipper and his table, the charge is read out and I have to say on this occasion guilty. The Captain asks you a few questions which you answer "yes" to every single one so as not to upset him. The word "no" must not raise its ugly head. The final bit is the punishment to fit the crime, the crime being adrift (late) under sailing orders. I was expecting the worst, as an offence under sailing orders is double trouble. In the end I was fined about £40 and had extra duties when in port. This was better than I could have hoped for and never did that again in my time at sea. I would hate to be in that situation again.

As mentioned before, there are some big differences between submarines and ships, some of these being that subs are not as spacious or comfortable as ships, we have to absorb more knowledge, we work more hours at sea and we do a dangerous job working under water. Because of these things we are given certain privileges. When we visit a country we are given a 4 or 5 star hotel to stay in for the duration. So when we are not on duty we are based in the hotel sharing a room. The one in Bermuda was fantastic – 5 star, near to the beach, pools, three bars, its own nightclub and paid for by the taxpayer. Thanks on behalf of the lads.

When we went to Gibraltar it was my first time seeing the Rock. That was what it was known as by the lads. The base here is very important as it guards the Mediterranean Sea. It is also a tourist attraction because of the Barberry apes or commonly known as rock apes. We had to go and see the Rock apes. Lovely cuddly things, not very big in stature. I was surprised. I was expecting bigger things as the word ape conjured up a large beast like I had seen on TV. When asking about this fact it was pointed out that these are the smallest apes in the world. You can buy food to feed the apes, which consists of mainly nuts. There is also a list of things not to feed to the apes. Some of the guys took this to the extreme. One guy had a picture of an ape with cigarettes all the way along its mouth. Don't worry the cigarettes were not alight. That ape could have been in the Guinness Book of Records for the first ever chain-smoking ape. I bet he gets cheap cigarettes.

Being young I had not been confronted with drugs before so when we were in Norfolk, Virginia, USA shopping in the supermarket for beer we were offered every pill under the sun. I knew they were not Smarties. I soon became cautious of the problem. I was not aware that the selling of drugs was so open. Norfolk is one of the biggest American naval bases on the east coast and has many facilities, legal or illegal. While I was there I got pickpocketed but could not find out who it was although I did ask around but no one owned up. I wonder why? We used to go to a bar frequently so made it our local and a good meeting place for the lads. I had made friends with a young girl who seemed pretty natural until one evening I decided to go back to her place. When I got there the place was nothing special but homely in a sparse neighbourhood. We had a romantic drink and I went into the kitchen to see what she was going to cook, I was feeling a little hungry. She was preparing drumsticks but what she was putting on them was not a normal powder. It was white and had a funny smell, nothing like mum's cooking at home so I made an excuse to go and left the house. Her personality came over as not being involved in that destructive habit. The girl seemed so nice that I decided to give her the benefit of the doubt and surprise her by going around one evening. When I got to the door I could see bikers smoking and drinking and the start of a party. I did not go in as I put two and two together and came up with illegal drugs, cocaine perhaps and other things.

One of the legal facilities is the PX (large superstore for service personal). Everything you can imagine is sold here, including lots of booze, and this was our regular stop off before going to the beach. The beach was a lovely golden colour, fairly busy with locals and holidaymakers. Once on the beach we made our little nest and proceeded to enjoy the sun and view of the topless beauties, after a while clearing a space around us being carefully watched by the beach police. We were doing no harm but attracting attention due to the large group. In the group of about forty blokes we filled two large oil drums with empty cans of booze. It was hot and we had mouths like Gandhi's flip-flops, which made us thirsty. So thirsty we were making sure we kept ourselves in fluids all day. By late afternoon we had quite a large gathering of males and females, no trouble just one hell of a beach party.

In America we used to frequent a topless bar for good night time entertainment, called the Inner Rooms. The bar was not too far away from our hotel so we went there many a time, sometimes after work. So much so that we knew the girls by their stage names and first names, just to be sociable. A few of the guys actually took root at the Inner Rooms as they used the place night and day 24/7. We must have spent loads of money behind the bar and on a good day the girls would give us a workout, keeping fit at the same time! By the end of our two-week stay the owner lent us his limousine and chauffeur for a day. We could go anywhere. The fridge was topped up with drink, blackened windows and a good stereo system. Excellent! We spent many hours just cruising around admiring the many streets and avenues, stopping every now and then for a spot of shopping or souvenir hunting. Every so often we had a few funny looks when fifteen blokes piled out of a posh maximum ten-seated limo. Very relaxed! When we did eventually go the girls were sad to see us leave as we had become quite attached to each other in many positions, oops, I mean ways.

A much prettier and safer place is Newport Rhode Island where they have held the sailing competition the Americas Cup. Very much a yachting island as the marinas bristled with top quality boats coming from all over the world. This was class and one of the restaurants was so upmarket it made a rich person look poor, if you know what I mean. It was an old paddle steamer turned into a high-class restaurant. From the outside not much had changed with an old wooden gangway used to get on and off the ship. We got as far as the door before being stopped but managed a quick look inside. Lots of tables being waited on, it would not surprise me if the ratio were one waiter per two tables, paying for the service. Everyone dressed very smartly with the light catching diamonds and gold every now and then, lots of shiny jewellery. If you wanted to impress a girl this would be the place to go, as long as she was paying. Newport Rhode Island is situated at the top of the east coast of America and stunningly attractive as the old town mixes with the new. The streets are very clean and hardly any litter around. The houses are worth lots of money and look it. Money is no object in a place like this – you just have to look at the yachts, powerboats and small cruisers in the marina to appreciate this fact.

Before I joined submarines I never realised how big they were until when in dry dock and maintenance periods. We went into Rosyth near Edinburgh for a refit to put some new attachments on to the sub. Manoeuvring the sub into a dry dock is a tricky operation. As the sub makes its way slowly through the locks ropes are thrown across to the jetty where they are secured until ordered to be moved by the controller. On the sub the Captain tells the casing party when to move the ropes along the sub's casing. This allows any movement of the sub from side to side to be negotiated so as no accidents occur. There are also tugs present to help in this manoeuvre. One time doing this manoeuvre we had some scaffolding around the fin and this was causing a few problems. We had to find a way of getting the ropes through the scaffold without causing any damage to the sub or us. We were coming into Liverpool for a run ashore to let off some steam before sailing the high seas underwater. There was quite a big gap between the jetty and the sub so the ropes had to be changed quickly and efficiently before they got too long and heavy to move. Taking a rope off I nearly fell in the water as I was getting a bit cold and the rope was wet and heavy. I managed to hold on to some scaffolding, I did not fancy getting an early bath. The water in any dock is never clean as the water gets used as a dumping ground for waste.

Anyway back to what happens when in dry dock. Once in the dock the sub sits on wooden blocks. These blocks are large and can only be moved by a crane. As the water level decreases the ropes that hold the sub in place are altered to allow movement. The sub must be level when finally resting on the blocks, and this is a tricky operation taking hours. Another precaution used are divers who check that the sub is sitting correctly on the blocks. The divers' visibility is not brilliant but enough to do the job. To see a submarine when standing at the bottom of the dock in all its glory is menacing. When the sub is floating in the water you only see a third above the water. The only time you get to see the whole sub is when in refit or dry dock. You can see all the sonars, hull valves and major fittings that you can relate to, but the sheer presence is overwhelming. It is like a large black machine of death.

Another part of life on board is storing ship with supplies for a long voyage. We always store for double the time away at sea in case we have to stay out for longer than planned. Onboard are large fridges and freezers, which are stored to capacity. For example say we are away for ninety days, we have three meals a day plus a snack at midnight, four meals a day for each person. If there are 100 persons onboard, that's a total of 400 meals per person per day. So for the time at sea that makes 90 x 400 = 36000 meals x 2 = 72000 meals are stowed onboard the sub for a patrol. Every crew member is involved with this, a large line is formed and items are passed or thrown from the jetty to the casing to their stowages. This usually takes all day, which is not surprising. Everything has to be accounted for and is thoroughly checked as there is a tendency to drop a few items or have a few go missing such as biscuits and cans of drink, by accident of course as damaged stock does not get returned. The Petty Officer cook knows this scam so is very quick to hear things drop or notice if from a packet one small item is missing. Believe me he does not miss a trick.

Some of the items are dangerous such as gash cans (rubbish bins). These come in thin metal sheets, which get folded into cans, and rubbish is compacted into them with a hydraulic compactor. Once when we were loading these, one slipped down the main access hatch, luckily enough there was no one underneath otherwise a serious injury might have occurred. The thin metal sheet actually went through the flooring by about 5 inches, the flooring being Formica, cork and plastic. Gloves must be worn to handle these, as the metal is so thin if one slipped a finger could be lost. The sheets are like razor blades because of their width and people always get cut, a hazard of the job.

I had been on HMS *Valiant* for about two and a half years when I was posted to Northwood in London. This was a shore base and headquarters to NATO; I was working as a messenger for FOSM (Flag Officer Submarines). The other messenger, a cook, was also a submariner so we got on straight away. We even shared the same house with two other people, a wren (female naval rating) and another male naval rating. The guy's name was Letts but got called Lil for short. We did have the choice of living in the barracks but there were many more advantages to living outside the base having your own time after work. For example you did not need to show your pass every time leaving or entering your home, no room inspections, able to have snacks any time night and day, the list is endless.

We had a party in our house and that was well attended. We said to people bring a bottle or whatever you want to drink. We had all the beer in the bath to keep it cool. We only invited people from the base as we did not want any trouble, we had a few local lads who we let in but when a few things went missing we told them politely to go and they did after some gentle persuasion from the lads. We had moved furniture around creating a big space in the lounge; we had a few rules one of them being no one was allowed in the bedrooms, as this was where all our personal belongings were situated. The party finished in the early hours, giving me a chance for some sleep as I had a camp bed in the front room.

The morning after was not good, but the girls did do bacon butties for us, bless their cotton socks. The smell woke us all up as it wafted through the house. I have never enjoyed bacon butties so much in all my life. The house itself was not very big but adequate and cosy. Now it was time for the clean up operation. Fortunately there were was no upstairs so only one floor to do. We did not do food so the kitchen was clean to start off with. The only food we had was crisps and nuts, nibbles. We did fill a couple of black plastic sacks with rubbish, mostly empty beer cans and bottles. When we surveyed the damage the only things missing or broken were the items that the locals nicked, small items of no real consequence. We also had a few gallons of alcohol left over so we kept this for our own use. We all felt so good after a morning's work that we went down the pub to wash the food down and have a quiet drink, this was well deserved as the house was now spotless.

On one occasion it was my flatmate's birthday so the two of us went into the West End and had a relaxing time pub hopping. We must have gone into many bars as we both got pissed (drunk). On the way back we got the Tube late at night and were glad for the rest, as we had been walking all night. I started feeling sick but did not want to throw up on the packed Tube so was trying desperately not to. I had my head back and was breathing deeply but the inevitable happened and produced the goods on the busy tube. I tried to disguise the fact that I was being sick but the diced carrots oozing through my fingers giving the game away. I did not have anything at hand to wipe the mess away apart from what was around me. It was not a pretty sight, my mate was asleep so missed the fun and games. We had to change tubes a few times; this meant possibly an open toilet, no such luck. I could not hide the fact that I had met Ralph. The smell could not have been pleasant, as I could smell myself from a distance. When we got to the later stages of the journey my mate, who was now awake, noticed my multi coloured top. He told me to take it off so as not to arouse suspicion of our wild night out. What he forgot to notice was that my shoes had changed colour and my trousers needed a wash. Had we got away with it! We made it home somehow and sneaked into seperate beds. His girl-friend was not happy with me the following morning because when we got in he crashed out and snored all night keeping her awake. Boys will be boys. She did not speak to me for days because he did not want sex for a while but just wanted to be left alone to recover. At least they will never forget that particular birthday. I never realised there were that many pubs in the West End.

I had been at Northwood for about six months and it was now summer time. The base had its own barge or narrow boat, which could be hired out to go up and down the canals from Milton Keynes. We got a coach from Northwood to Milton Keynes to meet the canal boat on a lovely hot summer's day. The boat itself looked new from the outside with a flat roof to sunbathe on, inside just as good with a cooker, shower and all the amenities. We had a curtain separating the male and female quarters at night time so there was no peeking. Our office decided to have a bit of a get together and bonding session so we took up the offer and we spent four days at sea. We took supplies, mainly beer and food with us and it just so happened to be my 21st birthday. Weather wise you could not wish for better – sun, sun and more sun. We took it in turns to cook, one of the girls made a pot mess (casserole), which was gorgeous. Food is always better if you don't cook it yourself. While she was cooking the food we went for a swim and collected a dead fish. There was a window just outside the cooking area so that the cook could enjoy the view. This was a perfect opportunity to start the bonding process between the girls and boys after only hours at sea. We dangled the dead fish at the window tying it securely so we could get down below to see the reaction of the girl. One of the guys said look at that lovely swan outside the window, she looked seeing an ugly fish with a funny eye. She screamed so half the world could hear, at the same time the stirring spoon came out of the pot spreading the casserole over a large area. Everything in this area was casseroled; it was not surprising when some of the casserole went over us, as she hated fish. What a waste of good food but we did finish what was left.

For my 21st birthday celebration we decided to go out into town after some beers on the barge, this made the evening cheaper and we would be in high spirits before hitting the town. We tied the barge alongside (berthed) as we had been doing every night and proceeded ashore. We found a real ale pub, just right for the occasion. Imagine the scene   you're sitting outside a pub, real ale in hand, lovely summer's evening, good social gathering with your friends, not a care in the world, music playing from the stereo. Heaven. We had a good bonding session talking about everything and anything, even telling jokes.

During the trip we had a serious moment when our Chief Writer fell overboard. We were about to tie up alongside and go ashore to do some shopping and stock up on supplies. We had tied up next to other barges to make it safe for us and the barge so that nothing could go wrong. We were getting off the boat one by one with the Chief at the back making sure everything was locked, when all of a sudden our Chief disappeared over the side and fell into the water. The thing was that the water was not deep and at the bottom was silt and dirt, not a solid base to push oneself out and to safety. We could see that the more he was struggling the worse the situation became. We managed to throw him a rope to pull himself up and back onto the boat. Pulling him up took a lot of strength, as he was knee deep in silt. As we pulled him up and the silt or quicksand let him go the bottom of his legs were jet black covered in mud and oil. That was actually quite a scary moment, as the quicksand could have dragged him under causing drowning and death, but we saved him.

Our Chief Writer was a skimmer (served on a surface ship) and we used to wind him up sometimes about submarine pay. Skimmers don't have the benefit of submarine pay because their conditions of work are better than ours. In terms of pay he was on about the same as us but he was a higher rank; we were ABs (able seaman) and he was a Chief Petty Officer. That sometimes caused conflict. We got on with the officers and staff well; friendly banter (extracting the urine) was common. Some of the officers were involved with the submarine service as well; this was good for me as one of the officers got me a draft onto my second submarine.

One of our weekly tasks was to take confidential rubbish to a large industrial incinerator; for this we had to collect the rubbish from all over the camp. The largest producer of rubbish was the operations centre (the Hole). This place was like Fort Knox, so many secrets and protected by Royal Marines and dogs. If I told you what went on down the Hole I would have to be shot. This place was built underground with the metal walls being 3 foot thick in some places. Once the rubbish was collected from all parts of the camp it was then transferred to a large van before being taken on to the incinerator. We had to make sure that all the bags were completely sealed so as nothing fell out. If it did this could be a major leak in national security. The journey itself was about one hour so not too long. The incinerator site was the biggest in London catering for every type of rubbish, from plastic to rubber, metal to paper and so on. Once there, the smell was sweet and unmistakable, we had to transfer the rubbish into trolleys to be dumped into a large collecting area, we quickly unloaded the van and made a sharp exit, as you could taste the smell after a while. On the way back to clear our throats we always popped into the pub for a cool sharp Harp. The trouble was we had to work in the afternoon so we had to limit our intake of pints. Maximum three pints but certainly no more as we did not want the sack.

Back to the Hole, with solid and very thick steel doors that were bomb proof, guarded by the best security money could buy. Even if you did get in you could not get out. Once I was on guard duty. The dogs are kept at the back of the building in a small yard with kennels. I went to get something from the yard and I forgot that the dogs were there. As I went past a window a loud bark and thud could be heard and a dog's face at a steamy window scared me half to death. It was like a cartoon when you see the eyes popping out and the body trying to escape from the skin. My colour had also deserted me. When I came back to the guardhouse the Marines were laughing and thought it very funny. They forgot on purpose to tell me about a dog they were exercising out in the yard behind the guardhouse. Marines and submariners get on very well with each

45

other, as they are both part of our elite fighting force. Being at Northwood (NATO Headquarters) from time to time we have ceremonial duties, as many of the officers are very high ranking. You cannot get much higher in the Navy than Flag Officer Submarines and he was my boss.

Because I was a sailor we had to be guard at a ceremony where high-ranking officers would be present, this meant dressing up in No. 1s (uniform only worn for ceremonial duties). With this we wore white gaiters (ankle straps), white gloves, white straps on our rifles, white belts, looking the bee's knees. We had to train for this twice a week but it was worth it in the end as we got time off work to practise our drill. I have to say the smartest uniform on parade must be that of the Royal Marines. When they wear their ceremonial dress uniforms they look splendid, every detail in presenting their uniform is carried out with pride. We also had to be inspected by high-ranking visiting officers and I have never seen so much gold braid sparkling in the sun. Although I was nervous trying not to make a mistake it was an awesome site of colour, discipline, pomp and pageantry, which the British forces are famous for. You do feel special and very proud to be part of the armed forces.

Northwood was a perfect location for the West End of London and concerts. While I was in London I saw Spandau Ballet at Wembley Arena. I had a few of their albums liking their style of music. I was disappointed with them live as I had seen them on *Top Of The Pops* and they sounded good but live the singing was not special and it took a while for them to get their vocal chords in tune. They played to a packed audience who made lots of noise getting very excited when it came to their well-known own songs. At that time my music taste was a mixture so I was just happy to see any bands or singers live, mainly for the atmosphere.

I also went to an open-air concert at Wembley stadium. This was going to be a full day with many artists such as Elton John, Kool and the Gang, Vapours, Paul Young and Nick Kershaw. The only problem would be the weather – if it was held in sunshine it would be a wonderful day, if not the concert could be cancelled or it would mean standing around in wet clothes and I might get a cold, nothing worse than a summer cold. The day came and bright sunshine all day, the stadium packed to the rafters with people. This was brilliant especially as I stood near the front hoping not to be squashed. Being at the front has its advantages and disadvantages especially when you want to get something. The more you drink your bladder fills up and must be emptied at some point. Going to the toilet was fun, as you could never get back to the same place. You could only hold on for a certain length of time before nature took over. In the end I came to the conclusion that it is best to stay round about the middle, best of both worlds.

I have always been keen on sport and one of my ambitions was to play on the sacred Wembley turf. My uncle was a fantastic footballer playing for Scotland at a junior level. When I was growing up he used to tell me football stories of his playing days and all the players he had met. As I grew up football was my sport and I tried to play it every day at school or for local teams. So a chance to walk on the sacred ground could not be missed. I took off my shoes and socks, rolled back some of the matting and stood on the hallowed turf pretending to be playing in an FA Cup Final; my dream had come true, I had a story to tell my uncle. I had played football on the Wembley turf.

My favourite artist I have seen live is Prince, at Wembley Arena. He was such a great entertainer and showman; he could do anything with instruments and wrote some great tunes as well as dance fantastically well. I had his video 'Purple Rain' and watched that over and over again. His entrance was awesome and had me jumping around very early on as the whole arena erupted.

Another favourite was Culture Club and Boy George, a good singing voice and always in tune dressing up in some outrageous costumes but keeping the crowd entertained. His voice was the thing that got me, it's something that is very hard to reproduce and not many people can. He actually sounds like the record, the quality is the same if not better.

I got on well with the officers when at Northwood, so much so that one of them asked me to play chess with him in a tournament. I had played for a number of years and represented my county when still at primary school. When at primary school I played chess most days so had a good knowledge of the game, achieving a decent standard of play. A combined services (Army, Navy and RAF) tournament was taking place. An officer and myself went along to represent the Navy. We went by car leaving early after work and what a journey it turned out to be. The officer had an old Mini, which was strange as the officer was over 6 foot tall. It was a wet and stormy trip going through many puddles, one deep puddle too many. The car broke down due to the engine being flooded, which meant we had to push the car for miles to find a garage; luckily it was only a Mini. At the time I was fit using the gym frequently, but not that fit to push a car in wind and rain. It seemed like an eternity pushing this car up and down hills, although going down was OK. Don't forget it was also raining heavily which made it slippery under foot. When we got to the garage after about two hours of gruelling exercise I was in need of a new body and water. I walked between the Mini and another car just to be quick, just when I got clear I heard bumpers colliding. I turned around only to see that the spot where I had been standing was no longer a space. I then had a horrible thought, what if my legs were still between the cars, and it doesn't bear thinking about. So after a rest and some work on the car we made it to the barracks and our beds in the early hours of the morning. We did not have a chance to practise so we were going in cold to the competition. Needless to say we did not do well and came home empty handed.

Whilst being a messenger working on a shore base I was itching to go back to sea. I missed the lads and being on a sub under the water. So I had a word with one of the officers on the FOSM staff and he got me a draft (posting) to HMS *Torbay*. The officer's name was Commander Christmas, a name that you will never forget. The sub was still being built so I had to join the crew in Barrow-in-Furness. I had been at Northwood for about one year. This was good in many ways as I would be on a new sub but the same class as HMS *Valiant*, with mainly the same equipment but updated with a few new pieces of hardware thrown in especially in my specialist field of sonar detection.

Barrow-in-Furness is situated on the west coast of Northern Britain in a remote part of the world, always cold or wet or windy but more often a combination of all three. I was based at Vickers shipbuilding yard, which was a massive complex of hangars and warehouses, building hardware for the Army and Navy including military tanks. My first place of rest was above a pub called the Blue Lamp. Above the pub were some rooms where submariners stayed, which gave me a chance to meet the lads. One night after being out I was just dozing off when I was woken by some nocturnal sounds, creaking, groaning, rustling, a few high-pitched noises. You've guessed it. One of the lads was giving a local species a lesson in behaviour of birds and bees during the silent hours, or a shag. He was a northern lad and was on the same sub as myself, all I could see was his white arse bouncing up and down stopping every set of strokes for a rest. He needed the practice as his rhythm did not make a merry tune.

Because the sub was under construction we did not have much to do, so we had lots of time off, such as finishing at midday or having a make-and-mend (afternoon off). We spent a lot of time down the pub or watching the Barrow rugby league team play. Some of the team worked at Vickers and on the sub, working in a number of trades, so we knew some of the team quite well. Barrow was a variable rugby league team in that every year they would go up or down in the league, too good for one league but not quite good enough for the other. Our daily routine would be to go to a working men's club in the afternoon, as it was cheap beer, finishing up in some nightclub in the early hours of the morning, hopefully with a bird in tow. The girls in Barrow knew the score so it was not a case of trying too hard. A lot of the girls wanted to meet a rich man and move away from the area. So when you went out the girls would come to you. The girls also knew that submariners had more money than the local boys so a better life was in prospect if they could marry one of us. We were aware of this and used the fact to our advantage.

One afternoon I had to get something for the sub from one of the hangers. Knowing what Vickers did I should not have been surprised with what I saw. Inside the hangar there were large pieces of metal lying around waiting to be assembled. In one warehouse they were lots of large metal rings, these rings were menacing. Standing beside one was dwarfing, towering above me like a large wave of destruction. These were going to be a submarine when welded together. I had always wondered how submarines were put together, now I knew, joining rings together by welding to form a tube. I was surprised as I would have though it would be safer to have a complete unbroken tube for our personal safety, welding under water pressure can crack. I suppose to do this you would need such a vast amount of space and materials that it is not physically possible.

The rings got me thinking and so many questions needed to be asked and answered for my own piece of mind. Here goes thinking aloud, if I confuse you let me know.

QUESTION: If the shell was an unbroken tube for the safety of the crew how could the decks and accessories be put in place?

ANSWER: At a guess you might be able to put them in at the same time, but there would be no room for error. An easier process can only be achieved if you can gain access to the inside of the shell, hence the rings.

QUESTION: Why not cut the shell into two pieces?

ANSWER: If you did have the shell cut into two pieces the machinery needed to raise and hold the second piece to weld together might not be available. The weight of one ring alone must be incredible.

Once the structure is complete how they know what goes where is amazing, it looks so complicated. Once the shell is complete and the decks, accessories put on the sub, the sub gets launched into the water down the slipway. Once in the water and tied up alongside the wall the Navy takes over, the sub becomes our responsibility. Now comes the messy bit, you can imagine how many different tradesmen, for example electricians and carpenters, are involved every day in fitting their pieces of equipment throughout the many areas below decks. I have never seen so many electrical wires and cables in all my life going through a small area. I did not count them, just one massive bundle of confusion.

Every worker has to have a pass to get on and off the sub so we know who is who, a pass or permission is also needed for dangerous work to be carried out. For example if a welding job is being done there has to be a firewatcher standing by with an extinguisher in case a spark causes a fire. Before any work is done a thorough check of the area is completed, checking for any potentially dangerous hazards. When the jobs are complete and the systems on board are up and running we have to operate them every so often.

One system controls ventilation, this changes the air flow around the submarine compartments. This is important especially in the reactor compartment as constant monitoring and readings of the gases are kept. The reason for this is that a gas is made up of chemical components, if there is a build-up of one particular component and the balance of the reactor is upset this could cause an explosion. I was changing the ventilation system but before this you must check various compartments of the sub for any workers. I did this and started the pumps and fans, then went for lunch. Unknown to me one of the workers had gone into a compartment after I had checked. This compartment is the one to avoid when running this system; it is very noisy and contains pieces of machinery necessary for the airflow. The worst aspect is that once the fans start the air pressure is so great you cannot open the door to escape. The guy who had relieved me while I was at lunch had to face an unhappy deaf and pale faced worker as he had been trapped for about twenty minutes inside this compartment.

Barrow is full of working men's clubs, which stay open all day and night. You can drink for twenty-four hours if you wish. So we used them for some light relief and keeping up our social skills. Then to work off all that sugar in the alcohol we used to play sport, especially football, and played in combined services tournaments. We did well at the hockey, getting into the Combined Services Final at Chepstow Army Barracks by the old Severn Bridge. We lost 1–0 but it's the taking part that counts; what a load of rubbish as winning is everything. We had a very good team, as we were able to keep fit and train during the week. We did some sport every day, even the officers joined in. We also arranged games against local sides to work up a thirst.

On board the sub it was back to duties and looking after the girls and boys. I had a nice surprise when I was told that I would be flying out to join HMS *Turbulent* in Florida for two months. It was doing day running. This procedure is where the sub goes out to sea for five days, in port for one week, out to sea for one week, in port for four days and so on; I had a total of one month off as not all the crew were involved full-time with the daily routine. I certainly made the most of this opportunity. I had the best and longest lasting tan ever as I spent most days on the beach watching the posers strut their stuff trying to attract the women. What made me laugh was that the submariners were all sorts of shapes and sizes and were having more success than the posers. Our biggest pulling power was our British voices, the girls loved to hear us talk.

The parks around Florida are so big and interesting. You have Wet and Wild, Sea World, Bush Gardens and many more. If you have never been to Sea World you must go. It is for every age and what the sea creatures do is a joy to behold. I saw the biggest crocodile or alligator, I'm not sure which, but this thing was massive. The head alone was longer than me and I am over 6 foot. You also have the shark encounter, if you're lucky you can see them being fed. For this you are on a conveyer belt travelling through the tank, above your head is a reinforced glass horseshoe-shaped roof. You can eyeball a shark and they can do it to you. You can imagine what a shark is thinking when he sees human meat in front of his very eyes – food.

We also went to Boston and found the Cheers Bar, which was used in the American TV series of the same name, which is shown in the UK. The bar is not used any more for television but has not changed much throughout the years. We stayed there for a while before doing some more exploring and found the place to be, very welcoming with lots of good bars and restaurants. We did get a little worried once when we walked into a bar in the Irish centre and felt we were being watched. We noticed on the walls lots of flags and support for the

IRA. We had a quick pint and left in case the black box came out. This was for donations for the IRA and if you didn't put in, watch your back. We had to be extra careful, as we were service personnel so the last thing we wanted was trouble.

That night after spending the day in Boston we got back to Coco Beach and met the boys in a bar, no one was sober apart from the bar staff. When it was time for the bar to close, about four in the morning, everyone piled into our hired ten-seater van. Only trouble was that there were about sixteen of us and no-body fancied a long walk home. As we all clambered in one lad took a run and jump into the van but caught the top of the door and cut his head open, nearly denting the doorframe. Two of the party were medically trained. They were only trained in first aid because their job onboard was to look after the health physics (atmosphere in the sub) but we called them medics. Some Americans came over to give assistance but were told to go away politely as we had the situation under control. They would not go until one of the medics was going to punch them, so they took the hint. We got this lad back to the hotel and put him to bed but after a rest he came back out to party the night away. This is a typical submariner as they do have a reputation for being party animals.

That was our second self-inflicted injury. A lad who got badly sunburnt caused the first incident. He was in bed for one week, and with the amount of skin in his sleeping bag you could have made another human being. He had spent hours asleep on the sand with no cream to protect him and having not been exposed to the sun for months. Because the sunburn was so severe he could not carry out his duties. When he was better he was punished for a self-inflicted injury and fined, which seemed a bit harsh but rules are rules. He had 9's (you are not allowed off the sub and must report to the officer of the day every 9 hours). This is probably one of the worst punishments, as you cannot go out and must stay on the sub at all times. You get more duties and your uniform is inspected every 9 hours by an officer who will always pick up some fault.

When in our motel, which had a pool, we could relax and enjoy our time off. As long as we were good we could do almost anything. We were having a pool party during the day and the cans of beer, or grenades as we called them, were on a table getting warm. We did not have enough ice to cool them down, but the pool was cold so we threw them all into the water, which seemed a good idea at the time. The trouble was the amount of cans floating on the water, probably four crates worth, was a little over the top. When he saw them the pool attendant went daft. We did offer him a can but he said no. The motel arranged for the duty officer from the sub to come down and speak to us about the situation. As a result we took the cool cans out of the water and carried on somewhere else. The motel did try and get the sub to pay for a new pool filter but with no joy, it turned out that the filter they had was old and in need of repair. The Captain, in no uncertain terms put a stop to that nonsense straight away. Whatever the Captain says is correct.

On the work front we were doing torpedo firings and being assessed on our performance. The torpedoes we were using were very accurate and a new design. They were to replace the old MK 24, which were not reliable. When a torpedo is being fired you have a ram that pushes water into the torpedo tube causing the torpedo to be catapulted forward thus giving it initial thrust. Once moving forward the propulsion system in the torpedo takes over, driving it towards the calculated target. When the hydraulic ram is in operation you can feel the whole sub shaking due the force of the movement. The torpedoes never missed so the operation was a success.

After the firings I was due to go back to Barrow when the boat sailed for Nova Scotia and Canada. One of the crew had to be flown home so I stayed on the sub. This was good news because my girlfriend at the time was over in Nova Scotia. I had not seen her for a year. She worked as a waitress around the hotel, we got talking and I asked her out. To my surprise she said yes and that was the start of romance.

Pamela is sitting down on the front left, everything you could wish for in a girl, starting on the inside working out. To this day I still think of her and what could have been.

In Nova Scotia we had a week off to relax, which we did. We had a game of rugby arranged against a local team. We started off well managing to score a try, on paper we had a good team – couple of lads had trials for big name football clubs, others had trained at Portsmouth for the Royal Tournament field gun race, others were just kamikaze pilots on a rugby field. After twenty minutes our fitness levels dropped leaking a few tries, we lost by quite a large margin in the end but enjoyed the pain, we should have stayed in the night before saving our energy. Some guys were feeling that rough they were sick on the touchline, making room for more beer later in the bar.

We had another function, which I could not go to because I was duty on the sub. This was another game of rugby against a local side. My girlfriend went to see if I was there, I had tried to swap days off but could not manage it. I was so frustrated because I knew what the boys would be up to. If I was not there she would be the centre of attraction, she was very beautiful with a tremendous body to die for. She was quite shy, not used to being surrounded by a pack of wolves. The boys were winding her up and telling her many tales of women and me, none of them true. When I saw her the following day her face looked as if she could have killed. She was asking me all these questions and believed some of the stories told by the lads. I did manage to talk her around. From that moment on I tried to keep her well away from the lads as they were all over her like a bad rash.

On the morning of our departure Pam phoned. We had to be on the coach by 08.30a.m. sharp, no excuses for being late. We were talking and time was moving on, I was aware that the coach was about to leave but could not drag myself away from Pam. I missed the coach on purpose and was so close to doing a runner (leaving the Navy all together) and staying with Pam. I knew that this was impossible; I would have been hunted down and sent back to the UK when caught. I would still have to complete my time in the forces probably at a naval detention centre, prison. The only option to get back to the sub was either a taxi or a lift from Pam. Pam came around to the hotel and she gave me a lift on the back of her bike to the sub. Her bike was very small, only a scooter but I was so glad to spend more time with her. We got to the sub as the last of the crew were boarding, we said our goodbyes making the most of our last moments together. I did not know but this would be the last time that I would see her. I left it to the last possible minute to leave her; I then quickly went down below and got changed because I was late. I really did miss her and we kept in touch for a while but then drifted apart. I wonder what she's doing now?

After this visit I left the girlfriend behind and we set sail back to Barrow. During the crossing we detected some whales under the water on our sonar. We could hear them outside so they were close and getting louder. Whales are attracted to warm-blooded creatures; a sub being warm will attract them. To move a sub takes some doing but we actually felt the sub move as it was nudged by a whale. It must have been a whale of large proportions to manage this. We could hear the whales and their high-pitched squeals being more vocal as they surrounded the sub. If only we knew what they were saying to each other; a very moving experience.

When I got back to the cold winds of Barrow, HMS *Torbay* was near to completion. Before we could go to sea and start work up, the sub and crew had to be commissioned. The crew is inspected on parade by the captain and FOSM (Flag Officer Submarines). I was part of the guard (tradition on ceremonial occasions to have a guard of honour). I had done this before at Northwood. We had practices to make sure on the day everything was spot on. During practising we had a few laughs as the guard was made up of many departments (there are many different specialised jobs onboard) and usually only the sailors did the ceremonial parades. So to some guys marching and drill was not part of their job description. One particular lad could not stop tick-tocking, this is when marching, and your arms swing the same time as your legs, on the same side of your body. Simply that if your left leg swings so does your left arm, which is really funny to watch.

The commissioning day was the day that the sub became part of the fleet so we invited our parents and friends down to the occasion. We had a large grandstand for all the visitors so they were protected from the elements; also the sub was decorated to add some colour to the proceedings. A splendid sight as all the metal was gleaming and our uniforms immaculate. We would be facing our entourage seated in the grandstand; they could be honoured to be present at such a moving display of force. After the inspection and parade we had nibbles

A proud and moving moment in front of your parents.

laid on at the Town Hall and a proper meal and dance in the evening. This gave our parents and relatives a chance to meet our colleagues and officers to ask any questions. I must admit we did look good, even the sub was decorated with colourful flags from front to back in the background, which made it take on a friendly appearance.

After that it was back to business and the sub needed ship's divers, even on a sub they are called ship's divers. I have always liked scuba diving and fancied giving it a go. We had to go to a warehouse where all the suits were laid out. The first thing you put on is a woolly bear (this is a green woollen suit to keep you warm in the water), then you put on a dry bag (all in one diving suit for heavy-duty work), not bad so far until we had to go on a slight jog to the quayside. This slight jog was an endurance exercise – we had to run through mud, do press-ups, sit-ups, at least the weather was cold so we did not overheat. By the time we got to the quayside we were out of puff and wanting a rest, but no such luck. Once at the quayside we were split into pairs, buddies (diving term), before putting on air tanks and a one-piece mask. I was second and watched carefully as my buddy went through his paces. As it was approaching my turn I was getting butterflies in my stomach and wanting a large meal to appear in front of my face as nerves always make me hungry. My turn came and I put the gear on ready to jump into the murky cold water. Then came the order to jump in. It was not a large drop from the jetty to the water but the jump was a test of your bottle. Once in the water we had to let some air out of our suits before giving the thumbs up signal that we were happy before going down on to the dock bottom and the sea bed. The water was not very clear at all, in fact you could not see anything apart from muddy water in front of your face. All I could see was a thicker cloud of mud coming up as I hit the bottom with my flippers. I had probably only submerged 15 feet but with visibility down to nothing I was only guessing my depth before returning to the surface. It was the next bit that I found difficult. We had to clear water from the inside of our masks but I could not get the mouthpiece back into my mouth after the water had gone. I had to abort the mission. I was really disappointed as I had always wanted to be a diver but not to worry, I can always dive somewhere else in clearer, warmer water at the same time attracting loads of fish.

Preparations were going well and everyone was in high spirits as we were about to go on work up (to test the sub and crew in emergencies such as fires and floods). This is always the hardest period in any submariner's life. Every-one on board hates this aspect of getting a submarine to sea after a long time alongside or against the wall (jetty).

I almost forgot, by now I had passed my part 3 and become a qualified submariner. For this you have to go in front of the Captain to collect your dol-phins, a proud moment for your personal achievement. Every now and then comes a moment in your life that will stay for you forever as a great milestone, earning respect from the crew and officers of the submarine service. This was one of those moments. Back home I made the local paper which pleased my parents who could boast to their friends about their son. Below is the picture and article:

BERMUDA MISSION

A sailor from Newbury who is serving in the Royal Navy's nuclear powered submarine HMS *Valiant* has left the English winter behind and is now in the sunshine of Bermuda. The boats visit follows exercises in the North Atlantic.
He is Able Seaman David Picton, aged 19, whose parents live in Culver Road, Newbury. He joined the Royal Navy two years ago and has served as a sonar specialist in HMS *Valiant* for 15 months. HMS *Valiant* is one of 12 nuclear powered fleet submarines in the Royal Navy. She is 280ft long, displaces 4,500 tones and has a crew of 110.

Staff from the work up team were travelling with us on board armed with smoke canisters and thunder flashes which give off a loud bang and scared you to death. The trouble is the work up staff throw these anywhere, when you least expect it. I am the world's worst for waking up and once I had to be woken by my mates as I should have been involved with the exercise but they covered for me. I must have looked rough as I literally got out of bed, put my clothes on and into action. Being ill is not an option, you have to get on with it.

The food is brilliant and is supplied by Vickers Shipbuilders. Vickers has many contracts with the military so money is not a problem so the sub is well stocked with a top quality range of food. We ate like kings having such delicacies as lobster and thick juicy steaks; no expense is spared. With the food that is left after a trip on the sub we had an option what to do with it. Normally it is given back to the suppliers but on this particular occasion we had lots left and the fridges had to be emptied. Perfect opportunity for the crew to take large quantities of food, and they did, back to their own freezers at home. There were large plastic rubbish bags with so much food in them the sides were splitting. I did not take much as I have never been one for cooking.

Once work up had finished and the staff were satisfied that submarine and crew had reached the required standard, the operations branch were put through their paces in a simulator. This is where we have various contacts on different sonars and must analyse them correctly coming up with the correct solution. We also deal with attack situations such as torpedo firings where we have to avoid being hit, so every aspect in a possible confrontation is rehearsed should we go to war.

On one occasion in the simulator I found it very hard to move or raise my arms because my body was so stiff after a session in the gym with my mate, who at the time was training hard to do the field gun run at the Royal Tournament. I had been stupid as I pushed myself far too much trying to keep up with my mate. My muscle fibres were so badly torn that I even found it hard to eat or drink, my muscles were so tense and sore to touch. When asked to do things it took me longer than normal. On one of the sonar sets you have to stretch your arms a little way, but even this was a painful experience and I had to hold onto a bar in order to keep my muscle stretched, in case I had to analyse a contact such as a ship quickly. With all the training out the way we could proceed to sea, our first duty was to Torbay harbour for a public relations exercise.

We anchored off in Torbay harbour and went to see Jim Davidson, who is a forces supporter, in concert. He had made a surprise visit to the sub earlier on to hand out tickets for his show and to invite us back stage afterwards. Before the concert we went out in Torbay to a few watering holes and became happy and in good spirits before making our way into the theatre. During his concert Jim did introduce us to his audience so we got a loud cheer. Everything was rosy until one of our lads got a bit loud and he needed shutting up. We tried but he thought he was funny and clever when in fact he was being a pain in the rear and started to annoy Jim, so Jim said to him, "I can remember when I had my first pint" which got a very loud cheer from all the theatre. I have never seen a guy shut up so quickly. We just fell about laughing, it was a funny moment and when back with the crew he had the urine extracted from him.

At night time in the bay we had to plot our position whilst on watch on a chart to make sure that we were not drifting on the anchor. We used the periscope to fix our position. The periscope has a very powerful lens used for setting up targets before firing the torpedo and for target classification so you could see inside people's windows late at night. You'll be amazed what goes on between 3 and 5 in the morning especially Friday and Saturday nights. This bird watching kept us amused during our early morning shifts; we saw a few red breasts and blue tits.

One of our P.R. duties was to go along for a day to a centre for handicapped children. Myself and four other lads volunteered or were asked nicely. No was not an option so off we went. I did find this very hard going as I felt sorry for the children and wanted to help them but sometimes this would be doing more harm than good. We took them various presents from the sub and at the end of the day our visit was appreciated. I take my hat off to people who care for the mentally handicapped as I found it a strain. The children had serious disabilities. Most of them had serious mental problems so they needed constant care and supervision. Meal times were hard work and we were expected to eat with them, which did put me off eating my meal. When we finished I had to go for some food with normal people to get back to the real world, more important a few pints to relax and de-stress.

This illustrates how handicapped the children were, the main thing was to make them happy and cheer them up taking their minds off their problems.

When anchored offshore we had regular visits by the police to make sure we had not been burgled or abducted by aliens. The police used to enjoy this as we made them welcome showing them around the sub getting on their good side. When the police left the sub to go on to dry land they used to take us ashore by fast inflatable patrol boats. We used to sit on the front and they opened up the throttle and off we went bouncing along the water, great fun. The only problem was that by the time you were on dry land you were wet from the sea spray; this was a good excuse to go into a pub to dry off on the outside. Sometimes as well if we wanted a lift back to the sub and they were going that way we would hitch a ride.

Back to sea now and supporting NATO. Exercising, playing the Cold War game, a few trips to Russian waters, this was not going to be a holiday. I can't say where we went otherwise I will be have to be shot as I have signed the Official Secrets Act. My strangest moment came when we had to go under the ice pack. This trip was a possible disaster in the making because the ice is never silent because it is always on the move and forever splitting. The noise it makes is a continuous series of high-pitched tones and it is very hard to navigate only by sound; on a sub there are no windows. If we did have a situation where we had to surface we would have to smash through the ice, picking a spot where the ice was not too thick. Also the temperature was well below zero so if we had to evacuate the sub we would be freezing our nuts off. The worst occurrence would be that the Russians would find us as we were in their waters and be able to gather information about our sub, this would have been difficult because some hatches were welded shut. We did manage to get ourselves in and out without being noticed, completing our secret mission.

The Russians have a class of sub called a Typhoon, which does not have to leave Russian waters to hit most military targets anywhere in the world. It can go down deeper than any other sub in the world and has hardly been detected. To give you some idea of the size of this monster take one and a half football pitches and join them together then put that underwater, or put a British aircraft carrier under the water. We tried to find this sub, our mission was to detect this illusive beast, gathering and recording as much information as possible without being detected ourselves. We searched for the Typhoon but with no joy coming back empty handed. It was obviously scared of meeting a Hunter Killer class submarine of the British Navy, but then again we were not happy about meeting the world's most powerful sub either.

By now the Cold War was coming to an end and the barriers between East and West were coming down. We were due to have a few days in Germany and see the Berlin Wall. I had never seen this before but it was a piece of history dating back to the end of World War II. Everything had been worked out for us to see checkpoint Charlie and meet the soldiers, we would stay overnight in barracks having a good chinwag and exchanging stories. There was only one snag, the German government. They do not usually allow nuclear subs into Germany and wanted a large amount of money from the UK for this to happen. Margaret Thatcher and the Queen, our boss said NO, don't be so cheeky. So we never got to see checkpoint Charlie. As you can see life is an adventure in being in the Navy and on submarines, every move you make is being meticulously monitored.

Here are a couple of short stories involving the lads; submariners do have a reputation for being wild and unpredictable. This dates back to the good old days when seafarers were sailors in wooden ships and enjoyed letting their hair down and causing havoc on shore when on a night out.

We were at a particular hotel in Barrow-in-Furness and it was late. Most of the boys were up so we decided to play some games such as dance of the flaming arse-holes, a famous game for Forces personnel to play. This is where you put paper up someone's bottom and light it. They must then get to the other end of the room or course without it burning the cheeks, a tricky manoeuvre. To make this fair for everyone the length of paper had to be the same for each person. One of the ends pointed to assist in up the bum. The course itself is not difficult but designed to test your skill in swerving around things, designed to slow you down.

After a few red cheeks we played another game with disastrous consequences. We had two teams in a relay race, a broom handle and a bunch of really drunk sailors, a recipe for disaster. Once at the broom handle you had to go around four times and back to your team for the other guy to take over. Getting back is not so easy as you are disorientated, swaying from side to side. It would be only a matter of time before someone hurt himself or did some damage to the room. One guy just happened to sway a bit too much and smashed into a glass service area causing a bit of damage, £250 worth. If you are going to do a job do it properly. As you can imagine we were not invited back again.

When based at Rosyth and going into Edinburgh we only had one car between seven of us. The car had four doors and a boot. I made the seventh person and had the option of the boot, so I took it. The ride would only take thirty minutes and it was cheaper than a taxi. It was actually quite comfortable and I managed to catch up on some sleep. It was quite a smooth ride for a boot. What I did not know was that they had decided to drive around Edinburgh for an extra half hour. I could hear everything they were saying so they disguised their intentions well. When they eventually let me out of the boot we got some puzzled looks from the people walking past. One person was counting the bodies emerging from this five-seater car. When I climbed out of the boot one person was staring with his mouth wide open probably expecting luggage. On the homeward journey some of us stayed and got the train back to barracks.

After the Royal Navy I spent a couple years on minesweepers in the Naval Reserve at Tower Bridge London. We had our own small unit to practise various drills and have tuition on explosives to clear mines using models in the classroom. We got paid a small amount of money, the incentive being our bounty. For this we had to spend some time at sea on ships and minesweepers. I found the routine really stupid as submariners have a simple approach to watch keeping (hours of work) and found it hard to grasp the system. The routine in my mind seemed silly, you never seemed to have a set time when on watch, three hours here, two hours there and so on.

At this particular time women were up in arms, they wanted to go to sea instead of staying in shore bases doing clerical work. The Americans have done this for a number of years so why can't the British. I will give you an example of why. On minesweepers the work is heavy and demanding in all sorts of weather conditions. You cannot wear gloves for safety reasons. During an exercise we were trailing a wire with explosives on at the aft (back) of the boat. The girls found it hard going and were not physically strong enough to do the manual work. Often times they had to be taken off the task, leaving the job to be finished by the man. To have an efficient fighting force you need everyone pulling his or her weight. It is well known that the British Forces are a superior fighting force, one of the best in the world because of their professionalism and discipline. There are no distractions from the opposite sex, and we cannot carry passengers. The Americans have a problem with a mixed ship, causing ill feeling between the troops. Pregnant girls are the main cause of this, nobody knows who the father is.

Another time we were doing a firefighting course in the Naval Reserve, being taken through compartments towards a fire. We had to start at the top of the unit, go down ladders and finish up fighting the fire. We were in a long chain holding on to each other so as not to get lost. At the top of the ladder the girl in front of me froze and was in tears, she was scared to move in any direction. She would not go down into the fire. I was last in line and the heat was making the metal compartments very hot, I could feel the rubber soles on my boots getting hotter. The girl went down in the end; the instructor gave her no option. He had to manhandle her down the ladder. Can you imagine this situation especially on a submarine, as time is important to stop the fire spreading. Lives could be lost because of one person. On ships it is not so critical as the spaces are less confined. Depending on the trial period with women on board ships the next step would be submarines. This would never happen.

I spent two weeks on board a frigate, HMS *Nottingham*, to get my bounty. I was part of the sailors' department. Having spent a bit of time on ships by now you would have thought that coming to terms with the watch keeping system would be easy, but no. On subs you do six hours on watch six hours off watch, simple, and you get time to relax. On ships you always seem to be on watch. Whilst on board we had a few days in Amsterdam. Needless to say the first place of call was the red light area and a bar called The Bulldog. This is a regular haunt for sailors of all nationalities. On the wall was a large African shield which one of the lads thought would look very attractive in the mess (living quarters). After many beers and being persuaded by the lads one of the crew was trying to rip the shield from its mountings on the wall. I left at this point so as not to be arrested and met up with the others later, minus the guy who was hanging from the shield. In the morning I woke up and standing in the mess was the shield in pride of place. How they got this home I will never know, you could not put this ornament up your jumper or in your pocket, not only that but the hole or space left on the wall in the pub standing out like a dog's bollock, I reckoned that they came to a compromise and he paid for it.

The following night it was window shopping and looking for bargains, one particular sprog (very young crew member) was lost for three days spending time with the girls of the night. I bet his parents don't know. I must admit there are some lovely girls and all gagging for it, but no bargains unless you wanted to pay lots of money for the privilege, although I was tempted once or twice. On the plus side you know that the girls are clean and will do what you want, they'll bend over backwards for you and that's only for starters.

The red light area is controlled but not by the police. The underworld has complete control so any misbehaving by the workers and they get a quick re-minder of their position. However the police are there and have a station in the red light area. The other thing that is in abundance besides girls is the selling of drugs. It is like going shopping in Sainbury's. You would be approached every day to purchase some Smarties disguised as drugs. By now I was used to the drug scene and ignored them concentrating on the girls and window-shopping for some entertainment.

I had been to Holland before but had stayed well away from Amsterdam in a quiet and beautiful old town with a clog and cheese-making factory. The cheese-making factory was wonderful, as you could sample the different flavoured cheeses, which were one to four years old. They had shelves in a windmill where they kept the cheese at various temperatures. My favourite was a nettle flavoured three-year-old cheese with a fine taste. They showed us the whole process from the milk to storage on the shelf, watching all this being done I got very hungry.

The clog making was fascinating as we watched a clog being made from an ordinary block of wood. They did have modern tools but still used some of the authentic chisels used in the olden days before the invention of lathes. This to me was the real Holland. In the town they had the usual small shops for tourists but not too many. The town itself was unspoilt and very clean and picturesque, the locals very friendly and some still wearing authentic Dutch costume, very colourful indeed. At the time my sister was collecting dolls from around the world so I bought her one dressed in Dutch costume. I would definitely go back there again but cannot remember the name of the place or how to get there.

Chapter 2

OLYMPICS

If you have never been to the Olympic games and you enjoy sport this experience is a must for anyone. I was fortunate to win a first prize in a hockey club raffle, which was an all expenses paid trip to see the final week of the Barcelona Olympics in 1992. I purchased the winning ticket by getting a fine because during the hockey match I had changed the formation of the team, which was voted silly by the players in the clubhouse after the game. I had played a new system, which I called the Christmas tree, with the month being December I had a formation where the goaltender would be the fairy on the top of the tree, then two defenders, three midfield, four attackers and one roaming player. The fine was that you had to buy some raffle tickets.

The winning ticket was for two people so I took a mate and we had a fantastic time. He was a very good footballer and we both had the same mentality for sport, it was part of our lives. We were given T-shirts, bum bags, hats, and all sorts of goodies with the sponsor company's logo on. We had tickets to go and see the wrestling, show jumping and hockey but not the athletics. However we did manage to get extra tickets for the athletics when out in Barcelona. I can remember watching at home the build-up to this special event and seeing how much organization went into this sporting pinnacle. We were situated about forty miles away from the nearest venue, our original thoughts were how will we get to the various events, but to get there was simple putting our worries behind us. We hopped onto a train into Barcelona central and getting to the ground could not be easier, every stadium was sign posted and buses, trains were running all the time ferrying people to and from events. Talking to some local Spanish they were saying how many old and rundown parts of the city had been flattened and new buildings appearing in their place. All the stadiums were brand new and built from scratch and a credit to the effort put into the organisation and running of this four-yearly event by the Spanish.

The hotel we stayed in for the week was 5-star with pools, bars and entertainment. The food was great with lots of choice on the menu. The beach was a stone's throw away across the road but we did not spend much time there as we were always at various events.

We were having a relaxing morning on the balcony chilling out as we had had a busy day previously and did not have to leave until the evening. The balcony was not very big but the most disconcerting thing was the surrounding wall was not very high; my mate was OK as he was only a few feet tall. My friend was sitting on the wall when I accidentally kicked it and a large chunk of plaster fell off into the garden below. Fortunately no one was underneath. We stared at each other and our faces went pale as the boulder hurtled towards the ground shattering into little pieces as it hit. We avoided sitting or leaning on the 4-foot wall from then on. My friend's waist was only slightly above the wall when standing up straight but I was over 6 foot so I did not feel safe and our faith in Spanish builders had gone. We had seen a programme; *Builders from Hell* back home – could this be their doing!

We also hired motorbikes for a day and did some exploring, finding beaches and birds, of the feathered type of course. Once after a hard day in Barcelona we went to a bar and had a few jugs of sangria, when I say a few I mean three or four each. We were so chilled and relaxed we could have stayed there all night and almost did. By the time we left everyone had gone, including the staff, apart from some old guy who was cleaning up and a few Alsatian dogs who were very friendly towards two total strangers. We were so relaxed we were no threat to them, although if they had bitten us they would have got alcoholic poisoning. I don't remember leaving the bar or getting into bed but I'm sure I was disco dancing all the way home – John Travolta, eat your heart out! The atmosphere wherever you went was electric but friendly and warming. There was no aggression or violence between the different nations; everyone was there for one thing, the sport and spirit of the Olympics. We were even partying with the Germans and French.

The first event we saw was the wrestling, nothing like the WWF (World Wrestling Federation); it was more of a cross between judo and wrestling. Real wrestling originating from the days of the Roman Empire where the person who was stronger and faster won, this sport was the Olympic ideal and not introduced to make money. It is very hard to understand the rules, even when they are explained in the programmes. The stadium was very impressive inside and out, brand spanking new and nothing damaged. Although not very full you still could sense the atmosphere coming from the mixture of nationalities.

During our next day we did a bit of sightseeing as we had a day without any events. Barcelona is famous for its football team, but what else were we going to discover? Walking around the shops and having a look inside, having a browse at what we could not afford. The best bit was people watching. The old timers were contented with what they had, all they wanted was a simple life. We were heading towards a fort overlooking the city where the view is incredible; you can see the harbour and most of Barcelona. I never realised the scale of what had been done to the city. You could see most of the new buildings that had been erected for the different sports. This was nothing like a major city back home as the layout was so different.

We also tried to change our tickets to go and see the American basketball team, the dream team. The Americans had taken all of the superstars and put them into one team, players like Michael Jordan, James Barkley and others who got paid vast amounts of money, which meant that they were professional and not amateur putting them into a modern day version of the Harlem Globetrotters. Needless to say they won the Gold medal easily, creating a real buzz amongst the fans showing off in every game. Good to watch, very entertaining but this to me is not the idea of the Olympics as every competitor should be amateur. The professionals have World Championships, which is their pinnacle, which amateurs do not have. The only sports that I can think of now that are amateur are hockey, along with track and field athletics. The Olympics now has got so commercialised and a real money spinner that to buy tickets was like gold dust and on the black market the money was very high, too high for us. We did manage to get tickets for the athletics, which was a bonus. It meant that we would see Linford Christie, John Regis and a few finals on the track. We were indeed lucky as we saw Christie and Regis in the same heat.

On the following day we were in for the surprise of our lives. Sally Gunnell should have completed her final the day before but it had been postponed until today, the day that we had tickets for the track and field events. She was favourite but with stiff competition from the Americans. We had a good seat just on the final bend so we could see the race unfold. On the way to the stadium we could see the Olympic village from the outside. The site used to be full of derelict housing and rubbish but was transformed into a modern state of the art complex. So here we were at the stadium, watching people coming in and the atmosphere building, the Olympic flame burning brightly in bright sunshine. Judges looked like parrots in their different coloured uniforms and flags from different countries were blowing in the slight breeze.

The sprinters came out for the first race, 100 metres hurdles, followed by the steeplechase. Then a chance of a medal with our 200 metre sprinters. Then came the race we had been waiting to see, the woman's 400 metre hurdles and our Sally. I had been following our athletes on television in the build-up to the Olympics, especially Sally, as she had become the World Champion in a very fast time beating the Americans. She was competing against them again. She was in great form, probably the best form of her life. Could she do it again? As she was introduced to the crowd a tremendous cheer went up and Union Jacks proudly flying in the wind. Time now to settle down for the race, a hush came over the stadium. The gun went off, tremendous roar and the athletes were away first time. The crowd was restless and as the athletes came off the final bend there was not much to choose between them. This is when the atmosphere took over and Union Jacks were appearing from every corner of the stadium. I could see that off the bend Sally was in the lead so she just had to hold on to win. I could only see the back of the runners as they crossed the finishing line. Sally Gunnell had given everything and was exhausted, I did not know who had won as she was recovering and showing no signs of joy just fatigue. Then the big screen re-ran the closing stages of the race and showed Sally crossing the line first. Four years of hard grafting work had resulted in her achieving her ambition. I was dancing, screaming, shouting, shaking hands with everyone. I even felt a lump in my throat. Then came her lap of honour and I felt proud to be British and witnessing one of the finest moments in our sporting history. I was getting a bit carried away so both of us made our way to the fence as she came once more around for her lap of honour. To get a good photograph I had to climb onto the fence. It was a touching moment. She has been my heroine ever since. That night was a major celebration. Being a trained athlete myself! I could understand her joy as four years of training hard had paid off. We celebrated for days and nights toasting our Olympic Champion, World Champion and World record holder.

The women's Olympic 400m hurdles champion doing a lap of honour.

Next came the show jumping. I have only seen top class jumping on the television, people like Harvey Smith and David Broome, always watching the Horse of The Year show when a kid. When you are there at the event it is such a different spectacle. The setting, atmosphere and colour all add to the occasion. The biggest difference for me was the size of the fences and horses. The horses are well groomed and look fit, healthy and very muscular. But when jumping, the power they demonstrated made you gasp with admiration. The fences too were scary and when a man stood next to them he was dwarfed by the size and span between the sticks at each obstacle. The horses managed to put on a fantastic display of jumping making the fences look easy.

The fountains near the stadium had been specially designed for the Games and worth the time and effort. At night time the colours would change from reds to oranges culminating in every colour in the rainbow. The fountains were all the way up the steps on your way to the athletics stadium. During the day they came on in the morning with lots of water being used to create the effect of a waterfall. The fountains created many different patterns, on display night and day, giving a relaxing atmosphere to everyone who passed them. The fountains were a good meeting place for the thousands of spectators discussing the day's activities.

One of the fountains on display during the day.

So on to our final destination, the Olympic hockey tournament and the final stages. We hoped to see some quality matches and individual skill to admire. My mate had not really seen nor played hockey before so he was waiting with anticipation to see the best players in the world. I had been telling him about the aggression needed when playing the beautiful game of hockey. He was a footballer through and through and I was not. I always thought of footballers being ponces (blokes with a feminine side) trying to pick up points for diving. I was trying to convert him into seeing the beauty of hockey. The ground was again purpose built but this time you could see the old town surrounding the stadium. The town itself had very little to offer in terms of bars, restaurants and nightlife. This was the first time we had come across new and old being obviously contrasting. The pitch itself was sunken below ground level and made from a water based astro turf surface. The spectators were near to the action.

We saw the semi-finals and final, both games living up to expectations. The hockey was amazing to watch, the ball was never still and as for the skill level, if I could do half of that I would be happy. The four teams in the semis were Holland, Australia (current World Champions) Germany and India. One of the first goals scored from the push back (start) was an aerial (lob) to the wing who on his second touch reverse stick (stick being turned around) into the bottom corner of the goal giving the keeper no chance, the whole sequence took just seconds. The final took place in the evening between Australia and Germany under floodlights, numbers 1 and 2 in the world. We joined the Australian supporters and had some tinnies (cans) of Fosters, mate! G'day. The Aussies were in high spirits as their team won and became Olympic Champions. A very hard-fought game with neither team giving much away. One of the German players was famous for lifting the ball in the air nearly the length of the pitch and he did this a few times. We had a great time with the lads from down under. Playing hockey myself I can appreciate how fit these guys must be. Astro turf has made a big difference to hockey, making the game much faster and more skilful, as was demonstrated by the teams taking part. The tournament surprised my mate by the excitement of the games and the speed at which the game is played, and the honesty shown by the players. In hockey it is impossible to cheat or fake a dive as the game is played with honesty between players and to fall on astro turf is very damaging to your skin as it burns and takes a while to heal.

I can recall a story about one of my friends after a game. He had fallen over during a game causing some damage to his knee. The skin had been burnt and cut; the person was not in a vast amount of pain until after a shower. It was stinging and every time he dried his knee puss would appear causing it to weep non-stop. This meant that he had to wear shorts to be comfortable. While we were in the bar with the team having a social drink discussing his wound one of the guys had an idea. The guy was drunk by this time so could probably feel no pain. The idea was to put some salt on the wound to dry it up, good idea. We explained that you might be in some pain but don't worry. We got him some neat salt and on it went. Not much reaction at first until the salt got into the wound. He had a few drinks in front of him, which he polished off before becoming a total freak talking gibberish. This was worth the pain because a few days later the wound was a black scab. This player was one of our top scorers and lived for hockey so it was all part of the game.

Chapter 3

FOOTBALL

I started my playing career when literally hours old when my uncle put a football at my feet when still in my mother's arms. My uncle was fanatical about football and a very good Scottish player. He was short but made up for that by his tigerish manner and aggressive play. As soon as I was able to walk he took me into the garden and I kicked a football. I used to annoy the parents, especially mother, by breaking the flowers and a few windows, but not on purpose. We also made two bare patches of ground either end of the garden where no grass would grow, which also annoyed my mother. Because my uncle was Scottish he supported Rangers and to wind him up I would support Celtic. Whatever he did I had to be different. We used to have some good tussles in the garden and one time my uncle could not get the ball so he hacked me down. My mum went mad at him but he was Scottish and getting frustrated at being beaten by a small boy much younger than him did his ego no good at all.

I joined the 1st Wash Common cub pack and they played football on a weekend. We had a very good team and hardly ever lost. I played in goal, which at the time I hated, but looking back on it was probably my best position. Our biggest win was 22–0. We also had training sessions taken by one of the dads and every week one lad got hit in the face with the ball. It was always the same person; this person was not really a footballer but an enthusiastic player. I used to love the six-a-side tournaments even though we never won. We came close a few times but were beaten by lucky goals according to me, the goalkeeper. I was always disappointed in not winning a six-a-side game because in an eleven-a-side game we hardly lost so confidence was high.

We had to play once on a cow field. The field had to be cleared of cows but unfortunately their excrement remained. The cows did come in handy, at least we had spectators. Once the pitch was cleared of cows we were ready to play, the only problem being that cowpats were visible and more than a few in my goal area. It was a case of selective diving, choose your spot. Another time the goalmouth was full of glass so I did not dive once. I used my feet, hands and inch perfect judgment to save shots.

The first International match I saw was England v Wales at Wembley Stadium; this was a complete surprise. I had finished school and my dad met me in the car. On the way home he did not let on about the match until I told him I had no homework, I did have some but not to worry, it was not important as it could wait to be done. He then produced two tickets for the match, I was so excited, and he was the best father in the world. I would be seeing top professionals and players I had only seen on TV. Players like Mick Channon, Emlyn Hughes, Colin Bell and many more who were my heroes. Wembley stadium was awesome and the atmosphere overpowering for a lad of ten years of age. I came out of the stadium with the biggest grin on my face, bigger than the Grand Canyon.

I played for the school football team occasionally, mostly in goal and for local clubs on pitch. I was getting bored in goal because my team were winning most matches and the defence awesome so I wanted to see some action. I was not a fast player but more of your midfield workhorse.

When I was in the Navy a friend of mine used to go on a football exchange involving the Americans. He lived in Eastleigh, Southampton and the American team was from Temple Terrace, a district in Tampa, Florida. So he invited me along, this was the start of a good and long friendship. When over in the States we had a total of five games arranged. One of the guys on the Tampa committee was Chief of Police for the Temple Terrace District, so he got us into the Rowdies stadium playing a match on the pitch as part of the exchange programme. The Rowdies were the local national football team for that area, the manager being Rodney Marsh the ex England and Manchester City player.

A family looked after each player and we were taken everywhere by them. Barbecues and social events were arranged but the main theme was football. Football in the States has never been big but at the time organisers were trying to push the sport to make it into a national game. It made a change playing in good weather rather than winter conditions. The Americans had some good players and most games were close with substitutes being used on both sides. Loads of water needed to be taken by the players to stop dehydration. The Americans had thought of everything and brought with them gallon containers of water and sponges. Before one game we had a rainstorm so the pitch was slippery. This was good for sliding tackles and for players who were not that skilful but fit and could run about all day, also the rain made the evening cool. During the match I was going like lightning for a fifty-fifty ball and came a close second place when the opposing player got his foot to the ball a split second before mine. I skidded for miles or so it seemed, getting points for style and presentation. We all played in most games but the highlight was definitely playing at the Rowdies stadium. After the game we met the Rowdies players and manager, old Rodders himself. We had a chat and some beers, a good bunch of lads who made us feel welcome.

After one important game between Temple Terrace and Eastleigh we made the front-page news in the local paper. We were being sponsored by a local fast food chain that had arranged for the press to come down. After the game some of the players were interviewed and had their pictures taken in the restaurant.

Guess what, I was on the front page eating a hot dog with two other friends.

We also had some fun nights out after the matches had finished. We went to a Reggie bar, which was open until the early hours of the morning. We went with the Chief of Police so we did not have to pay to get in. This was a real basic Caribbean place, no mod cons neither any money spent. There were no tables or chairs just planks of wood and tree trunks. Everything was outside so the floor was just dirt and grass; there was a rickety bamboo stage, which looked as though it would fall down any second. A variety of food was served so if you fancied alligator or fried bugs you were more than welcome. I had never seen those on a menu so did not bother tasting such delicacies, I tried to dare my mate but even he refused. The music was Reggie all night, three live bands that sounded like Bob Marley, each coming on at various intervals. During the breaks a DJ would take over playing Bob Marley and other Reggie performers so by the end you were so relaxed and a cool man. You felt like a Rastafarian. I loved this place and could recommend it to the world, I have always been a fan of black music especially Reggie. I wonder if our milkman was of dark skin?

The Tampa Bay Tribune

From left, soccer players David Picton, Lloyd Paddock and Malcolm Phillips from Eastleigh, England, sister city to Temple Terrace, enjoy hot dogs at Mel's on Busch Boulevard after a soccer match.

One of the hosts had a friend who had a speedboat so one sunny afternoon we went to a lake and had a go at water skiing. It looks easy when you see it done but it's not. Standing up was hard enough and it took me the best part of one hour to master this. Even then I was only standing for a split second. For the ones who could do it well they made it look like a piece of cake with icing on the top. When we were not in the water we would cover ourselves with bite cream as the many trees surrounding the lake attracted flying insects. The lake itself was popular with water skiers all helping us if we needed advice, I certainly did. We did come prepared for the day with a cooler full of soft drinks and food cooked on the barbecue. With all this exercise the food was most welcome. The food was in abundance and did not go to waste; there was everything there, chicken, steaks, pork, clams, oysters and others. The following day my fore-arms were taut as I had been holding on to the bar tightly. As you might have guessed by now I like my food, so on the way back from the lake we had arranged to eat at a steakhouse.

By this time I felt really hungry and so did the others. We all had lots to eat and ate everything that was put in front of us. On the way out I noticed a challenge in big bold letters saying, 'TRY OUR 6LB STEAK CHALLENGE can you eat this IN 1 HOUR 15 MINUTES'. I have always been a large rub-bish bin when it comes to eating so we decided to investigate. You had to eat as the notice said 6lb of steak in 1 hour 15 minutes. You could stop twice for two 15-minute breaks, so if you wanted to walk around or spend time in the toilet you could, but if you were sick the challenge was lost. What the notice forgot to mention was a small bowl of side salad, baked potato and one piece of bread. We had to have a go because if you didn't make it you had to pay $24.50 about £18, well worth it for all that steak. So training started two days before, lots of exercise, cutting down on fizzy drinks and our food was carefully monitored. I felt good about this, we were in serious training. The moment arrived and into the restaurant we went, we stood waiting to be seated and had our picture taken.

There were two notice boards in the reception area. One contained pictures of those who had failed the challenge, which was full, and one contained the pictures of those who had passed. This had seven pictures, people all bigger than me by about 18 stone. So we sat down at our special table and they an-nounced us to everybody in the restaurant, cowbells ringing, music and all that hype. We were announced as two guys from England here on vacation trying our 6lb challenge. You could see heads turning around trying to spot the guys. They were expecting two guys of large proportions weighing in at 20 stone-ish. I was about 13 stone and my mate 16 stone, but it's quality not quantity. Then came the embarrassing bit, the room went silent and the lights dimmed, then came a posse of staff carrying our meals, making lots of noise. The only thing missing was fireworks. When everybody saw the size of the steaks a loud gasp and wow could be heard throughout the restaurant. We were certainly the talk of the restaurant and as people came up to see the size of our tray we offered them a mouthful but they had to decline, as this was not in the rules. People were taking pictures, I felt like a real film star with all that attention. The steaks came on a tray and folded over, 6lb of pure meat about 3 inches thick. I started wading through and about half way felt good, I stopped and while I was standing up walking around, the steak was being reheated. This was good because it meant that the steak was always cooked and not red inside. I was determined not to give up; with 2lbs left I had my second wind and could see a glimmer of hope. 1lb left and my stomach was about to burst, too much salad I guess. I was finally beaten with less than 1lb left and half a baked potato but I ate more than my mate. I made a promise to myself saying that in future I would order my steak in ounces not pounds. I was amazed that I had kept everything down and the following day I was not in any distress. Woke up in the morning, first port of call toilet and solid lumps cascading into the depths of the pan. A picture below of me eating half a cow:

Cow today gone tomorrow.

We were also taken on to the police firing range to shoot some amazing weapons. We had a go with a colt 45 pistol, one of the most powerful handguns in the world at that time. The kick is fierce so you must hold the gun firmly with both hands, leaning slightly forward. We also fired an original World War I rifle. How the soldiers managed to fire these things accurately makes you wonder. They were heavy and with a single bolt action took a while to load. No wonder so many guys got killed as they had no chance of loading their rifles and firing them in a quick time when being shot at or machine-gunned by the enemy. We had to put on ear defenders as the noise was deafening and goggles in case of hot empty cartridges flying into your eye. I had fired guns before so looked forward to this challenge.

On one of our days off we had a barbecue, the Americans can certainly barby. There was enough food to feed an army – an amazing spread. We had clams, oysters, burgers, sausages, steaks, salad; I'm feeling hungry thinking about it. To open up a clam a large knife is used to get in between the shell to prise it open. The person doing it wears a large thick glove in case he or she stabs their hand, a dangerous task, that's why the men usually do it. There are parks especially for barbecues with facilities for team games and amusements for the whole family. We arranged a game of softball between the Americans and Brits; it was quite funny when the Americans started putting on these large gloves on their wrong hands. To us this was like cricket but with a bigger ball. Softball is very similar to rounders so we understood the rules perfectly until someone was out. This always caused friendly banter, not quite cheating but on the verge. It would be good to have these in Britain but we don't have the blue skies and hot climate but it is a fantastic day out. In Britain we do have large parks but cannot guarantee that the sun will shine upon us, even if the weather forecast says so. As you can tell I am getting extremely excited telling you about a sport called Softball, a very sociable sport, good clean fun for all the family.

Anyway back to the football. My ambition had always been to join a proper football club with a stadium, floodlights, training three times a week. My chance came when living in Barrow where I had the opportunity to play a lot of football. I went along to a game one afternoon and spoke to the Barrow FC manager. Barrow were then in the Goala League, the old Division 5. They were playing Manchester United reserves the following Saturday. The manager and myself had a chat and he invited me to a training session. He also had me shown around the ground and its facilities. The best bit was when he invited me to the dug out with him and the team during the Manchester game; I felt part of the set-up already and was lapping up all the attention. After the game was over I went into the clubhouse to meet the backroom staff. What I did not know was Britain's first £1 million player was there – Kevin Reeves, ex Manchester City. It was such an honour and privilege to meet the best player in Britain at that time. I felt as if I had met royalty and walked out of the ground with a great big grin on my face and feeling so good. It was as though I had just signed a multi-million pound contract myself, I had hit the big time. All I had to do was play football and impress the manager to give myself every chance of succeeding.

The training session came. I was determined to do well but had never been in this situation before so this was my big chance of getting into the big time and making a name for myself. After the session I went away feeling that I had not let myself down and had demonstrated all that was asked of me. I was now hoping for a phone call and to my delight it happened. I had impressed enough to be included in the squad but was not able to sign a contract as I was still in the Navy. So I would play only when called upon which would be a limited number of chances. As it turned out I did not get on the subs bench once but came close on a few occasions.

While I was there they had two managers, the second one being David Johnston, the ex Ipswich, Liverpool and England player. On my day off I was having something to eat in a local café when in walked David and the assistant manager. They saw me eating and joined me so we chatted about tonight's fixture and David said, "I want you at the ground tonight I will be picking the team with everybody there." I felt like a real professional with my head swelling by the second.

We met at the ground before kick-off and David picked the team in the changing room before the game. The team had not been performing well and in danger of being caught in the relegation battle so the team would be picked on merit not reputation. I was sitting there with everything crossed awaiting my big chance but was not picked. Instead the players left out watched the game from the stands. You could see what David was trying to do, create a team spirit taking one game at a time with no favouritism towards players.

Training was fun most of the time, having small games and practising set pieces, like a real football team. This particular session started off cold and sleeting, typical winter's evening up North. The temperature dropped even further down the scale, the sleet turning into driving hailstones, the stones being as big as pebbles on the beach and as hard. During this session we had to find shelter as our bodies were getting bruised, such was the ferocity of the stones. When running into them it was torture for our faces and we had to turn our heads to avoid injury. Once the shower had ceased we went back onto the pitch to find no sign of grass, just large droplets of ice forming a white blanket.

Barrow finished up fighting for survival that season but did not go down. I was sad to go but the Navy called and the sea waited. My little fling with the big time was over but good whilst it lasted. I had a sniff of the professional footballer's life and loved every second; I could definitely do this for a living without a shadow of a doubt.

When I left the Navy I thought of getting back into football and went on coaching courses with the FA. I got my preliminary badge at Bisham Abbey where we were given some expert coaching skills from top coaches. This is the first step to becoming a fully licensed coach with a Football League club. We had to work hard and demonstrate various skills with a football; we were kicking a ball around most of the day, which I had not done for ages. So I used to do some additional practice in the garden or in the local park. We were also given coaching assignments such as to take a coaching session demonstrating passing a ball along the ground accurately. We would then go away and the next week coach that session with a group. I enjoyed this immensely because it gave me knowledge and confidence in my own ability.

Bisham Abbey is where the England football team train before a game and there was a rumour that the England team would be arriving soon so we could watch a training session including Gazza and friends. Unfortunately the rumour was wrong and to our disappointment no one turned up. We were looking forward to a game against England and hopefully scoring a goal or two. Can you imagine telling your sporty friends that you have playing against England today and you had to mark Gazza, if only it was true.

We had one full day four times a month to complete our course. Each day would be a full day from 9am – 6pm, most of that time practical work on the pitch. I passed the course getting good feedback from the tutors. My task now would be to find a local club to exercise my knowledge of the game; I was itching to progress to bigger things but this was easier said than done. I tried various local clubs but with no joy, this was partly due to the season coming to an end so no new coaching or playing staff was needed.

The next step is to go on residential weekends, this gives you a chance to meet other players with the same goal, excuse the pun, enabling you to have complete concentration for that weekend course. You eat, drink and sleep football. If you have any difficulties you can practise the correct way as much as you like. When the examiners think you are ready they will put you forward for your full badge. At the end of the course you get feedback and analysis, which you take on board for next time. The pupils on this course were of a much higher standard than before, nearly all the pupils were attached to various league clubs, there were even girls from Arsenal Ladies. Our coach this time was Mike Pejic, ex Derby County and England. When I was younger I can remember him playing on TV under Brian Clough, what a player. Coaching was now much more involved taking in the finer points, we were coaching eleven-a-side games putting across points such as creating space in the last third of the pitch. Sounds easy but much more involved and more concentration needed. I now definitely had to get coaching experience and eventually managed this at various schools in the area under the regional FA coaching scheme.

I had all the kit with tracksuits, waterproof jackets complete with FA prelim coaching badges, cones, lots of footballs. This was all well and good but I needed to work with adults so I tried various local football clubs again for coaching experience, I even wrote to Southampton and Reading FC but none took me on. Without coaching experience with adults I could not continue, as I could not put into practice what I had learnt. That was the end of that dream.

My next step into football was really a shot in the dark, refereeing. I was always amazed how much verbal abuse was aimed at referees, so much so that I wanted to change players' attitudes and make football a fair game. But I was not prepared for how impolite and aggressive football players are. I took my course and exams in Newbury, my local town, in the dark and wet evenings of the winter. I found the course easy but interesting, seeing things from the other side of the law. Once I had passed the exams I bought myself the black kit, got the badge, whistles and cards, I was now ready to take on the world.

My first game was running the line (linesman) with a very experienced team of officials; this was a game between two topsides in a local League. Before the game the referee had the officials in his room giving us some tips and advice. He was very calming and reassured me, putting my mind at ease. When we went out on a cold misty day my first duty was to check the goal nets for any holes or danger. These were OK, after this running towards my touch line position. The game went well and I had hardly any abuse, I even had time for some banter with the fans. The crowd were very good-natured and the players played hard but fair. A good start to my career as I had enjoyed the game. Next game was a bonus, I found some money on the pitch during inspection before kick off, I was honest and asked the ref what to do with the loot, he said keep it and add it to your match fees.

I started refereeing in the middle for the local Sunday League. I had a superb start to my refereeing career but could it last, no. This game was not much fun because I did get abuse and the players were still drunk from the night before. The players were not gentlemen but thugs. During one game I had some mud thrown, hitting me on the back. I turned around and it could have been one of several players. I did a few seasons but for £10 a game plus expenses it was not worth the abuse or travelling. I also found that because referees were in short supply in my area so many weekends were taken up and I had no time on my hands for anything else. I would be refereeing three times over the weekend, sometimes four if doing an evening five-a-side competition at a local leisure centre. This meant I had no time to pursue my interests. After a few more games in the middle, football left me with a bad impression of the sport – how could they call this beautiful? More like murder ball.

The FA have tried to help referees by using the approach made by the Rugby Union code which states that an offender can be punished by giving away 10 yards. This was tried but never really instigated; why I don't know. Another good rule from Rugby Union would be that anybody deliberately cheating by interfering with a goal being scored then the goal should be given. When these rules are applied in rugby no one argues. The only trouble is that if these rules were applied in football you would be left with a five-a-side match. Footballers have no respect for authority and need to be taught a lesson, in rugby you never see referees being escorted off by police. In football it is a common occurrence, what chance do referees have of survival on a football pitch. Heavy fines should be introduced to stop indiscipline, the fines imposed now are a joke, for example a top pro earning millions a year gets fined £2000, that's about two minutes on the pitch and will not make the slightest of difference to him. If you were to fine him £500,000 that would make him think. I have been to see a few games where on the pitch the players have started having a go and through no fault of his own the referee has lost control of the situation. The players are in his face hurling abuse and he is surrounded. It would be nice to see all those players sent off and donating half their wealth to charity. They would not miss half a million pounds given to a good cause. Once violence starts on the pitch it escalates to the terraces, not that a small percentage of football fans need an excuse, but it gives them one.

I went to see Cardiff City play Swansea at Cardiff's ground, Ninian Park, in the Welsh Cup. I was only a youngster going with my dad and granddad. The game itself was not particularly violent nor was it dirty but the fans started fighting and it was not a pretty sight, but I had to laugh when the Alsatian dogs were let loose. I have never seen so many so-called fans (thugs) move so fast over the fence. They were scampering and scared, not very tough now. The dogs had won a convincing victory. Then came the charge of the Light Brigade. The police horses scattered the crowd, some of the people did try to hit the horse but the horse could look after itself. Shortly after this the police regained order, by this time we had gone hopefully avoiding the thugs. That was the first time I had seen dogs and horses being used to control a crowd, definitely a deterrent.

I went with a friend to see West Ham play Spurs, mainly to see Glen Hoddle. We were in a mixed area of fans sitting down on the hard plastic seats; we knew before the game that the West Ham fans could be a bit volatile so we thought choosing the seats a good option. This was a safe way to avoid trouble or so we thought. Spurs outplayed the Hammers early on scoring a fine goal to take the lead, so we cheered. Spurs scored again and we cheered again, this time we got some harsh looks and evil glares from some kids in front of us. One of the kids kept on making eye contact with us so I was glad when West Ham made it 2–2. Then disaster struck, Spurs got the winner, the excitement got the better of us and we both cheered. The ringleader then turned around with some other kids and threatened us with violence. As we left we could see them waiting for us outside an exit, but we knew which one so we avoided them. This situation could have turned very nasty for us; it would have been two people against ten. I wish I had a dog and horse at hand and take no prisoners. It makes me so angry to think that people can get away with needless violence watching sport. Football is the only sport where you can get away with undisciplined behaviour. Playing rugby you can now be cited by TV or videos for foul play and have the necessary punishment; football should be the same. How often do you see families going to watch a game? Never, this is because of the violence and bad language used by some of the thugs and players spoiling football.

Chapter 4

HOCKEY

My first introduction to the game was at school, the secondary school used to be an all boys school so the main sport was rugby which I did enjoy but not as much as hockey. I played for the school and played in the half back position and scored a couple of goals. From there I played in the Navy for various bases, submarines and the combined services. The combined services team is always good because it is an amalgamation of the three Forces. My only achievement whilst in the Forces was getting to a Navy Cup final as mentioned before but loosing 1–0.

When I returned to Newbury I joined the local hockey and cricket club and played for the fifth team, which was a winning team and had a few ringers in, but a fantastic team spirit. Some of the match reports written by ourselves were out of this world and the goals we scored were just sensational. For example, "Newbury continued to squander chances, which were created by the outstanding wing play of Picton".

When in the shower I was shampooing my hair after the game with the lads. I was wondering why my hair was still full of soap despite being under the shower to wash it off. I must have had half a bottle of shampoo added to my hair, which was the cleanest it had ever been. I could not open my eyes to find out who it was as my whole head was covered in a rich soapy lather. The boys were sneaking up adding shampoo to my mop of hair, a good team spirit. This was still the days of playing on grass so it was more a case of hit and hope rather than skill, which brought everyone to the same level of performance, this made games more competitive at a lower level. The ball would jump over your stick more than once, especially as the game went on and the grass got churned up.

Every year at the beginning of May, Newbury hosts a hockey festival, which is a good money-spinner for the club. Teams are invited for the weekend and come from as far a field as Holland. There is a separate girls and boys section, games are played during the day working up a thirst for the evening. All the teams meet Friday evening at the clubhouse for a drink and a chat and get thoroughly out of their heads. A bit like National Lampoons Animal House. Saturday during the day we play friendly hockey and sweat pure alcohol making room for some more. All day is a party as the hockey is not serious but the

79

drinking is. Saturday night a marquee is put up and a disco takes place inside with a live band. No one stays sober and drinking games resume so wear your oldest clothes and be prepared to drink anything from tomato sauce to warm larger out of a sock. The boys and girls are not shy. After the disco it is back to the tented village for some afters. The tented village is where most of the teams stay and is a makeshift campsite; it never sleeps. Then on Sunday it's hockey during the day with two serious games taking place between a festival's eleven and the men's and ladies first teams. Then the night time swansong at Newbury Racecourse, a sit down three-course meal with wine, which usually ends up in a food fight.

Once we were sitting down at the table having wine and being very sensible eating our main meal. The table was round which meant that everyone could see everyone. We had gone through two courses, nothing wrong so far with only one course to go, until the profiterols came out. We knew the self-destruct button was about to be pressed. One of the guys said very convincingly that we should eat our desert with no hands. Everybody agreed to this, why I don't know, maybe everybody was waiting for the chance to do something messy. A few of the guys did this thinking it was an eating competition. The term red rag to a bull springs to mind as seconds later one lad had his face pushed into the desert; this was the start of flying objects. The worst thing about profiterols is that they can be thrown and they were. Profiterols are also covered in chocolate and cream, which does stain very well on white clothes. The tables are quite close together and one of our guys missed his intended target hitting another person leaving a mark on his jacket, so now two tables were involved, then it became three and so on – you can imagine the absolute carnage. By the time the profiterols had been used up with none being eaten people were in the toilets trying to get the chocolate bullets off their clothes, but with not much success. It was a case of before and after the Lord Mayor's Show.

Every year each visiting team is invited to do a short sketch, one team made me laugh so much I was actually crying. We were all sitting down at our tables. By each table was a TV. Before the action started we were told to watch the screens but do not adjust them. The screen started off blurred and nobody paying much attention, still talking and drinking, but as the picture became clearer we could see a few wires and pullies. We were still not really paying much attention until one of the girls shouted out "A MAN'S WILLY". Yes a man's Willy was wired up and being pulled in many directions. We could not believe our eyes seeing such a beast. The girls were getting closer to the screen not believing what was in front of their eyes, the guy actually had a hook through the fleshy part of his willy and was pulling it around like a snake. What a brilliant idea I thought to myself. The guy that did this must be able to withstand serious pain. In fact the guy who performed this wonderful feet of skill was always doing crazy things involving his bodily parts, being at the same time a superb hockey player.

Another time we did the Rocky Horror Picture Show and caused a right mess. We were all cross-dressing for the occasion having borrowed various clothing from the girls. We got ready for our show going over the last moves making sure everybody knew the dance steps. The music started and we were on. We started off slowly with a few songs getting the crowd going, lots of people were standing on tables and chairs waiting for the finale. The final dance came; the Time Warp, and we had not anticipated what could go wrong when doing this well-known dance. One thing we forgot to take into account was the low ceiling. Every time a certain chorus of the Time Warp came on the ceiling tiles were getting punched and smashed. We had not planned this and the organisers who were hockey members just looked in horror. By the end of the song only a few tiles were left intact. It was a very drunken affair and the day after the dinner the club had a bill for the ceiling. I went along on the Monday to help clear up the demolition; pieces of tile and food were everywhere. It was like the Somme in World War I. I was half expecting to find someone still asleep under the debris. The worst thing was that one of the committee members for the festival was one of the Racecourse Managers – oops! Explain that to your boss.

It has always been a tradition at the Newbury Hockey Festival to run a few furlongs along the racecourse, naked or not it's up to you. Naked is more fun as you feel free but you can never find your clothes at the end as someone always takes them and hides them for ransom. To make it more interesting you can run a furlong over the sticks but it is wise to make sure that if you do go over hurdles that the meat and two veg are tucked in because the fences are made from strong sticks and rather sharp. You might get a nasty rash. I was amazed how long a furlong is, especially on two legs and not four. By the time you finish you need some nursing back to health by the many females present. This is a good spectator sport as you can see the run-in from the restaurant. There is always a side wager as to who will win the annual event, which is well supported by many spectators of the opposite sex, especially when the runners are naked.

Another year one guy managed to climb onto the sloping glass roof of the main bar area which is very high, and difficult to get to. There was a stir from the crowd and a gasp. All you could see was the outline of the guy lying on the glass. An amazing feet of acrobatics but very dangerous. I did not notice him at first until people started looking up at the roof. This was the same guy who had his willy wired up the previous year.

It is the tradition that every year at the end of the dinner people go down the escalators head first, so much so that this has become a challenge amongst the adventurous and daring. There are two escalators side by side with a small gap in between. The sides of the escalators are made of rubber so when you come to the end you will stop and not go through the glass. The people that attempt this always have two lines rubbed onto their shirts to keep forever as a souvenir of the occasion. Like anything it starts off as a game but then gets more daring as people egg each other on. But touch wood I have never seen any injuries. A few near misses where people have come off faster than expected, only to be saved by their mates catching them. This is something that I did not try myself.

On the Monday everything winds down and by the evening there is a sense of calm and the event is all over for another year. Usually the weather is always good and hot so everybody is in a playful mood and in a relaxed state. Monday morning games are played but by the afternoon no one is bothered as people have to drive back home or are recovering from the previous night. Other sports are played or invented as teams pack up their belongings. Many teams come back year after year and go home with a smile on their faces; the weekend has been so non-stop you feel at a loss after such a high.

When we tour ourselves we usually have many a story to tell. I have been to Guernsey once and Ireland twice. At Guernsey we took the girls' hockey team as well. The girls took with them on the plane a wheelchair, pink bloomers and granny clothes. We just took some girls' clothes. The girls are probably worse than the boys for horseplay and will do most things for a drink and a good night out.

During our first night on the town the girls were wheeling a wheelchair through the streets of Guernsey dressed in granny clothes with hats and brooches to match; they looked the part. You can imagine the faces of people in pubs suddenly seeing twenty grannies ordering vodka slammers from the bar and drinking them down in one. The grannies were taking it in turns to be wheeled from bar to bar. A couple of our guys who were wearing women's clothes were dancing on the tables though not in the same pub. They had the full sexy gear on, stockings, suspenders, make-up, if you were the other way they were not safe, but they could run fast, even in high heels. We watched with anticipation as one guy danced with a fan directly above his head, the fan was rotating like a helicopter blade but we did not tell him as we were waiting for him to catch the fan or use it as a prop to show us some amazing tricks. These separate events all happened before we got to the nightclub and both parties came together.

At the nightclub the girls were again in superb form but this time dressed in pink bloomers and pink silky tops. They certainly had all the boys paying them much attention, but what was under their home-made bloomers? How they were made only a few people knew. They definitely stood out in a crowd, the girls were also fined if they lost them. Don't forget about tour rules, whatever happens on tour stays on tour.

One of the playing positions to avoid is goal tender. This is where you have a cricket size ball hit at speeds of 90mph from close range coming towards you. You are expected to get in the way and save it. The person trying to score can hit the ball high or low, hard and fast. Because of this not that many players are willing to fill this position, as injuries are quite common. Being on tour we all had to choose a playing card to see who went in goal, palms were clammy and brows sweaty as no one wanted to draw the card of death. I drew the unlucky card and had my first taste of being a goaltender. I was slightly nervous. I had a few tips from the boys and they warmed me up with a few hard shots aimed at my testicles, thanks! That certainly got my eye in. A short corner can be advantageous to the attacking team, a short corner is where four defenders are behind the goal and have to rush out when the ball is pushed or hit into play from a marked spot along the dead ball line.

At a particular short corner during the game my defence stayed behind the goal on purpose allowing the attacking team time to tee the ball up and pick their spot. I was saying my prayers and cursing the guys. The shot came, I stuck my foot out and saved the on target attempt. My counterparts and the other team mobbed me as I became an instant hero and kept a clean sheet during the game. That particular game was beginner's luck and I even saved a few more attempts on goal giving me a reputation of being a future goaltender at the club.

When the event was held in Dublin, Ireland, we had a good flight across in the afternoon and arrived at the hotel containing most of the hockey teams. So we dumped our gear in our rooms and headed for the hotel bar to get the juices flowing. From that moment on there was only one way to go, and that was down. The first order was twenty-two pints of Guinness; we only had eleven players and felt thirsty. The first pint we took in turns to down in one large sip. After that it slowed down and a modest pace was set. At the bar was another team wearing a snorkel, mask and rubber gloves. We had a great time finding out what the snorkel, mask and rubber gloves were for. So as not to waste any of the Irish black velvet, the Guinness we had left when the bar closed we took to our table to accompany our solid food.

We knew we had to eat before the evening started or face the consequences; we did not want to be ill. During the meal we had a few pints left over so we played drinking games to finish off the remainder. After the meal we adjourned to the hotel bar and carried on socialising. We were not allowed to go to bed as this was one of the tour rules, to go to bed you had to be ill or have permission from the chairman. Other teams had arrived, whom we knew from the Newbury Festival, so we had a good chat. As the evening went on I was getting more and more talkative and while I was chatting to some young and pretty girls at the bar the boys did something to my laces. I did not have a clue what it was as my beer goggles were appearing. I thought that I was doing really well until both girls seemed to step back and laugh at something I was saying, but what I did not have a clue. I must admit by this time I was having trouble understanding myself, suffering from sleep deprivation.

That evening I went to bed but because of a few pints fell straight to sleep. In the morning I woke up feeling terrible, did not want to get out of bed. I had a headache, mouth like Gandhi's flip-flop and had to turn up for breakfast otherwise I would be fined, and being fined with the state I was in was not a good idea. When I was getting dressed and putting on my shoes I noticed tattered laces that had been considerably shortened. When I say shortened I mean hardly any laces left. I did not think much of this but it made me re-live some of last night's happenings. Still not being able to crack the crime I had to ask questions at the breakfast table putting them across tactfully. I kept wondering until some-one said, "How's your laces?" and told me what had happened. Apparently they had set my laces on fire while I was chatting up the girls. There were flames coming from my laces, which the girls could see and smell the smoke. The boys just stood watching my feet on fire. I must have been so engrossed on trying to score (shag) the girls that I became blinkered. I did not hear, see or smell a thing but could only admire the boys' cunning followed by searching for my laces; I now had one pair of laces between two pairs of shoes.

Another shock I had was to learn that one member of the team did stairway diving, which is a very dangerous pastime. This is his party trick and not to be copied, I'm sure the beer numbed the pain. We were walking along the corridors coming from our rooms when some stairs appeared and one of the guys decided to dive down them. I watched in amazement as the guy bounced down the carpeted stairs, thank God for that, reaching the bottom easily. He got up as if it was all in a day's work and continued walking towards the bar, unruffled and not a hair out of place. It looked like something from a spoof movie or spaghetti western. If you thought that was bad, wait until you hear the rest.

After the bars have shut in the main hotel a smaller bar opens downstairs and remains open until the last person leaves. This bar is always popular, as many people want to stay up late, having no intention of going to bed early, even though by now it is 2.30am. Evenings or should I say early hours of the morning always seem to end up taking the same pattern when fuelled by alcohol. The more you drink the more dangerous the games get; well how about this – one of the guys took a run up, dived and aimed to head-butt a metal tray, held by one of our guys, with no safety net. The metal tray was examined afterwards as a thud was heard during his circus act. He had certainly hit the tray as a dent was visible. He was a member of our team and a Welsh International hockey player. He did us proud and the death-defying stunt worked. His aim was to impress a female and score with her; I don't mean a score from the judges either. He went to bed with a female hanging of his arm.

As the tour went on, our bellies were getting larger and larger with even larger amounts of Guinness being consumed. I have always said that when in Rome do as the Romans do, the Romans being Irish Guinness drinkers. The Guinness mixture does not travel well so we had to fill up in prime Guinness drinking country, any excuse for a pint. We must have averaged fourteen pints a day, that was with food and exercise, sounds a lot but the amount was consumed over twenty-four hours. Because we were all expanding outwards we had a competition to see who had the most impressive belly towards the end of our gruelling tour; it was a close call between a few guys who were certainly up for it. My belly was growing but not up to their high standards, yet!

When at Corinthians Hockey Club, one of the top clubs in Dublin and who were hosting the tournament, we decided to take off our clothes. This is a typical tour occurrence but one guy did it in style. It was a hot day and we had just come off the hockey field. We got ourselves a pint of Guinness and sat down to enjoy the afternoon. Another team behind us were playing party games and having fun when one of our guys ran off to go behind a hill, disappearing from view. We knew something was afoot when clothes such as his shirt, shin pads, socks but nothing too outrageous are being thrown into the air leaving us to wonder about his Marks and Spencer's underwear. Then he appeared at the top of the hill with his underwear on posing before he disappeared again. Then his underwear appeared sticking to a hockey stick being displayed for all to see. The question for the gathering audience was would he appear naked. For the finale he appeared on top of the hill in front of an audience, which he loves, he appeared not quite naked, he was wearing his socks. He received a standing ovation for his efforts and did a lap of honour around the hill, still doing the full Monty before getting a pat on the back when he finally returned to the waiting public and us. At these events there are no Police around or CCTV cameras on during the day's play, just some ambulance people who are used to seeing flesh.

On a few occasions some of the lads got debagged (underwear taken off leaving them exposed), not a pretty sight, but one of the hazards of touring. One of the lads was not having this done willingly so we had to hold him down. This was done by the biggest bloke on the team who sat on his chest. This served the purpose, as the guy did not move for a while, as one of his ribs was almost, but not quite, broken. The guy who sat on him had a very good knowledge of bones diagnosed this medical condition, as he was a vet. So when on tour always take a spare pair of underpants just in case one gets torn away by accident and a doctor or vet.

I had this done once and had scars on my arse cheeks to prove it as I was dragged along the astro turf pitch. These were guys from a different team who we got on with, having a laugh joking around. We would play a trick on one of their guys so to get even they would get us back, they got me back. It was half time, I had a good half helping our team to a slender lead. Leaving the pitch for refreshments, I was being ambushed with no exit door when they started to rip my shorts to get at my undies. I put up a struggle so they decided to drag me. By now my undies were almost off exposing cheeky flesh. When they dragged me my cheeks took the brunt of the coarse carpet, now I know how Baboons feel. There was one good fallout from this behaviour besides skin and blood; it produced a good chat-up line and an icebreaker for later on in the bar.

Back in England I have also been to a few mixed tournaments, these are great fun and the weather nearly always wet so come prepared. We usually pitch tents or sleep in cars. I slept in a mate's car one evening and was dying for a poo. It was torrential rain outside so keeping dry was going to be a problem. My first attempt of relieving myself was the toilet, I found a jacket then made my way through the rain and muddy ground to the toilets, they were locked. When I got back to the car I was a drowned rat. By now the turtle's head was touching cloth (dying for a poo). My only hope was that in the car there was some paper, all good touring players come well prepared, luckily I found some toilet paper in his car. Stuffing the toilet paper under my jacket I tried to find a dry area but without any luck because it was raining. All I could find was a tree. So I had to relieve myself outside in the rain under cover of darkness and the branches. During this call of nature things were not going well as the toilet paper was getting wet, in fact everything getting wet. I thought I had not made that much of a mess under the awful conditions. When getting back to the car I had to change, there were no visible signs of a struggle, phew! When the morning came it was a different story. I did not sleep well that night so when it was first light and the clubhouse opened it was into the showers and an emergency washing of trousers, my aim had not been good. The hot showers were not working so cold water was the only option, I had to rub hard as chocolate stains are hard to wash off and that was the only pair of trousers with me, I had to wear shorts for the remainder of the tournament, even when going for a drink in town.

One particular mixed tournament was played during the Rugby World Cup, which meant the final was played during our matches. We usually have a few South Africans with us and it just so happened South Africa were in the final against the All Blacks. The matches were suspended because of the interest. The bar was packed and a great atmosphere, lots of noise amongst all sorts of nationalities. South Africa won so the South African contingent was happy, making even more noise. The bar ran out of beer as we had major celebrations so we had a donation from various drinks left on the table creating a green mixture, we named this drink a cocktail called Bok Snot, as Bok is another name for South Africans. This mixture looked horrible but tasted not too bad. When we were clearing up we found a few coins in the bottom of the jug, all sparkling and clean, hours later it dawned on us that these coins started off dirty in a real state of neglect. None of us felt well but if the mixture did that to coins think of what it's doing to our insides. Just as well I have a cast iron gut. A good remedy to stop you feeling rough is to dilute the mixture adding no alcohol, practical but not probable.

During my time with Newbury Hockey club we had a chance to see how good top professionals were at playing the game. For a couple of seasons we had Paul Barber join us, and we went up every season he played. Paul Barber won a Gold medal in the Seoul Olympics with the Great Britain team, so he had a very good C.V. He could hit a ball so hard and accurately it was frightening. I could actually remember the winning goal that he scored to be a champion. As a person he was not big-headed but down-to-earth and a friend to all of us in the club. He would bring his family down after the game to the club and stay for a while.

While playing one game for Newbury he ran into the area and hit a ball into the top corner whistling past the keeper's head missing bodies in a crowded area. He had to be very accurate not to cause serious injury. His position was defender so he had to be strong with his stick work, he could take the ball off you so easily with one hand. During training he made us work hard and his fitness level put some younger guys to shame. His training methods were very positive and direct, he would teach us new skills and by the end of a session we were glad of a rest but our results improved throughout the club, as all teams benefited. Because hockey is not a major sport he would not be recognised when walking around amongst the public.

One time he came to my flat and I had some friends around and none of them recognised an Olympic Gold medallist. Even when I have introduced them to him they were still none the wiser, none of them play or watch the beautiful game of hockey. I have played golf with him a couple of times and managed to beat him once. As you can imagine he is very competitive and a born winner.

Chapter 5

GOLF

I started playing at a very early age when staying in Scotland with my relatives. I used to enjoy the pitch and putt courses and crazy golf. Swinging the club was banned at an early age. My mother is Scottish and some relatives played golf so I was given a few old clubs to wreck the garden with. At school I played with my friends so I always had a partner.

I joined Newbury and Crookham Golf Club as a junior, which was a well-run section, supported by the members. Getting to the club was never a problem for the juniors because our dads used to drive us there and collect us at night. We used to spend all day at the Club, playing 36 holes in all sorts of conditions. I used to watch golf on TV and wondered why it was such a difficult sport. After all the ball is not moving and you have time to prepare yourself for the shot. At the time the junior section was very strong and in 1979 the club won the Thames Valley Junior Golf League without losing a match. We even won the match against the rest of the League, 7 games to 4. We had quite a few single figure handicaps in the team, my handicap was 14 and could only just make the starting line up. The handicaps were 2 ,4, 5, 10, 12, and 4 or 5 players around 14, so a very strong squad. The players who were in the 10–18 handicap section were very strong on their own and we only needed six in a team, we had strength in depth. One of the lads was playing excellent golf and could have turned pro he was that good, playing in national tournaments and beating players like Jose Maria Olazabal and Paul Way who both have played in the Ryder Cup. Olazabal is still a top golfer today. One of the junior girls, Karen Davies was very talented playing off single figures. She joined the professional tour playing for many years competing with the best.

Final Placings being:	P	W	D	L	PTS
Newbury & Crookham	6	6	0	0	12
Calcot Park	6	4	0	2	8
Reading	6	3	1	2	7
Henley	6	2	2	2	6
East Berks	6	1	2	3	4
Goring & Streetly	6	1	1	4	3
Badgemore Park	6	0	2	4	2

Thames Valley Junior Golf League Champions
From left to right David Rosier, Richard Mead, Peter Rodgers, Richard Holloway, Neil Birrell, David Picton, David Price, Kevin Dunks, Michael Roberts, Gary Roche, Ian Briggs.

I once played at Eton College golf course in a Berkshire boys open tournament, the course itself is only 9 holes but tricky and some water hazards. This was my first tournament where they announce your name on the tee. It is a nerve-racking experience, and you just want to hit a half decent shot and keep the ball in play. Referees are walking around with you during the match making sure that the rules of golf are observed at all times and you can ask for their advice at any time. On completion of the round you have your scorecards marked, with the referees present making sure there are no discrepancies.

I was on the tee after being announced, shaking in my boots and the shot I produced was one of absolute horror, I did not get the ball up in the air or very far, I only managed a duck hook (low shot not very far hooked to the right) into some reeds and tall grass and my ball was lost. This meant that what was now my third shot had to start again from the tee. My nerves were even worse now but I was determined to get the ball in play and on the fairway with no more penalty shots. I finished the round but did not come anywhere near the prizes.

I also played in a few pro-ams with my friends and had a great laugh in the process once winning a portable colour TV. This was with a very good friend of mine. Four of us went up to a course near the coast, staying overnight in a hotel.

We got to the hotel to have a few night-caps at the bar. We stayed up until the bar shut but before going to bed had some port, very nice too. We took the port up to our room; we were both sharing with each other so we did not have to be too quiet. We both slept well but not long enough. Waking up in the morning was an effort but I still had some port left in my glass so that was breakfast sorted. I felt good as I was excited and the port hit the spot putting a smile on my face. None of us played that well but my moment of class came when on a par 3 hole they had a nearest the pin competition for the amateur players. My mate the pro went first hitting his ball on the green near to the pin, I went third and nailed my 3 iron inside his. We measured it and put the distance on the marker. I might win but we were not the last group. The pro was quietly confident but I had my doubts. When the round finished and back into the clubhouse we looked at the prize winners and to my horror I had won. We had a port to celebrate.

My first ever golf triumph came as a junior when I won an eclectic competition (this is where you have a number of rounds and record the best score per hole). I scored 14 shots under the par for the course. This was keenly contested amongst the juniors as we all had a chance to win. Another rule in this kind of competition is that you must say before you play that this round is going to be counted.

While still a junior I also won a pro-am with our club pro. At the time I was hitting some form so had high hopes for our team of two. I did not tell anyone in case my confidence backfired. I can remember playing a chip shot and the pro was not going to score a point on that hole, we were playing better ball so the best score counted on that hole, in this case mine. The shot I was faced with was chipping onto a narrow green sloping down from the right, bunkers right and left. The pro was not paying much attention to my club selection as I got out my sand wedge for a lofted shot. He watched my shot as it went skyward landing softly onto the green with a very good chance of a par. He was expecting the ball to travel along the ground, as this was the safer option. He was not prepared for the shot that I produced. He stared at me not flinching a muscle; I was waiting for the repost. His voice rose mentioning the shot that he had in mind, much safer and less risk. Using the sand wedge I could have thinned the shot, taken too much ground and caught it heavy. He said it was lucky but I call it skill. I was only 3 feet from the hole.

I have always been an erratic player and never been scared to try difficult shots from impossible positions, just like Sevvy Ballesteros. One area of the game that I need to improve on is when working out percentages (making a difficult shot when the easy shot is available). I like the cavalier approach. An example of this was when playing with the club pro who was having kittens with some of my shots, but being bold I won the day.

My first ever set of clubs was bought from my headmaster for £5. He had a half set of mixed clubs and a bag. As Christmases and birthdays came and went I added to the clubs and eventually had a full set. Because golf balls have always been expensive I go golf ball hunting and at the moment have a good collection. So I have not bought a ball for years. I have been on golfing holidays to Spain, Portugal and Ireland. The best thing about playing golf abroad is decent weather so waterproofs and brollies are not needed. It is always an effort taking them off and on and putting brollies up and down. In wind brollies always have a mind of their own and tend to make you frustrated when you are trying to keep calm.

I had another winning experience in Portugal, this was my first golfing holiday and I was playing OK, but nothing outstanding. It was probably the fact that I was playing on good fast greens, no waterproofs, lovely hot sunny day in shorts and T-shirt. We played a maximum of five rounds to count for our scores. The scores would be calculated by a Stableford system (points scored on each hole e.g. par 4 hole, get a par and you score 2 points). On the final day I was starting in third position so needed a good round to win the competition. I did not start off playing to the best of my ability but, as the round went on, I improved. I improved so much that I started to hole every putt on the greens and striking the ball off the middle of the club straight down the fairway. When your game suddenly clicks into place and every aspect goes to plan it is so invigorating, you just want to keep on playing. I finished the round with a score of 41 points, which no one could match. The second and third place golfers came in with moderate scores but none to challenge the champion.

During a different trip but still in Portugal we had good weather all week, so good that we had to put loads of cream on to stop us burning. After a round people would have the T-shirt, shorts and sock tan. This looks so funny especially when sunbathing. We had our own patio so no one could see our silly suntan marks. After the round we all got ready for a sit down meal in the marina, this place was a frequent haunt for our party with superb fish dishes. Before we went out one of the guys was looking very red and had a bit too much sun, we kept an eye on him throughout the meal. After the second course he went for a walk but got as far as the middle of the floor before fainting in the restaurant. The funny thing is that he was only a short person and had small red rings around his neck, legs and forearms, most of his body covered. That was our first contender for the 'Wally of the week' prize. He was a very good single figure golfer but he never played well after the sunburn. He spent most of the time in bed under doctor's orders.

Fish is one of the main dishes in Portugal, caught fresh every morning, the different kinds of fish on the menu mouthwatering. We had a guy who when it comes to fish eats everything including the small bones and heads. I was sitting next to him in the restaurant and I could not keep my eyes of his plate being demolished. He started off with a whole fish, eyeballs, the works. Cutting away the white fish even sucking the bones dry. By the time he had completed the disassembly all that was left was the backbone of the fish with his fingers still in one piece.

In October all the boys go away abroad to play golf without the girls and we have fun and games. Some of the guys find it therapeutic, as they do not get nagged for being at the Golf Club too long and spending most of the weekend avoiding jobs around the house. We also have a few nights where we eat together as a group. We all fancied an Indian meal so we ordered various dishes. I was really hungry and one lad bet me that I could not eat a meal for two people. What he did not know is that when I am hungry I could eat for Britain. So I ordered my two portions and I must admit I love a good curry. It came in a circular dish with the rice in the middle, all the trimmings and different dishes around the outside. It was a feast and I ate it all, one of my best curries ever. I did not have a starter but had a nibble of his; this was his attempt to make me full before my main meal but I saw right through him.

We had fun going out with some of the older guys who were a bit set in their ways. We hid a guy's Toblerone chocolate bar. He had been saving this for a couple of days and was really looking forward to a bite or two after a round of golf. He did not see the funny side of this especially when he found an empty Toblerone wrapper on his bed. The guys in his apartment bought him another one after he had sulked and had done the washing up as part of his punishment for being childish.

Back on the golf course we had an incident with a buggy. For the older guys this was a great and worthwhile option as some of them were not in the best of health. Walking a long way made the old war wounds play up. One of the four balls (four people playing golf together) consisted of four retired businessmen. One of the four always had a simple approach to life; always enjoy it, with age being no barrier. He had many friends younger than himself enjoying the outdoors. With friends all around him he had his younger days back. As they were going along the fairway he would always volunteer to drive the buggy. When out of view of any onlookers the games would start. They would race each other to the ball or deliberately hide something that made the buggy difficult to start, like the keys for example, they were up to no good. A particular person in the party was playing motorised buggy dodging with his playing partners. The idea being to play chicken with the oncoming buggy coming straight at you, jumping out of the way at the last moment. Instead of missing the buggy he hit it and a large flap of skin was hanging from his arm, he carried on playing for a bit seeing the funny side of things. When the rest of us saw the arm it was hospital time. It all ended happily as he was still able to play golf after some first aid and a bandage. Can you believe four grown men playing such a dangerous game?

Some of the courses we played were championship courses especially in Portugal at Quinta De Largo and Villamoura. At Quinta and Villamoura we had time-share houses on the complex so we could see some holes from the windows. I have played the courses about five or six times and because they are so well looked after you don't mind spending the money. Playing a good course the greens are the telling point, if the greens are good more often than not the remainder of the course is good. To play golf on such courses costs anywhere between £40–£50. There is also much greenery on these courses giving them another plus point. There is nothing worse than playing a top course and the fairways are bare of grass. These courses when walking on the fairways felt spongy and springy underfoot. A course in the UK, which is a good example of this, is Woburn Abbey as the course is well manicured with plenty of green keepers.

In Ireland we played on some links championship courses such as Port Marnock in Dublin, where they played the Irish Open a few years ago. We had to sign our names in a register before starting, I signed as the Reverend Ian Paisley. This course had the best greens I have ever played on in my life. They were like Augusta, Georgia where they play the US Masters, very fast but the ball could be stroked instead of hit, which suits my style of putting. The first hole is quite daunting with an estuary running down the right hand side. There is no semi rough, just a narrow fairway and water. This was my first experience playing on a links course; I found it difficult to get to grips with the wind as on parkland or woodland courses you are protected to some degree from the elements. You had to aim so far away from the target the ball became like a boomerang except the ball never came back if the wind dropped. You would have been better off taking a putter all the way around as the wind affected the ball so much.

Another course we played was Trim Golf Club. We were invited to play here by one of the boy's uncles. The day was very bleak and not at all good for golf. If we had not been invited to play we would have had a refund because the weather was so bad. Not many golfers turned up on the tee. We reluctantly started our round in rain and the course began to get waterlogged by the third hole. If the rain carried on there was a chance of the course being shut but we played 9 holes before a siren sounded. This was the signal for all the golfers who were on the course to return to the clubhouse. Not to our amazement, the course was shut. Instead of completing the round we had a complimentary breakfast with everything on a large plate including nigger's dick (black pudding), my favourite. Needless to say I ate all mine as the open air gives you an appetite and we had not eaten due to an early tee off time. When we had almost finished the breakfast a tray of chips came out. By the time we had finished the food and enjoyed the Guinness our stomachs were solid, the hospitality of the Irish was impressive and made us feel at home.

On the same tour one of the guys made me laugh. We were playing on a different course going out in fourballs. In our group of four there were two professionals, a single figure handicap and myself. So a bit of a needle match between friends and the need to win was a driving force as money was at stake. One of the professionals who is one of my best friends had the shanks (ball goes sideways off the club at a ninety degree angle). He did this three times in a row and actually went around the green. His face was getting more and more annoyed and redder by the second. We gave him so much friendly banter he hated us for days afterwards; the best thing was he was not my playing partner. In golf having the shanks is the worst affliction you can have. It shatters your confidence when chipping and that part of the game is so important. To all you non-golfers it is like climbing a mountain having a fear of heights, you have to get over it somehow but it won't go away.

I have played many courses around the world but Woburn Golf Club in Southern England is one of the prettiest. I got the chance to play there when one of my relatives invited me up. On television I had seen a few European tour events played there involving top players. I was eager to have a bash at the course trying to reproduce the quality of my mentors. I definitely had a bash but played to nowhere near my potential. I was wayward of the tee, playing shots from impossible positions in the trees. As soon as a ball hit the tree it would go about 2 yards straight down into thick rough. But the good thing was that you could relate positions on the different holes to shots that the pros were faced with. I played different shots trying to emulate them and execute the same shot. They had made it look simple with a silky touch and attacking the course with amazing results, easier said than done.

For scenery St Enodoc Golf Club in Cornwall is one of the best and takes some beating. Some of the holes are near to the cliffs and actually scare you because of a shear drop down to the sea but on a clear day you can appreciate the view and the contrast in colours around the course. One particular hole is just awesome. You stand on the tee looking down onto a dogleg (a bend on a hole) par 5. The hole is completely open, giving no protection from the wind. Out of bounds is the sea, cliffs and beach, which is situated about 10 yards off the fairway. Luckily for us on that day the wind was not too strong and I managed a 6 on my scorecard. Another hole which I will never forget is a par 3 with a raised green (green which is raised above ground level), you hit the ball over a hand-made stone wall and a few grazing animals, you get the feeling that you really are in the countryside

The great thing I find about playing golf is that every course is totally different and a challenge, if things go wrong there is only one person to blame and that's you. It's also a great opportunity to see the natural beauty of the countryside and visit different places and countries around the world. You also meet many business people making a few deals or contracts here and there. By joining a golf club, if you find that you need a favour, no matter how big or small it will be done.

A friend who plays at Sandford Springs near Basingstoke invited me to a society day; this is a local course to me as I live in Newbury. This course has three 9-hole courses so you never know which two will be chosen. We played two rounds of singles golf with lunch and dinner provided. We used a Stableford system of points scoring. Before we went out coffee and bacon butties were provided, this was great as the day started off not looking promising when looking towards the heavens. In the morning my partner and I were in contention for the prizes playing average golf but in the afternoon we burnt up the course and played better than our handicaps suggested. This is known in the golfing trade as a bandit (playing much better then your handicap suggests). We made a clean sweep of the prizes. Being a visitor meant that I could not collect the first prize, which went to my friend but I won the best guest competition winning some golf balls. So it was a good day for us as we won both competitions. We also made one important discovery, how fantastically tasty Guinness and a Mars Bar is when taken together. That could have made all the difference as we had this for lunch as well as a buffet snack.

The Hockey Club had a society day at Haddon Hill Golf Club as quite a few members played golf as well as hockey. The course is near to Didcot power station. The morning was 9 holes, just to get us warmed up for the main event later on. In the afternoon round our first tee shots had to be done with a hockey stick to make things interesting. This is again difficult but looks easy. Out of twenty-five blokes not even half made it past the ladies' tee; if you did not make it past the ladies tea there was a fine, which was to play a hole with your zip undone and dick out. This is done on a hole where there are no ladies present. The hole is also selected by the length and location, when saying length, length of the hole.

In Newbury there only used to be one golf course for many years but over the last ten years more and more have sprung up. There has been a new 18-hole course designed in the centre of Newbury Racecourse with a driving range attached. I used to work at the range during its early stages giving me time to practise and my golf was improving slightly. We used to try many different things like with a driving club hitting a ball of a tee peg on your knees using different clubs to see who could hit the ball the furthest; good clean fun. To pick up the golf balls we had a small buggy with nets around it as protection for the driver. You could guarantee that when you got close in, near to the golfers, someone would aim for the buggy – as I did when I was practising. You would see white flashes whizzing past your driver's seat or hear a loud thud; both were scary. This was a perfect job to improve your golf, if this facility was available when I was a junior I could have played off a single figure handicap not just scrapping around in the teens.

For a time I worked as an Assistant Secretary at Sonning Golf Club in Reading. A friend of mine offered me the job and I accepted the post after an interview with the committee. This was my first look at things behind the scenes. I love golf so thought that running the competition side of things would not be difficult as I had knowledge of golf and how systems worked. I also helped with the members' section and daily running of the Club. The girl who I was taking over from had been working there a number of years so knew the procedures well; I had a lot to learn. I lived at the Club for a while as it had rooms for the employees so made friends with the staff. As a result I was invited to private functions with Reading Football Club. Our catering manager was a good friend with the Reading manager and team. He invited them up frequently for food, drink and a chat. I played golf on my days off as it was free to play, perks of the job. If the weather was nice that was a bonus. I got on with most of the members playing in some weekend competitions. I was always the first out as I had to collect the scorecards making sure that they had all been filled in and signed by a marker (the golfer's playing partner).

On one occasion there was a big function at Reading Football Club after the new Madjesky stadium had been built. One of the staff could not go so I went in their place being given a free ticket, which I was very excited about. This came as a complete shock to me having little time after work to get ready. One of the girls drove there but not back, there would be free flowing wine all night. We parked the car and went swiftly into the large open-plan foyer, the girls did not want to get their hair in a mess. A smartly dressed person was waiting to take our tickets. Looking around everything sparkled, having that fresh new sense of expectation. When you get inside the lounge area there is a big window which overlooks the pitch. The floodlights were on, making the stadium look out of this world. The view was panoramic with nothing in the way to obscure your pleasure. The guests were celebrities of TV and sport, some of whom I recognised. This function was in support of cancer research and when we sat down to dinner we had waiter service and a three-course meal. Afterwards we had a bit of an auction bidding for various prizes. The bidding was way out of my league, starting off at hundreds of pounds carrying on to thousands. To be fair though the prizes were a chance of a lifetime costing lots of money. I had to sit on my hands; on my measly wage I could not afford to bid. I just took in all what was going on enjoying the free meal and very tasty free unlimited wine. After the expensive bidding had ceased time to let loose and dance, shaking down the hospitality. They then had live bands playing, the main band being the Bootleg Beatles whom I had seen before. Everything about the occasion was done to impress, I knew that to get the Bootleg Beatles took some substantial cash. So we danced the night away and got a taxi home into the sunrise.

I did get well looked after by the Sonning Golf Club catering and functions staff being invited to many functions. Being an Assistant Secretary has its down side as well; you have to be careful what you say and how you say it, some members take offence to discipline and try to manipulate you and don't take no for an answer. For example when running a Winter Stableford competition playing from tee of the day one card had not been signed. When playing in a competition all cards must be signed by the opposite team. It happened that one card had not been signed and I was reported to the Secretary for not checking that all cards were correctly completed. That person happened to be the Men's Captain who was always interfering, we never saw eye to eye. The Captain was in the wrong and was told so by the Secretary. The unsigned card did not count towards adjusting the golfer's handicap because when starting the competition the tee of the day was used. Therefore the competition did not count towards handicap adjustment. Also the golfer's position in the competition was not challenging for any honours.

They also had a snooker table at the club and when I was invited by the members I took part in a game. Again I don't think this went down well with some members. I lasted six months there before deciding to leave the institution. I did get on well with all the staff socially and made some good friends and working relationships but the important members have the final word.

Another victory at golf came at my home club, Newbury and Crookham. The Newbury and Crookham Bogey is the oldest competition at the club with a solid silver cup to be kept for a year. The competition is played in a medal format where every shot counts. I had a reputation of being a bandit, this is where you have a handicap that does not reflect your ability, and your handicap should be lower. The thing was that I could not produce the goods when it mattered in competition, but this time everything went according to plan and I finished my round playing to a handicap of 7 when it was 15, quite a difference. My name is on a smart large wooden board in the clubhouse, displayed forever. I just had one of those rounds where every part of my game came together at the same time, playing like god.

The same year I came equal first in a major competition at my home club but lost in a play off. I was absolutely gutted, I hate losing at the best of times but I played so badly that I did not do myself justice. On the day of the competition I can remember coming up the last hole having a short iron into the green and pulling my shot left into a greenside bunker. From there I took 4 shots to get down making my total for the hole 7. When I heard there was a tie for first place I could not believe how stupid I had been on the last hole. To this day that still sticks in my mind because with one shot less I would have won my second major competition that year.

During those days I never had a matching set of clubs, my first ever set was when at Sonning Golf Club. I thought of treating myself and had the professional measure me up for a set. He recommended various sets and told me to try a few out. The clubs that I had been playing with were all wrong, grips too small, clubs too short, shafts not stiff enough, the list was endless. I have now a set of Wilson Fat Shafts and I swear by them.

Quite a lot of my golf friends are professionals and I went to the Ryder Cup one year. One of my friends had a spare ticket so I jumped at the chance; to be there is definitely better than watching it on TV. The atmosphere is electric and every time a roar is heard people on the course are wondering has Europe won or lost a hole. For all you uneducated non-golfers the Ryder Cup is a competition between the European golf tour and the American golf tour played every four years. To watch the best golfers in the world competing is a joy, just to see how they can move a ball in the air or play shots from impossible lies and end up a few yards from the pin. I have played a few championship courses myself having to manufacture little chip shots around the greens, most of the time not to the same outcome. Some places where the ball lies to rest are complicated and demand your full attention to produce the required result. The pros make these shots look easy but they practise them for hours. But saying that if you had the talent and played every day with a coach you would probably be able to play much better.

Golf should be such an easy game as the ball is stationary when you strike it; surely a moving target is harder. There are many factors that come into play when hitting a ball correctly. One such factor is a repetitive swing, to achieve this you need to practise the correct motions very hard and not allow bad habits to creep in. To hit the ball straight down the fairway every time you play on a course is the end result of many hours of hitting balls the correct way. If you have a bad shot it is the end product of a bad swing.

I used to be a very keen junior golfer and play in all weathers but now only play if it is dry and sunny. As golfers know playing in the wet and wind is a real pain, as you have to take waterproofs on and off, the grips get all wet through and you cannot hold the club. It has been known for golfers to see the club flying out of their hands after they have hit the shot because they have no grip. I was playing with a friend in similar conditions when he teed off finishing his swing with just a grip left in his hand. The rest of the club was following the ball down the fairway. His face was a picture of surprise and horror as he had a perfect finish to his swing before realising what had happened. We both laughed, taking us ages to play the hole and retrieve his broken club.

Chapter 6

SKIING

My first ever experience of skiing was in Andorra with a large number of mates! One of my friends organised ski trips and invited me along. I knew most of the group from either playing sport or down the pub and I was not the only first time skier in the party. Before we embarked on the trip we had various newsletters sent to us giving regular updates on the amount of snow that had fallen. All of this was above my head; to me snow was snow. It was my intention to gradually learn skiing on the mountain under expert tuition.

We were leaving from Newbury early in the morning so we had a get-together in the pub before we left to discuss the finer points. If we wanted we could buy matching sweatshirts and T-shirts emblazoned with the slogan Piste Head Posse. This was to look good and stand out on the slopes, so I did purchase the goodies on offer. We hopped onto the coach wearing our matching sweatshirts making us part of the Piste Head team. The journey seemed to take forever, having to get on a coach, plane and coach, but it was worth it when we got there. We got to the airport in good time heading straight for the refreshments. At the airport we stood out in a crowd, a large group wearing loud sweat tops. The plane journey was only a few hours but after that was the hard slog to our resort. Along the way and going up the mountain we did not see too much snow until near the top but there was enough to begin skiing on. Some of the lads had their own skis and boots; I was going to hire mine, don't forget I was a total novice so might not adapt to it. The snow when we got there was average for skiing but the weather forecast for the week was sunny with little chance of snow. That meant that to get good snow you had to go higher up, in other words the higher you go the harder you fall. We checked into our rooms and made ourselves comfortable before getting our skiing equipment. When getting measured for skis the taller you are the longer the skis, which means the faster you go. Being 6 foot 2 inches I had long skis, don't forget first time ever on snow in skis and boots going fast down a hill, I can feel a broken leg coming on.

Finding boots was fun as I have big feet, size 12, and people around France and Spain generally have smaller feet. No shop had a pair big enough so they had to get some sent from the next resort in a special box. Then I had poles, what do you do with these? Carrying all this gear back to our digs was good fitness training and took hours; mind you we did stop at a few watering holes on the way. When we eventually arrived back we dumped our gear in the room.

With all the equipment needed for skiing, our room was lacking space. Space being the key to sleeping arrangements and an extra person in our room, it was like trying to fit a square peg in a round hole so someone had to sleep on a mattress on the floor – that was me. A good thing was that the accommodation was not far from the slopes.

In the morning we all awoke, some easier than others, definitely not looking our best. The first timers or beginners had a ski school meeting at the bottom of the mountain at 9am. I did not know what to expect, having not had the best preparation, too many fizzy drinks and lack of sleep. In our room was another guy having lessons, at least I would have a friendly face to laugh at for the gruelling day ahead. Once up and semi-conscious we had to get dressed, it seemed as though we were about to embark on a polar expedition. Trying to walk in ski boots on different terrain, carrying skis and poles ending up at our meeting point was draining on our energy supplies, our sugar levels zapped. The first task was to stand up and stop. This took me the first part of the lesson. The button lift I found really hard to negotiate, the instructor told us and demonstrated how to safely use this funny shaped bit of kit. I tried very hard to overcome this torture but my legs would not work resulting in a large bruise on my bum following several falls. I always seemed to fall on the same side, finding solid ground. As the week went on I did improve having had one or two scary moments.

On the nursery slope, nursery because it is a tiddly widdly slope on a slight decline, I managed to hit a shed. This was midway through my lessons, I still did not fully understand how to stop or slow down. I was heading straight for this abandoned shed, I had a total panic attack and memory loss and could not at any point remember how to stop. There was a bank of snow before the shed, which I hit and this slowed me down until I disappeared into a gully. I had to be rescued by the instructor who pulled me up onto my skis. That was no use to man or beast as I found my skies on some wooden boarding surrounding the shed. I tried to walk out onto the snow but fell down again, I was getting so frustrated and wound up that I took my skis off slamming them down on the snow. After I had stood up and dusted myself down I turned around and the others were having a good old chuckle. Then, in the evening, news had got back of my adventure so I was the topic of conversation. The first person in the group to hit the only shed on the mountain that was off piste.

On another occasion I was skiing down the first main run and lost control, heading towards a metal cable car stanchion. What happened next was a miracle – I suddenly had to do two quick turns in a row avoiding certain death. I managed to gain control, do two parallel turns and stop behind the stanchion which gave me the encouragement to keep going. When I opened my eyes and saw what I had done I thought about writing to Ski Sunday; it looked impressive to the watching public as it happened directly below the ski lift. I listened for applause but not a hint. To do that in five days I thought was impressive.

Because of the weather being so hot there were a few red faces in the evening. One particular lad was so red you could warm a kebab on his head and face; mind you he was not the only one to look like a baboon's arse.

Then of course there was the après ski. In all the resorts you always find one popular bar that is used for this purpose. This bar gets packed with skiers from all over the world with a brilliant atmosphere. I must say after one week of skiing and après ski you sleep for a whole day when you return home. When I go skiing I try and do everything, ski all-day and party all night as do the others, so we never stop until we are on the plane going home. Our room had run out of beer and wine, so to stop us from dehydrating we went shopping and bought almost a trolley full of booze. We forgot to count the cost as we raided the shelves, hoping we had enough money between us. We got to the counter and we had exactly £27.85 in our pockets. The bill came to £27.85; how lucky can you get! When we got back we replenished the fridge and had a party that night before going out to play. The fridge took a hammering because we had to stock up again the following day.

The parties we had before going out into town were excellent and saved us money because sometimes we did not go out but stayed partying for hours, playing card games and drinking games. One of the girls one night actually fell asleep so we put her to bed. She had been joining in the fun playing most of the games getting more and more inebriated so it was not a surprise when her eyelids finally shut.

When I came back from Andorra I was black and blue with bruises, having fallen over that many times. Because the snow was melting and the weather at night still cold, the nursery slopes were becoming icy so when you fell it was a hard landing. The biggest and most impressive bruise was the size of a football and all colours of the rainbow.

My next adventure on the slopes was with most of the lads from Newbury Rugby Club; this was in Solden, Austria. I had a cold before we went so my parents had given me some glycerine and honey medicine. A friend of mine also had a cold so we started off by drowning it with water. When this had run out the only thing left was the medicine. We finished the bottle between us and never even had a sniff of a cold again; from that moment on we became the best of friends. The coach trip passed really quickly as we were talking so much and laughing at anything that happened, especially our instant cold remedy. When we arrived at the resort there was plenty of snow and by this time I had become an intermediate skier, which meant that I could go higher up the mountain where the snow is more plentiful. We got up late this particular morning and most of the people had gone skiing so we decided to have a quiet day. We went up the mountain doing a bit of skiing ourselves looking for the others. We could not find them but by this time we had been to two or three bars, having a drink in each. So we decided to have a bar crawl on the mountain working our way down to the bottom. We would see a bar and ski down to it, after a few drinks your skiing improved because you were so relaxed, you will also be surprised how many bars there are on a mountain. In the bars females tend to sunbathe, sitting outside lapping up the conditions. You see some lovely sights in the snowy regions.

We met up with the others eventually when it was time for a shower and food. Going out that night we had loads of gossip to talk about, as we had not seen each other for the whole day. We had to discuss the skiing and major wipe-outs (falls). During this session in the bar we had punishments and awards to give out, this would be voted for by the team, to do this we needed to set up a courtroom situation. If you were found guilty by the kangaroo court (court made up of friends) you would be punished. This meant doing something daring or unusual in the company of others. Your outcome or punishment being decided by the court. Things like standing on your head while singing a song or walking around the bar with your trousers down. I was up for a court hearing; my mate had dropped me in trouble for falling over while stationary in slow motion. My punishment was to climb a Christmas tree; not a harsh punishment so I did this with ease.

Also on this trip I decided to buy myself some ski boots. I had been told that the most important thing to get were boots that fitted comfortably, I hunted high and low for a pair and eventually found some, size 12 and big; I didn't need skis with those boots. This also meant that when skiing again I did not have to worry about waiting for hired gear so could start skiing straight away wasting no time if the snow was good.

We went skiing again the following year but in a different resort. Before the

Good snow

trip started we all had new sweatshirts and T-shirts given to us. The name this year was going to be TMIY (take me I'm yours). We were all ready, willing and able, even the girls. At the start of this trip with almost the same group of people as before, we again met in the pub but this time very early in the morning and helped ourselves to bacon butties and a hot drink before setting off on the coach. The journey was fab and we arrived in the resort when it was dark. We had to wait until the next morning to ski. But before we went to bed we treated ourselves to a nightcap, just the one, this time I mean just the one. This other lad and I decided to get up early and have some good snow before the crowd spoilt the piste. We were on almost the first lift up to the top but as we got higher up the mountain the fog started to come down and visibility was not good. You could see but not that far in front so we decided to go anyway because the chances were that the runs would be clear. However the conditions got worse and the fog closed in, the only thing to do was to ski down the mountain hoping that the visibility improved. I followed my mate for a while until he disappeared; he was there one minute and gone the next. It was like something out of a cartoon. All I could hear was his rustling and laughing; he had taken a wrong turn and missed the piste completely. By now visibility had got worse and a white-out (when everything around you is the same colour and your eyes have no definition) was taking place. The trouble with a white-out is that you cannot see what turns or bumps are coming up; it's like skiing blind. We found each other in the end and went for a coffee until visibility improved. In the cosy bar I ordered the coffee talking to a lovely girl, trying to put the charm on. This went wrong when she handed me the coffee in a cup and saucer. I took the saucer in one hand, my hand shook violently, a tsunami in the cup. I quickly put the saucer down – how could I control this? I tried for a second time, trying to be relaxed, but it was like struggling against a gale force wind with gusts up to 120mph. By now my mate was getting thirsty but had pleasure in watching me struggle. One thing for it, two hands, one saucer and concentrate moving slowly to our seats, this worked as only a mild swell appeared, hands trembling. My mate said having a coffee with loads of sugar was just what the doctor ordered, we both had the shakes due to the fact that we had not much sleep and our sugar levels needed topping up.

We met the others for lunch and finished early in the afternoon to have some sleep, all trained athletes need sleep. I improved my skiing greatly and by the end of the trip I was ready for another challenge and did not want to go home. On the last night a mate and I were the only ones with cash left so we decided to go on a bender (drinking all night). We managed a fair few pubs ending up in this nightclub and we were the last to leave. While they were clearing up we slid a bottle across the bar and into the bin, a good shot helping them out. We were asked to leave by the Australian bar staff and my mate said no. He told them that we were leaving in about four hours time on a coach, could we stay for a few more drinks, please. They had a change of heart and said yes but when the staff go you go, that was fine by us.

On the way home to the hotel we saw a poster of a stunning girl which was half ripped, the bit that was nearly hanging off was her bottom half so we took this to show the boys, she did have a stunning pair of legs. Also while walking back we passed a garage with some big flags flying outside. We decided they would look good as a duvet or bed cover, so we pulled one down being careful not to alert the police. Fairly easy process as the garage was shut and it was dark. We took the poster and flag all the way home as souvenirs. We got back to the hotel just in time to pack and catch the others on the coach. I do not recall most of the journey back, as I was so tired and took any chance to sleep. I spent most of the journey horizontal.

My next holiday was at Le Plagne in France, one of the best areas in the world for skiing connecting most of the French Alps. This was brilliant with so much snow you could ski anywhere on the mountain. I had been skiing already that year so I would not have to start learning again which meant that my skiing would improve and I could try more runs and go higher than before up the mountain. The people who I was with this time were not drinkers so I would be sober and able to have early nights. We stayed in a chalet with Blue who was our host along with another lad and a girl. They were good fun and the food was excellent. Blue and the girl were from New Zealand so we had something in common, rugby. He even showed us how to do the Haka, a famous traditional Maori dance performed by the All Blacks before a game of rugby. He took us skiing and entertained us the whole week with his wit and Kiwi sense of humour. They awarded the guests prizes for the week and I had a prize for the best wipe-out (fall). I was coming down a narrow tree-lined run, not very fast, when my skis stuck in something but I carried on and did a full stretch dive ending up in front of them leaving my skis behind me. I was at the back of the group, they had all stopped and turned around as I arrived literally at their ski boots. They gave me 10 points for style. I had a sore chest, good job I was not a female.

While in Le Plagne we spent a day in Val D'Isere and Tignes famous for the Olympic games and World Cups. I had seen the resort on TV and always wanted to ski it. I went with three really good skiers – three instructors and an experienced skier, and then there was me. I was determined to ski with them as much as possible especially doing the Olympic and World Cup downhill runs. Until you actually do them you cannot appreciate the steepness of the slope or quality of skiing the professionals have. When they fly through the air they cover a lot of distance in a short space of time. We were at the top of a run and the other three wanted to try a few difficult slopes so we parted company. They went one way and I went the other arranging to meet up at the bottom. The way they told me to go was steep and a mogul (bumps) field, I hate mogul fields at the best of times. It must have taken me ages to get down because the moguls were like small hills or so they seemed, bigger than anything I had tackled before. I was more concerned about my limbs staying together than hurrying down to meet the others. By the time I met the others they had been down the mountain and up again. No matter, I was happy to be alive.

One thing I do enjoy about skiing is when you have finished for the day you can sit in a log cabin up the mountain with an open fire and have a drink. Doing this you must make sure that you give yourself some light to see outside before you leave the warmth of the cabin, as you have to still complete the run to the bottom of the slope. When you eventually arrive back at the chalet, food and hot drinks are laid on, coffee and cake. It was very sociable being entertained by the chalet staff and telling Blue where we had been up the mountain. He knew the mountain like the back of his hand so could tell us where to go tomorrow for some good snow for everyone to enjoy.

With skiing you are bound to have some injuries and I had two, both my fault. The first was when I was learning to use a button lift. When coming up to the top of the hill I let go too soon and started to go backwards, at the time not wearing any gloves because I was being lazy and it was a long walk back to the hotel to collect them. I had let go on the upslope and as you know you cannot ski uphill so I fell backwards onto the button lift track rather than to the side. The next person behind me, who was also a beginner, went over my hands with his skis. All I could see was lots of blood over my hand so I put my hand in the snow to numb the pain and stop the bleeding. The snow was getting red and the instructor came back with the first aid team. I was then given a piggyback down the mountain by an instructor, who must have been strong as I weighed about 13 stone, carrying me into the first aid station. Once the staff saw the blood I saw the doctor straight away and he stitched me up, put some bandages around my fingers and sent me on my way. When he was stitching me up I could not look as I saw the massive fishhook he was using and pulling my skin all over the place without any aesthetic. I was in a lot of pain by this point so a bit more would not make any difference. He did a very good job because you can hardly see the join now. All I was worried about was could I ski again? The doctor said yes but be careful, try not to fall over and break the stitches. He had put the bandages around my fingers in such a way that I could put a glove on and hold a ski pole. I went back to see the troops, had a vodka pain killer and carried on partying and skiing all week.

My next injury was in the resort of Val Gardina but this time I was not allowed to ski again during the trip. Four of us went together and stayed in a small lodge being hosted by three girls and one boy. We had been skiing for about a day and a half and done a fair amount of piste bashing when we decided to take a short cut. We had been down black runs and the Olympic run. This was a very short piece of snow and should have posed no problem. The run passed through a small piece of snow with rock either side, sounds so easy. I managed to miss the snow and hit a rock with my hand; my friends said that I dived for the rock ending up both hands around it cuddling it like a pillow. I doubt this very much as the pillows I have are soft. Getting up carefully I noticed that my hand was painful but could slightly move it. I thought just a bruise so carried on skiing but found it hard to grip anything especially when going up on a button lift. At the time I did not realise that my hand was broken. When we stopped at a restaurant near the end of the day situated by the gondola (cable car) I took my glove off and a large lump appeared over my knuckle. I realised that I could not move my little finger without being in a lot of pain. The good thing was I managed to do a whole day's skiing. I went back down to see the doctor at the first aid centre, by now knowing the procedure.

While I was in the waiting room a lady was brought in on a stretcher and put into a room with first aid workers around her. You could tell by the noise that she was in distress and not very comfortable. The door was left slightly open so I could see what was happening and hear what was being said. She had a broken hip and they were deciding if it was worth putting it back in place there and then. As the girl was in pain anyway they decided to go ahead with the plan. All I can remember is hearing this almighty scream and then silence; it must have worked because by the end of the week she was walking on crutches.

I went in to see the doctor and he X-rayed my hand showing a clean break, no complications. Just then my mate came in and could see the results displayed on the screen. My mate was a trained first aider and had himself seen the doctor on skiing trips. The doctor, who was a local lad and could speak English, used him as a decoy to distract me while he put my bone back in place, I was determined not swear although it did hurt, I could feel the bone being moved around. When the doctor finished I looked at my mate and went OUCH. The doctor then took another X-ray to show that the bone was perfectly back in its original position. The next step was a cast on my hand to keep the bone in place so no more skiing. I asked if the cast could be set in a grip, just right for a ski pole to fit into; not possible. I had to spend the rest of the holiday with the chalet staff who took me shopping and topless sunbathing, I did not mind going topless with a stunning view of the mountain peaks, these ones not covered in snow. This was the first time that I had any fingers broken so some things were a nuisance, like for example having a shower. I had to keep the cast dry so I had my hand stuck up out of the shower in a plastic bag. Eating was fun, as I had to get the staff to cut up meat for me or ask one of the boys. I didn't think asking one of the boys was a good idea in case they tried to feed me as well. The one good thing was that I am right handed and it was my left hand that was damaged. The right hand is used for one very important and skilful manoeuvre, wiping your arse after an explosion. To find out how difficult this is have a go yourself with your other hand, I bet it is not 100% successful.

One of my friends got really jealous when he came home early from skiing on purpose to find me sunbathing with the girls on the patio displaying their fine assets. His eyes lit up seeing this wonder of nature but when the girls spotted him looking they covered themselves up; he was disappointed but I told him all about tit (joke). He was after one of the girls and so was I. One night we met each other about 4am on the stairs waiting for the girl to come home from the bar. We had to toss a coin in the end to see who was going to bed alone. I went to bed leaving him to his tricks. I was not bothered, as I would be seeing her and the girls tomorrow whatever happened, covered up or not.

Sharing the apartment was another couple who joined in with the fun and games; he was an airline pilot and just as daft as us. In the evening we played cards and games after tea. One of the games was called 'hand knock' and very funny as I was wearing a cast. The idea of the game was to follow each other's knock around the table using your hands. Every time I had to knock my cast hit the table so hard that it sent things flying around people's heads.

After a night out my mate left early to go back to the chalet to see if he could have his wicked way with this particular girl. The girl was very pleasant and by now had become a friend of mine. I arrived later on only to find my mate on the floor half naked with this girl, I was a bit surprised as he had a wife back home but was still into female company. I had turned on the light only seeing two hands not belonging to the same people. He quickly said turn the light out and shut the door. You can guess the rest as he was very reluctant to leave her and denied all knowledge of a shag. The others and I knew the score; he was the sort of guy who would never look a gift horse in the mouth.

When you have finished skiing on the piste and you get to your hotel feeling tired, never sleep on the sofa in the lounge by reception when you are with twenty-nine other people; someone will do something, and they did. What we did was to paint a guy's face with ladies' make-up and left him there for all the other guests to marvel at the work of art. Imagine the shock when he looked in the mirror – he had lipstick, mascara, eyeliner and lots of different bright colours. We also told the reception staff not to tell him when he woke up, he was asleep for quite a while and pictures were taken as evidence for the Kangaroo court later on in the week. By the time he woke up his face was just a mess as the make-up started to itch after one hour.

One time I was sharing with three other boys, I knew the lads well and often socialised with them back home. It was not a nice day outside but raining so skiing was off the agenda. One lad went for a poo but forgot to flush as the other lad was waiting. The other lad went dropping his log, when he had finished commenting on the masterpiece that was being sculpted. We all had a look at the shape of the brown clay and decided not to waste it but increase the quantity, we had a poo stack in the making. By now three people had produced and not flushed, it's a smelly affair. Not to be tried if you are not good friends or you want to marry someone. But we were young lads and wanted to bond and cement our relationship. I was the last person in, so now was the time for the finishing touches. I gave the lads one last chance to see the finished work, this was modern art at its most creative, next masterpiece could be going into the Tate gallery. A big drawback was that by now the first thing you noticed was the odour clearing your nostrils. You are probably thinking how rude but we did flush afterwards so as not give the cleaners a heart attack.

If you want to go skiing, the French Alps to me are the best, so much skiing to be done and runs to suite all abilities. I went with some people from Newbury who worked for Vodaphone under the name of W.I.M.P.S. 99, myself and three others went by car all the way crossing on the ferry, to get to the resort of La Tania. We met at the house of one of the guys. He was a manager at Vodaphone and had everything you could wish for – outdoor pool, tennis court, snooker table. The best thing was in his double garage – a jet ski, water ski's, golf clubs and lots more. I was definitely working for the wrong company. We left Newbury early in the morning taking it in turns to drive. I did not take a turn because I cannot drive, and we arrived at the resort about twenty-two hours later. As we were going through the various resorts we saw snow at ground level so going higher the snow would be tremendous with warnings of avalanches. They had a record-breaking snowfall just before we arrived. I could not wait to get my skis on and attack the pistes. From our chalet you could ski to the slopes. The slopes were part of the three valleys – Meribel, Courchevel and Val-Thorens going as high as 3266 metres. This area is the biggest expanse of resorts in the world, the pistes connect the resorts so you can ski somewhere different all week. There are more ski runs here than anywhere in the world. We skied off piste, or tried to in my case; with the snow being so deep if you fell you had a soft landing. You could literally ski anywhere on the mountain. All this skiing built up an appetite.

One night we were left alone but the chalet staff did say that we could help ourselves to what was in the fridge. We had the midnight munchies after messing about on the slopes on our bottoms using tyres and a metal tray. We had good fun doing this, reaching some incredible speeds before bailing out onto soft snow. So when we came in we had some food, more food than we should and drank most of the wine available. Red wine, so a healthy tonic.

The same night one of the guys who was a Vodaphone manager phoned the 24-hour call centre to see if a problem on his mobile phone could be rectified. There was no answer and when he did get through they could not help him. This was about 5 in the morning so by now he was getting more and more frustrated trying to work his new model mobile phone. He had finally had enough and he did not like his phone at all so he smashed it with a block of wood. He even put it in a bag and smashed that making sure that it would never work again. I was shocked as it was a new phone and very expensive. The model was only just out in the shops being miniature size but he could pick a newer model up when he got back to work. The section he was in dealt with customer care and complaints, I bet he did not complain to his boss when he went back with a brand new phone in little bits in a plastic bag.

On a different trip I was on my way to Italy again on a second visit, it was to the Dolomites at a resort called Tonale. The snow there was not very good so we decided to go to a different resort for the day where the snow was good at a high level. Where this resort was I have not got a clue. We got a coach to take us and bring us back. We stopped for coffee and a quick chat. This was to tell us the arrangements and times for getting back. It was now time to make our way onto the cable car, joking about somebody getting lost and being left behind. We had all been skiing before so this was highly unlikely. We arranged to meet at a restaurant on the mountain for lunch. After a good morning's skiing and lunch I left one group of people and found another one. I did this all afternoon so as to do as many runs as possible. When it was starting to get past mid afternoon I started to head back to the coach but took a wrong turning ending up on the other side of the mountain. I did not have a map with me so I was going by memory. The trouble was after a while most runs seem the same and had no idea of where the runs ended up. I got lost and found my way back to a resort, but not our resort. In the meantime the others were waiting, hoping I would appear soon. They waited for a while until they could not wait any longer as the driver had to return the coach to the depot by a certain time. I was missing.

When they got back to the hotel and I was not there they were about to phone mountain search and rescue when I phoned and told them the resort I was at. Luckily enough I had the address of my hotel on me. The resort where I ended up was over an hour's drive from the hotel. I had done so much skiing that day that when I took my boots off my feet were steaming. I had to be picked up by the holiday rep and a friend, managing to keep myself occupied by finding a bar and a warm drink. I did not have much money on me not expecting to be in this predicament. Standing outside alone in a ski resort seeing no familiar faces is bleak. I did not want to stray too far from the spot I was in as I knew where I was and familiar with my surroundings. When the rep and my mate arrived I was so glad, I had last seen my friends about seven hours earlier

When I arrived back at the hotel the boys and girls were eating so I had a standing ovation when I walked in. They gave me a silly hat to wear all the time for twenty-four hours because I had won the Dick Of The Day award. This was voted upon by the group and given to the person who had done something stupid during the day. I had won that hands down. On the slopes you must be loud in what you wear to be seen for safety reasons but there is also the posing factor. My kit has always been very colourful and many different colours not matching. But with all the colours I had on display I still got lost, so I was guilty as charged.

Other places I have visited are Solden in Austria and Sauze in Italy. Some of the views are so spectacular, taking you breath away. One time we were in the cable car going through the low clouds. Below the clouds was not an appetising day for the slopes but we were only here for a week so every second counted to ski till you dropped. When we got above the clouds it was a different world, lovely blue sky, mountain peaks covered with snow dotted around the skyline, I wish I had my camera. Coming down the mountain was tricky because we had to ski through the clouds, a strange sensation. It was like going from one world to another.

With skiing, the conditions can vary so much. In a particular resort you could not ski all the way down to the bottom because the conditions were dangerous. Rocks were being exposed due to the lack of snow. It was also freezing in the shade but not too bad in the sun. We were sitting down having a coffee at the bottom of a hill and a skier tried his luck coming down the slope. The slope was shear ice so you could not turn or stop on it. This skier just kept on going in the same direction and had no control until he went off piste and into the forest. This looked like a nasty crash but the skier escaped injury, sliding the rest of the way on his bottom holding his skis.

Most of the lift systems on the mountains have been updated and consist of button lifts and cable cars. When we got to one lift we did not expect to see an old T-bar design. This is a very old system that I thought went out with the ark. This particular route across the mountain was owned by one person. He charged a small toll for anyone using it to go on to a different part of the mountain. This was the only way across to where you wanted to go. I had never been on a T-bar lift before. A T-bar lift is an upside down T attached to a wire, carrying two people sitting on either side of the bar. I went on with an experienced skier who had used this system before and just as well. You have to actually ski, letting the bar push you along working together. I was at times not connected to the bar but had gone on ahead. It was like bumper cars as my mate had one hand on my jacket holding me back. We had a laugh doing it our way, a bit like Laurel and Hardy.

Skiing can also be nerve racking, especially when you have just started to learn. Many people see the snow and want to ski without knowing the basics, how to stop and turn. By the end of lessons for a week, if you have achieved something, confidence is high. Usually on the last day everyone goes skiing together and the beginners are taken up the mountain with the experienced ones. One beginner lost her nerve halfway up the mountain and would not move. She was sitting on the snow, skis in hand, crying and scared. One of the experienced skiers took her down to safety. I cannot remember her coming on a ski trip after that. That is the worst thing that can happen to a skier, to lose your confidence.

Another example of where you can lose your nerve is following an accident, which shakes you up a bit. A lot of skiing is to do with confidence, it's a knock-on effect, the more confident you are the higher you go, the slopes get more and more difficult but can be dealt with, your speed increases and so does the thrill and so it keeps on going.

Another time fifteen of us were going up on a button lift, which was actually quite difficult because it was long and steep but once at the top there was good snow for the beginners. We had persuaded most of them to come with us, as we would be their mentors not leaving their side. Looking at the button lift from the bottom some of the beginners were a little shocked at what lay ahead, to them this was like a Black run (hardest slope to conquer on the mountain). I have to admit it was steep. It was time to grit your teeth and go. Maybe the beginners were right, when we got to the top we only had ten people left, five had fallen off but we found them easily with no casualties. The best thing you can do in this situation is to try again and carry on. It's always good looking back at what you have just skied, it builds up your confidence. As I was saying before, the scenery is spectacular with so many different aspects and you get a real feel for space and freedom.

Once going back on the plane we had two guys on crutches with knee injuries and other guys who had a few near misses. Both the guys to whom it happened were very good skiers but I was undamaged this time which made a change. We had finished skiing for the trip and had about one and a half hours of daylight left so we decided to hire sledges. We were going down a steady slope used for the less advanced skiers when one of the guys put the brake on; the brake being a piece of metal that sticks in the snow on either side of the sledge to try and slow you down. But on this occasion the brake stuck in the slush. He was lifted out of his sledge and the sledge caught his chin. He was on all fours in the snow with blood coming from his mouth; he had bitten through his lip. The other guy came down the mountain veered off to the right where there was stone and rock and bounced along them leaving his sledge behind. It looked bad but he only had a sore back.

Chapter 7

WEATHER

I have always been fascinated by nature and especially weather conditions; I just find the underlying power in such things as whirlwinds, hurricanes, and avalanches incredible. You also never know when they might strike. When I was in Tampa, Florida, in the USA, we took a trip on a friend's boat and went around the keys to Coco Beach on the opposite coast from where we started our journey. During this voyage the sky started to go black and rain clouds gathered. My American friend warned us about this area being notorious for whirlpools and tornados suddenly starting from nothing and within minutes you could be in a life-threatening situation. The boat we were on had a powerful engine so we could outrun the danger should we need to. I managed to photograph the sequence of events which took place. From start to finish the sequence took five minutes. I recorded the whole process because the chances of seeing this natural freak of nature is minimal, a chance of a lifetime but I remained respectful of the danger. Looking at the photographs you can see the two peaks forming and joining together, you can also see the process involved where the water is being picked up by the whirlwind and the clouds returning the water to the sea, a simple but effective cycle.

I was going home after working on a cruise ship. I spent a day in Tenerife two days after they had had their worst flooding ever on the island. The flooding only took place in a small area called Santa Cruz where the cruise ships dock. The trouble was that Santa Cruz is situated at the bottom of a valley and is not designed to take large amounts of water in such a short space of time. On the day of the storm they had 270 litres per square metre fall in 2–3 hours. To you and I, a monsoon. I got a taxi from the ship to my hotel, which was situated near to the worst hit areas. Going through the town, water was still flowing with mud everywhere and cars buried under thick silt and rubble. I had never seen devastation at such a scale in my life. This must have been terrifying for the people; a total of six people died, two of them children. An eye-witness account told of a man and child trapped in a car. His car started to fill with mud and silt so he tried to escape by walking through the current with his child but to no happy ending.

Another report said of how, "he initially tried to get the door open which took an immense amount of strength as the pressure he was pushing against was much stronger than him. Once out of the car he grabbed his child but sadly the speed of the flowing current took their feet and they did not survive".

Don't get too near

I have great admiration for the people of this small community in the way that they got on with life as if nothing ever happened. Near enough all the shops and restaurants were open, with people clearing up mud and debris. They had lost electricity and water for twenty-four hours, some places longer. The low-lying areas were still under mud, rubble and water. If you ran the taps the water that came out was brown so you could not have a shower or clean your teeth unless you bought bottled water. From the photographs you can see the devastation for yourselves.

Total Devastation

Again the power of nature. Imagine as well the thunder and lightning, the cold water, really dark; and the noise must have been deafening and very, very frightening. Having been there and seen it for myself you can create all sorts of pictures in your mind especially when you see all the valleys and paths that the flowing mud and water would have taken. Everything was really dusty where the mud was drying out and the firemen were covered in mud laying hoses to suck out the water from shops and houses. The flood or mudslide went all the way down to the sea from the hills taking no prisoners; you could follow the path of the flow taking bits of mountain with it.

Sunsets are colourful and the one in Key West, Florida is meant to be fantastic. I saw that and I was not over impressed, I did not quite know what to expect but had heard and read in books about its beauty and colour. I had a picture in my mind of a bright orange or red sky making things glow in the vicinity. The only thing glowing was my body having had a few shots of tequila.

Key West is also the southernmost tip of America and to mark this fact they have a large concrete coloured post with markings on it. The markings are of distances to other countries, such as 90 miles to Cuba. Not much to see but a place you might never visit again.

The best sunset I have ever seen was when working in Lanzarote and Puerto Del Carmen. I was about to finish work and noticed a bright orange glow, so I went outside to have a look and, no joke, the whole sky was bright orange causing an orange shadow across all the buildings, I only wish that I had my camera because I will never see a sunset as good as that again. I just stood and watched the sky for ages until it began to get dark. It was like being on another planet and you could have painted the whole sky one colour. It was as though the sun was on a collision course with earth. Even the locals were out admiring the sky.

I live in a small town and I play golf whenever I am home. One afternoon we were going to play golf and on the way could see a storm approaching, driving to the club it seemed to be following us so when we arrived we decided to wait for the storm to pass before we played in case we got wet. Soon after the hooter went for all the golfers to come in from the course, this was going to be no ordinary storm for these shores. Big black rumbling clouds started to gather and everything went really dark, thunder and lightning, the full Monty. We were all inside watching the storm unfold in front of our very eyes. In the centre of the black mass was a bright circle, the eye of the storm. I always thought the eye of a storm was an unreal expression used to describe something that was make-believe, but it obviously was not. It was the way the eye was controlling the storm, always gathering, ever expanding. The clouds were circled around it and all the time it was gathering more to make a giant mass of dark black imposing cloud. I never expected to see a tropical storm in Britain. This was the sort of storm you see in Oklahoma, America.

Chapter 8

HOLIDAY REPRESENTATIVE

This is one job that I have always wanted to do because it is overseas and you are interactive with people and not restricted to 9–5 working hours. So I applied to Airtours and was offered a job. Before we started in a resort we had to go on a training weekend, this was such a laugh. These courses are more to see how you can get on under pressure and work with different characters. Every night we would socialise and get to know each other, a good bit of bonding, some luckier than others. We had everything there from homosexuals to lesbians and others, experimenting with sexual habits. After a day of classroom work we decided to have a bit of a party so we sent the girls on a beer and nibbles run to the off-licence. When they got back to the hotel they had to sneak the drink in and not make the shopping obvious. They came in with carrier bags clinking and about as discreet as a pork chop in a synagogue.

The work itself is quite demanding and does give you an insight into life overseas. You are put under the spotlight straight away and have to get on with the different situations that crop up. Out of the groups who had spent the weekend together there was only one girl who went home early. When the course ended we had all bonded really well, so it was sad to see the group break up. The ones who were going to the train station went together and when saying goodbye we would do impressions of flying geese running down the platform with sound effects. On the course they played a video at the start and finish, using geese to demonstrate working as a team. The first time we saw it we did not see the funny side as we were a bit nervous but the second time around it was so funny and we nearly wet ourselves, so this stuck with us and hence our final parting gestures. At the end of the course we knew that getting our uniforms meant success. There was quite a lot of uniform to be packed and taken back to Newbury for tailoring to fit my shape. We had just been given a box with sizes of small, medium or large. I had about two weeks to fiddle with my uniform, afterwards putting it into a large suitcase neatly packed before flying to my new destination. I had a letter sent through the door by Mister Posty. I was very happy I had been sent to Roda in Corfu.

I had been to Corfu many years before but only on holiday with a mate. So I arrived and was picked up by the area manager who showed me around the island and introduced me to the team. I must admit they were brilliant and made me feel welcome. I stayed in a room for a couple of nights before going on to my final abode, opposite a pub, above a Chinese restaurant, what more could a person want. I then had one week to be trained up before starting out on my own. Part of the induction was to go on the excursions because I was going to sell them to the holidaymakers and hopefully make some money. I was introduced to the hotel owners and staff who again looked after me, apart from one evening when the rep who I was taking over from had a weekly fun night. This was something that she did off her own back and a good way to keep on the good side of everyone, including punters. I was game for anything and joined in the spirit of things. I was happily sitting down minding my own business when volunteers were needed for a game. I was the first one to be dragged up standing in front of an audience with four other men. They had us strip off to the waist, it was hot anyway so I did not mind. Then they stuck a heated brandy glass over your nipple and left it there for a while. The idea was that the burning mixture of alcohol and air inside the glass would cause a vacuum not allowing the glass to be pulled off. You could not pull it off because it would burn your skin and you might smash the glass. The Greek staff knew how to take the glass off without causing damage and entertaining the crowd. I was the last person to have this done and I had the glass on my nipple the longest. When the glass does come off you are left with a large ring around your nipple. This does look very stupid, forming a multi coloured ring which does not look cool when trying to sunbathe and it lasts for days. That was my first real taste of being a rep abroad, joining in and having fun.

A popular night out was always the Greek night, with flowing drink and food all night, which was part of our guide duties. This was a good one for the reps to take part in because they could relax a bit watching the show, having food and drink. There was belly dancing, tricks with fire and lots of curvaceous girls dressed in skimpy outfits, a definite combination to make a good evening.

The only trouble was on the way back it was quite a long journey and more often than not someone would feel sick. We came prepared with sick bags but these hardly got used, as there was no warning just a splatter of liquid, normally red as the wine was free flowing. Being the rep in the coach I would have to sort this out with the coach driver who was not pleased and was not shy in letting out his Greek emotions. The coach driver was responsible for the condition of the coach so a smelly sticky mess was a big no. The coach driver had the authority to throw people of the coach if they caused trouble. This was easier said than done and could end up in a fight as most of the adults were drunk and badly behaved.

One of the things that I had to learn quickly was how to judge the Greek people, things like their temper and mood swings are in their blood and they have many aggressive tendencies of a similar nature. One good lesson learnt was to be honest with them and not to cheat nor go behind their backs; they will look after you if you look after them. If you get invited into their house it is an honour and this happened to me. I got on really well with the son of the family who owned the hotel giving him my time and effort with the customers. He appreciated this, creating a good bond between us.

Scuba diving was popular and I loved it so when the reps got invited down to sample the delights by a local sub aqua company I could not wait. For us it was all free with a picture to boot of us underwater in all the equipment feeling like James Bond on an undercover mission. If you look closely you will see my hair does not look wet, but it is, this is one thing that my friends found fascinating – waterproof hair. When the instructors were taking me down I was very buoyant so weights had to be added to my jacket. When I had finished my dive and stood up in shallow water I felt the full weight of my air tank and all the extra weight, which pulled me back down into the water. The fish would swim with you and come really close as they were used to being fed all year round teaching them not to be scared of people. You could also feed them yourself. The water is so clear you can see for quite a way.

James Bond in disguise, one thing that I had pointed out to me was the fact that my hair looks dry when in water?

Then there was the popular booze cruise; all the reps went on this as a party night, which was arranged every month for the Airtours reps to let their hair down. The boat was old but good enough for us. Some of the people were feeling a bit unwell not being helped by some of us eating egg sandwiches. We had a swim in the sea, diving for bottles of vintage champagne, which you cannot buy in the shops and a barbecue on the beach with one or two orange squashes followed. On the beach we played games and collected wood to make fires for later on. Where the beach was situated you could see across to Albania where there was a war going on. All that was visible were small fires, which looked like houses on fire, and the fires were scattered around a large area.

Because Roda was so small all the reps from all the different companies went to the same watering holes, which made it into a consolidated team of workers. You made really good long-lasting friends and when someone did leave the island it was always sad. I had a few hotels to look after and over the first month I had all sorts of problems to deal with, including domestics. In one incident a couple started fighting each other and had to be separated. It just so happened that the night before I had been out with them for a few social beers so that made it easier to diffuse the situation. I also had the usual things of overbookings, rooms not ready, people having cameras stolen and others. For the first two months I did not stop working, or so it seemed but I was still enjoying the experience. The life of a rep is never dull or boring.

It was party time again and we were told to bring a water pistol. In one of the complexes I was looking after one of the waiters used to work for a holiday company. He had collected on his travels a super soaker cannon, which fired out tons of water, quite powerful and a good range, just what the doctor ordered for the night ahead. He had no hesitation in lending it to me. The gun had two large round water bottles on the top, these could be replenished easily and quickly for maximum damage inflicted on the enemy.

We gathered in the pub beforehand to get acquainted with each other and our water pistols; we could not wait to start the party so no time like the present. It all started off very quietly with a few squirts being let off at close range and not getting any holidaymakers wet. Then the range got further and the big boys started to come out. Because I had the biggest soaker a few of them ganged up on me and I got wet. So I opened fire, managing to hit my targets and others so we ended up having a battle on the street until the coach arrived. We all got on the coach and waved goodbye to some annoyed wet people who did not want another shower.

In our first bar we had a whale of a time and my super soaker worked a treat, everything was soaked including the bar staff, never seen so many wet T-shirts in my life, but the girls did look good and came prepared in the correct swimsuits. On to the next bar and same thing again. The floor was becoming a swimming pool so my super soaker had to be locked away in the boot of the coach and never seen again that night. By the end of the night everyone was well and truly soaked and drunk, some of us carried on but were not allowed to carry our water pistols any further. By then most of us had lost ours or they were broken with all the firing. The coach went back at midnight so the rest of us got taxis home, getting into bed in the early hours.

We also had a night out in Kavos, which has a reputation for being a drinker's paradise; well it is that and more. All you have is one long street of bars and clubs. At the end of the street is a rocket and bungee jump for your pleasure. I have always said that I will never go on a bungee jump so I went on to the rocket with my partner. On the rocket you are strapped into a sphere and two bungee cords are stretched to their limits then released sending the sphere high into the sky. I was not sure if I would enjoy this but I did and would definitely do it again. My partner had a go on the bungee jump with the instructor and enjoyed it. After she had finished she tried to persuade me to have a go, she even offered to do it with me to give me some support, but there was no way on earth that I was going to have a go. On the way back walking to the coach through some of the streets people's bodies were littering the route, asleep or not feeling well and looking rough.

When the season is coming to a close we always have an end of season party. This one was different to the rest; it was going to be away from our beloved Roda. A special occasion to say thank you for all our grafting work throughout the season. This was arranged by the company managers on the island of Corfu. Roda is a nice place but a change of scenery would be a welcome change from our daily routines. The plan was to spend the night in accommodation so we did not have to worry about getting back to Roda for work the following morning. Part of the evening was to have a prize giving session. During the party various prizes were given out in the form of T-shirts, nominees were as follows. Me "I can't get no satisfaction", Brenda for "like a virgin" and June for "girls just want to have fun". All the awards as you can imagine involved sexual connotations; mine was for being fussy, only going for beautiful girls and not trollops. I also won the award for the "driest" season, as being fussy had not paid off with limited shags; but it was my first season.

This is where I first got the nickname RAVEY because I was out every night dancing or raving. After the meal and the awards we carried on partying and our final stop was a pub with a disco. By now all the participants were very happy and a couple of girls fell over trying to dance, we thought that one of the girls was hurt as she was crying and in pain, she did not want to go home and at the end of the night all of us took her back to our pre-arranged apartments. There was no room allocation so I slept with her and another girl, very cosy. Most of the night she was in pain saying that she could not move. It was only when the morning came and we had to go that she stayed motionless. It turned out that she had a broken rib, so we called the ambulance and she was taken to a hospital. She wanted me to stay with her so I went along for the support, it was lucky that her boyfriend was Greek and a doctor so she was in good hands and not long before she was back on her feet socialising.

Sometimes to relax was hard because you always felt that people wanted to ask you questions about work. On your day off the word work or anything associated with it must be avoided at all costs. So the children's rep and myself found this lovely secluded place to sunbathe away from the tourists. We had to get a bus into Corfu town and then a ferry across to a small bird sanctuary island

and a lovely jetty with only us on it. The water was clear and perfect for snorkelling.

It made us chuckle when a little old Greek lady ran with her shopping to get the ferry as it was leaving. She missed the sailing time but was determined to make a grand entrance, as it turned out a grand exit. With gay abandon she threw her carrier bags full of shopping aboard not caring about the contents of vegetables and proceeded to walk along the jetty holding on to the boat. All you could see was white knuckles, shoulders and a head followed by, nothing. She was there one minute and gone the next. She had run out of jetty and disappeared out of sight into the sea. It was like a scene from a Tom and Jerry cartoon. The both of us just burst out laughing and could not stop for hours. We did see her climbing out of the water so she was not injured.

The beach in Roda was long and sandy and very relaxing so it was a popular place to visit. One evening I went down to the beach after work and fell asleep. I was woken up by this cold soft air blowing in my face and a sniffing noise but very soft. It was quite pleasant so I opened one eye to see some fur and an eye looking into mine, then I opened both eyes to see a dog in my face. The dog was very friendly but a stray. When you go abroad to the Mediterranean one thing you see are many stray cats and dogs. Because there are many strays at the end of a season the local authorities lay down poison disguised as food to stem the tide. If this was not done you would have a serious problem with many children getting bitten causing injury and maybe disease. The strays will eat anything, even decaying meat, as the food is scarce. The animals usually only get fed by the tourists. Sometimes you do feel sorry for the puppies or kittens but you just have to turn a blind eye, although I did feel very concerned one time when waiting for customers.

I was meeting people outside their apartments for a welcome meeting and one of the young girls noticed some puppies stuck down a gutter under a drain cover and the very young puppies were making a high-pitched crying sound. I did feel sorry for them, but what can you do. You hoped the mother must be around somewhere to look after them otherwise they would die.

My next place of work was Mallorca and Magalluf, party country. I was introduced to my colleagues as RAVEY but that soon got changed to DAVE THE RAVE after a few weeks of clubbing. A good perk was that wherever you went, if Airtours ran an Escapades (18–30) programme in that resort, the beer was free. We had to produce identification cards until they got to know our faces. In one particular night club we got free drinks all night, we would be given cinema looking tickets by the PR guy swapping them for alcohol.

In the hotels where we worked we could eat in the restaurants free. The particular hotels I was looking after were of a very good standard and good value for money. This meant that the holidaymakers had hardly any problems during their stay. These were Sol hotels and they have chains all over the world. Because they are a Spanish company in a popular resort they have a very good reputation for customer care. In all the hotels I was looking after there were other reps from different companies. This was good because there was always someone to talk to if you were on duty and nobody else around.

The holidaymakers were excellently looked after because nothing would be too much trouble for the staff to make the holiday run smoothly and if the customer was happy the reps were happy, no hassle for us. One time I was asked to go and sort out a problem by the pool. This was late in the evening and the weather was dull and overcast. When I arrived at the pool all I could see were about twenty girls messing around, all topless and not much more on. I had a choice, do I go and speak to them asking them to stop with a 90% chance of being thrown in the pool, or do I stand and watch them hoping they will see me and get bored and stop soon; though not too soon. I came to the conclusion that it was best to be seen and watch for any injuries. I made myself comfortable and watched a great show of girls enjoying themselves, you could see that some were getting cold and had to leave; there are some perks to the job.

I was looking after two 4-star hotels beside the beach and a couple had won a prize in a national newspaper for an all expenses paid one-week holiday getting VIP treatment at this particular hotel. I was the rep so it was my job to give them everything they wanted and show them around Magalluf, not too many pubs more sightseeing. I took them to see a show called PIRATES. When we got inside I showed them to their reserved seats being courteous at all times, the idea being that when they got back to the UK they would write an article in the paper about their holiday. So Airtours wanted to create a good impression by making them comfortable.

This show is one of the best in the world in my mind as you get fed and watered watching World Champion acrobats. Reps are always welcome and even volunteer to work to see the show. When you arrive with your ticket at the entrance you are met by the acrobats. They come from a wide range of countries, the majority coming from Eastern Europe. There is something about them that is different from any other person in the world. They are trained athletes so their bodies are perfect. During the show they have to be flexible and very strong with lots of stamina. Standing by them you are intimidated by their greatness and confidence.

At the end of every season Pirates hold a party for all the reps on the island just to say thanks for selling their show and making them wealthy. With the party every year there is a theme, this particular year it was SEX MANIACS, which the reps entered openly. Some of the costumes were brilliant; two guys wore Hawaiian shirts, shorts and a blow-up doll attached to both of them. The doll was in a sexual position and on their shirts were pictures of girl's parts in splendid colour. The funny thing was that one of the guys was my flat mate so I had seen most of the pictures in the flesh. Sometimes, after a night out, I would walk in on his female prey and catch him in the act. She would be slightly shocked but he did not mind and carried on making honey. It was not surprising he was an

Escapades rep who loved to entertain the girls as part of the job description. At the party we had a few people dressed as Austin Powers, bunny girls, school girls and girls with not much on. With the booze being free all night, people were getting very happy and hot and letting their hair down or something like that.

I also used to assist with the Escapades (18–30s) programme whenever needed, especially with the bar crawls. This used to be a laugh as going around the bars our groups got smaller and smaller as people dropped out for one reason or another. This served its purpose as I now had experience in the fine art of drinking and shagging, not letting one interfere with the other, enjoying them both at the same time. That night after the party and still in fancy dress, we went to a club where again the reps could get free drink. The bar was packed and I had a result pulling a "real devil" and took her to our flat where we spent the night. Before we could go to bed we had to get the paint off her face, as it would ruin the bedclothes. So we had a shower and it all came off including her clothes. By now I was pretty sober and getting very excited building up a lather of passion. She had a lovely body as we dried each other caressing the parts other beers cannot reach. Time to hit the sheets, having no time to sleep as the sugar kept us awake, we had little option but to carry on. We even put the mattress on the floor to stop the noise, being considerate to the neighbours. In the morning we both had the day off so got up taking our time to get ourselves together. She had everything apart from her watch and tights, we could not find her watch and looked everywhere with no success. So when she had gone I went back to bed for an undisturbed sleep, recharging my body. When I woke up in the afternoon I went and had a wee wee and looking down at the pan saw a slight glint, I thought I was seeing things as it was still morning blues; it was actually her watch. I went fishing and retrieved the missing item, which was still working and telling the right time. I had to wash it with normal water to get the worst of the corrosive liquid off, I then left it on the side to dry before going back to bed again. When I told her where her watch had been she was not keen on the idea of putting it back on her wrist, I just put it down to one of those things. I left out the bit where I had pissed over it because I am a gentleman.

Still the same day I heard my flat mate come in and go into the bathroom. He then comes into the bedroom concerned about my well being. I was awake but not a bright spark but detected panic in his voice and terror on his face. He just looked at me, his eyes wandering looking for any injuries. He kept on saying "are you hurt, do you need to go to hospital?" I convinced him that I was fine but he was not as ease. He thought I had been bleeding or had a go at goat slaying, there was blood in the bathroom. We had a look and when I saw the carnage I rubbed off some of the marks with ease, it was the devil's red paint all over the shower, which was a good impression of a murder scene with lots of blood. The penny then dropped and I could see where he was coming from being a mate. He was relieved thinking that I had been bleeding out of control. I was out of control when trying to put out the devil's fire.

The flat we stayed in was in top condition with a cleaner coming around every week to do our washing as well as the housework; we did pay as she did a very good job. The flat was not normally used by Airtours staff as it was privately owned, given to Airtours by a friend of a friend. We had to look after the place, as it was a privilege to live in clean comfort with nothing broken. However we once broke the washing machine which we had to pay for, you'll never guess what the cause was, bearing in mind my flat mate was an Escapades rep. – a condom had slid over an opening to one of the pipes. He always carried condoms in his pocket in case the situation arose. We laughed and put it down to experience. The flat was certainly the best accommodation that I had stayed in being a rep and it overlooked the beach. To get to my hotels from the flat was easy as it was only a short walk. We had a balcony that was nice to sit out on after work enjoying a cool drink.

I had finished work late and left my key with my flat mate who is usually in before me, I had done this for him to get another key cut to give a key to a lodger who was only staying for three weeks. I'm knocking on the door for ages with no success, thinking to myself he must be in. I eventually have to knock on next door so that I could climb over the balcony to get in knowing that the bedroom balcony door is always left open for ventilation purposes. I climbed over aware that if I fell I would probably break a leg but had no choice. It was in the early hours of the morning, still in my works uniform. I had been asking people where he was but nobody knew. When I got into the bedroom my mate was asleep and nothing could wake him up, he was dead to the world. I was not amused as I was tired and had been knocking on the front door for a long time.

One year I had to move quite a few times over the winter months, my worst being three times in three weeks, some apartments good others bad. I can remember a particular time when I moved in with three other people. The bedroom I had was not ready and the mattress was on the floor, the room was very dusty and there was hardly any space for your clothes. This was a spare room turned into a bedroom. I gave the room a real clean hoping this would deter all the bugs from making camp. First night in bed I could feel things crawling all over me, I did not think anything was wrong at the time until I was getting ready to go out and saw a few bites appearing on my skin. Initially I thought they were heat spots as the house was warm. Instead of the spots going they were increasing and itching so I went to see the doctor, I was really embarrassed when taking off my clothes. He gave me some cream and I also tried sleeping on top of the covers so as not to be bitten any more. This did not work so I tried to sleep on the sofa, hopefully getting away from the root of the problem, again with no success. The itching was getting unbearable. I went back to the doctor, a different doctor saw me this time and he gave me some strong pills, hooray these worked a treat in clearing up the marks on my skin. I told Airtours and they arranged for the bug man to come in and spray the apartment. It took a while for the bug man to come so in the meantime my boss had the mattress changed, as

I could not suffer any longer. I could not believe that I had to suffer bites from fleas living in an old mattress before the mattress was changed. I later found out that the girl who had the mattress before was a right tramp having orgies with anything that had a pulse, dirty mare.

I enjoyed helping with Escapades, especially the bar crawls. We had to wear grey T-shirts and dance in most of the bars and play drinking and party games. One of the games was to get the blokes to strip. If the blokes were shy I used to start them off getting others to join in. On one crawl we had a rugby team needing no encouragement to show their working parts in action. As the crawl went on with lots of dancing my T-shirt always changed colour to a dark grey because it was very wet due to all the perspiration. I had to dry my sweaty top under the dryer in the toilets, as it did not look at all attractive. This had its perks as well; in one bar we did the conga with boy girl boy girl and so on. The reps joined in to give the proceedings a boost, the instructions were to put your hands on the bottom of the person in front, next the head and carry on down the body. When it came to the chest my hands fitted like a glove around a girl's chest, and as I have big hands you could not have designed a better fit: one of the wonders of nature.

I have also been on TV with *Escapades* when Airtours sponsored a programme called Night Fever, which was a karaoke competition between girls and boys. This was held on Magalluf beach and it was a glorious day with the sun beating down. All the reps had to wear tight fitting T-shirts and stand at the front of the audience throwing water bottles to the crowd. Suggs from the pop group Madness came on, he was the judge and main compare, followed by the contestants, Frank Bruno, Ricky from *Eastenders* and a girl from *Blue Peter* along with other celebrities. We all had a ball and the female co-presenter caught her hair in a tiny hand-held fan so filming was stopped until she was freed by cutting her hair, which she was not pleased about. When the show was resumed the camera panned round and I was on the end of the line. The cameraman asked me to do something stupid so I played the air guitar and it was that good I had a spot on TV for about 30 seconds on my own. I did not tell my friends back home but some saw the programme and recognised me; famous again. So that I did not miss my piece of fame for 30 seconds I asked my parents to tape the show for me. The thing was that on the same night there was the John Travolta film *Saturday Night Fever* being shown. Both shows with nearly the same name, an easy mistake to make, they taped the wrong programme. I have still never seen myself on TV. When I was back home Channel 5 re-ran the series and my friends came into the pub congratuiating me on my performance of a lifetime; worth an Oscar.

My first repping assignment in Magalluf involved having to look after a hotel working with an experienced rep. The hotel itself had the potential to be trouble but my partner was a girl from Glasgow who could look after herself. It was now Christmas time and winter, most of the bars in Magalluf close down for this period so the amusement caters more for the old. Staying at our hotel were some young lads who were idiots and out to cause as much trouble as possible. What they did not realize was that the Spanish youth don't tolerate that behaviour in the wintertime. Magalluf becomes Spanish and lager louts are not welcome. The young lads were involved in fights most nights and came second. In the hotel we had the police down on a regular basis and by the end of the week we were on first name terms. My partner was fluent at Spanish and Mallorcan. Mallorcan was the local language so she was able to control the situation. Once the louts went back home we had another lot for the Christmas period; it became the Bronx.

Christmas Eve I was walking to work starting at 9am. Not really full of the joys of Santa as it was dark, early and cold. Turned the corner and two of the louts are getting a beating from some Spanish lads, so I just carried on walking leaving them to get on with it. Got to work and told my colleague so we were prepared for trouble. One lad came in later with blood on his shirt, cuts and bruises but went straight to his room. When we saw him once he had recovered we told him not to cause trouble otherwise he could be thrown out of the hotel. When we got to work a few days later he had been causing trouble at night in the hotel with the police being called. The Spanish police have a reputation for being hard and rough. He then came to see us saying that the police had beaten him up, they probably had but he deserved it, so we had no option but to throw him out with nowhere to stay. He had to find his own accommodation, he moaned but rules are rules

We had complaints about drugs being used in the Hotel. We had our suspicions but could not confirm anything about the rumour. I do not smoke so my sense of smell is pretty good when it comes to any sort of smoke, cigarettes or drugs. A few times when in various places around the hotel I could smell drugs, my partner was also finding weird smells. It was a matter of catching them in the act to take any action. We concentrated on a group of young lads who did not look too clever, they just looked unkempt and unhealthy. Going to breakfast one day and the likely lads were in the restaurant eating small amounts of food, not enough to keep a pigeon alive. This is a good sign of drug abuse. I could not believe my luck when the lads were openly exchanging drugs in the restaurant. This is when I pounced telling them to find a suitcase and pack. So again we threw them out into the winter climate.

One of the worst incidents was when a couple of Asian lads had trashed their room and obviously had a chip on their shoulder about something. This is what they had done to the room; stuffed rubbish under and down the side of the fridge, broken a door of the wardrobe, used the floor as a bin, left dirty unwashed plates on the table and floor with some being smashed, had written loads of slogans saying we hate the Spanish and Spanish are ***** but not put as nicely and stuck them to a wall, pulled bedding onto the floor using it as rags to wipe things clean. When the police saw what they had done my colleague translated Spanish into English for the Asians. It was clear that if they were taken to the police station for questioning they would have had a severe beating. The police had read all the slogans in the room and were not happy. My partner was a true professional and very firm when it came to dealing with volatile situations, she was from a rough area in Glasgow. This is part of the down side of the job, playing piggy in the middle between the holidaymaker, Airtours, the hotel owner and police. The other down side is dealing with death.

I had a case where an elderly couple in their late sixties and early seventies went out for a drive in the country. They had hired a car for a few days to see the island. This particular day was hot and sticky, the air being not of a good quality. The couple pulled into a petrol station because the husband was not feeling well. He went to the toilet telling his wife to stay in the car. He had a massive heart attack which must have killed him instantly. I saw the lady a couple of days after the fatality as she was staying in my hotel. She was obviously still shaken but hiding it well from the other guests. Her late husband had done most of the couple's paperwork so she was not aware of the small print on documents. She was not sure about her insurance policy so I read it for her. I was surprised to read that her husband was not covered; the policy they had been sold did not cover him for death because he was too old. This meant that the lady had to pay for everything herself. I had to phone the UK a number of times to arrange with her bank to send out money. Airtours did help and did not charge her for various items. She was now on her own so I would spend as much time as possible with her making her comfortable and being a shoulder to cry on and a friend. She then wanted to have the body put in a coffin and taken back on a plane to the UK. To do this would cost her £2000, which she could not afford. So in the end we persuaded her to have the body cremated because it was practical and cheaper.

She wanted to get home as soon as she could which was understandable but there were no planes available for a number of days. She suggested having a friend come over and stay with her until a flight had been arranged. Getting a friend to come over was a problem, as she did not have many true friends, they all only knew her to say "hello" to and not much else. She was also only tolerated by people and not particularly liked in the social circle she had back in the UK. A relative finally came over and took her back on the plane. During their stay together they did fall out with each other having a few tantrums, it even got to the stage where objects were thrown at each other and her relative wanted to go back. I now had to be the peacemaker and persuade her relative to stay. That was hard for me in an emotional sense. I had been dealing with most of her feelings and she had confided in me and told some secrets close to her heart. I felt like the son she never had. I also had access to all her financial documents which if there were any discrepancies I could have been accused of stealing or worse. The lady was not that sort of person and had a heart of gold as I had trust in her. I also think that when she left the island there was a slight bond between us, which is very hard to explain. Being in a hotel, word gets around of any major happenings and a group of girls also became her friend, which helped me out giving me time to do my job.

After this interruption it was back to normal and the weeks passed. During a weekly meeting of all the managers and reps I had a surprise. A letter had been sent to the Airtours head office in the UK and a copy to me. It was three ladies who stayed at the hotel where the lady's husband had died. The ladies were staying with a different travel group, Thomson. Unbeknown to me they were impressed with my conduct and professionalism at dealing with the situation and felt strongly enough to sing my praises in a letter to Airtours. When it was read out I had a major head swell, feeling so good about myself. They made me out to be a national hero, which I was thankful for because I am.

Another death that I have had been involved with was when during the winter I was working as a Golden Years host, entertaining the elderly. We had a dance night and the large lounge was busy. I went for a drink then heard a call over the public address system for an Airtours rep. When I got there another rep was already at the scene and an old guy slumped on the seat. So we evacuated the room and put a barrier around the body. I did not know this but the procedure for a body in Spain is totally different to the UK. The rules are that the body cannot be moved until a judge says so. The judge could be in his bed and does not have to see the body but relies on the doctor. The doctor has to confirm that a person is dead first before any further action can be taken. The body cannot be moved, not even by the doctor, until the judge has passed the body clinically dead. While all this was going on the body was decomposing and turning literally white then blue. For the wife it must have been terrible seeing her husband asleep for two hours not wanting to believe that he was dead, especially after having a good night dancing. By now the judge had made his decision but the body could not be moved until the undertakers arrive. The wife was now coming to terms with the situation and she managed to leave her husband's side getting back just as an old wooden coffin was brought in by two lads dressed in normal clothes. We had to distract the wife while the body was carried away in what looked like a builder's van. The wife was then given tender loving care and time to collect her thoughts. I just thought it was disrespectful the way the body was left in the middle of a large room and not allowed to be taken away to somewhere smaller and private.

Now for some happier stories back to the "Bronx" in Magalluf. I was looking after the golden years programme and having party nights involving bingo, karaoke and general fun. Beside myself entertaining, there was a solo guitar player who played three nights a week. He and I got together and sang a few songs, I have not got a bad voice but not good enough to earn any money from singing, or so I thought. I was singing 'American Pie' with the words in front of me accompanied on the acoustic guitar with no cheating, I was singing live. After I had finished the song I got a good clap and one of the old guys who was sitting near to the stage said that I was very good and he meant it. I was so pleased my head swelled to such a size and the guy was sober which made me feel like a pop idol.

The old can be just as crazy as the young when it comes to enjoying themselves in a strange place. We had two grannies came for about three weeks for a Christmas break; they were old but acted like twenty-five years olds. They had each brought with them a full clown's outfit with frilly collars and cuffs, pointy hats and shoes, they also had in their suitcases a Santa outfit with the red skirt and top trimmed with white; they were "lovin' it large". One night they went out in Magalluf dressed as clowns and had a whale of a time rolling in during the early hours. They were out nearly every night and even throwing each other into the pool. They would also help me with the bingo dressed as Santa Claus; they were two girls who just loved life. They would sit on the old chaps knees in their short skirts putting life back into their contented bodies. They would kiss and cuddle and flirt with the more agile men. The old are sometimes worse than the young when it comes to partying.

We had a party night and I was after some volunteers to cross dress. A granddad with a walking stick could not resist the temptation; it was as though a miracle had taken place. He threw his walking stick down and ran to the front, I wonder what he did when he was younger? He started the ball rolling and more volunteers came forward. The idea was for the girls to dress the bloke in one team and visa versa in the other team. By now the sherry and booze was making for a happy atmosphere with no holds barred. I have never seen two people so eager to get their kit off in all my life.

Sometimes there are unexpected moments that are just really funny. One such incident was when I was standing up behind the desk and my female colleague was stroking the owner's dog, which was a cute white fluffy thing. She was saying things like, "aren't you cute and hairy, I could kiss you" and kissing noises plus a few others. One of the holidaymakers walked in and I smiled at him. He looked at me and I looked back at him but nothing twigged. All he could see was my top half and a woman's voice talking sweet nothings, what do you think he thought? My colleague stood up and smiled at me then looked at him. He stopped in his tracks. Then the dog walked out from behind the counter. He was so relieved and started to give a nervous laugh when the penny dropped, both of us realized what it must have looked like to him walking in seeing only me smiling and a girls voice talking seductively, no she was not giving me a blow job (talking with your mouth full) although I would not complain because she was very pretty.

At Airtours we performed a Christmas cabaret show so we did various songs and dance routines and games. This was put together by the entertainment team who were only amateurs but enjoyed performing. One of the guys mimed to the Robbie Williams song "Let me entertain you", wearing make-up, and got a big clap from the happy audience. This guy was a drinking buddy of mine and played a joke on me involving the holidaymakers. The night before we had gone out to the pub and I took this girl home thinking that no one knew about our nocturnal habits. I was one of the first to arrive at the cabaret venue because I was not supervising a coach. Unbeknown to me the boys knew about my adventure the night before and told the holidaymakers on the coaches. They even described what I looked like so I could not escape, tall, dark and handsome. I happened to be standing by the door welcoming in the holidaymakers when one of them asked if I was DISCO DAVE. I knew that something was up. They then asked me about last night and when I saw the boys they grinned; I was popular for the rest of the evening.

My name had now changed from DAVE THE RAVE to DISCO DAVE. I was known throughout Airtours as DISCO DAVE, even the managers and other holiday companies on the island knew me as DISCO DAVE. I used to walk into a bar and the DJ would announce me as I walked in, "DISCO DAVE IN THE HOUSE". If they wanted anybody to get the games rolling they would turn to me. A particular bar had a small stage and they played a game involving changing clothes with someone of the opposite sex. I was volunteered, as no guys would get up because it was early in the evening and people were sober. We had to go into the ladies toilets, change and come out again, make-up was optional. We came out and both looked good, as we were almost the same shape with a few obvious differences. The prize was a free cocktail if we changed back again on stage, we were both game and enjoyed our cocktails very much after building up a sweat. As you can tell, some games involved changing clothes with women. Being a man I don't not mind participating in these pleasurable pastimes, it brings joy to all concerned. Taking my clothes off was not uncommon.

One of the guys was leaving Airtours and the island but before he went he had promised the pub, which was our local, that the guys from Airtours would do the Full Monty. There were only four guys in the Airtours team and I was one of them. Initially we had to be persuaded with a few shots down our necks. We also had an awaiting public of Airtours females. So we went outside with four plates of all different sizes and gave the smallest size plate to the most well endowed beast; which was me. I was on the stage at the front and we had a few groupies (people who support and follow groups wherever they are playing) with us who were making enough noise for the whole pub. The groupies were the girls from Airtours so they were giving us lots of encouragement to go all the way. As we got down to our underpants we had our plates concealed. We then turned around and discarded our underpants so that all the audience could see was our bare bums. When we turned around we had the plates covering our manhood. A large cheer from the pub could be heard in the next resort as the audience were taken by surprise. We all grasped our plates tightly so they did not fall and our performance went down in history never to be repeated or forgotten.

However I was now well known so at the next year's Christmas party they had a disco and played the theme tune from *The Full Monty*. I knew what was coming next. As soon as the music started the DJ called my name over the microphone, I had no choice but to go on stage with the others. There were four of us, all Escapades (18–30) reps, not the same guys as before but proper "having it large, who dares wins" Escapade reps. We gave the audience a teasing performance, I was the last person to take my clothes off and by now an audience of hundreds of girls, some with cameras, had appeared in front of the stage. I had a difficult situation to face, did I tease or did I produce. The spotlight was on me, the expectation immense and the girls hysterical, I made the decision to produce and when I did the captivated audience were in awe of the raging bull. The cameras were flashing frantically which made my confidence rise. One of the girls showed me a picture she had developed from the party. I was impressive, not one negative comment.

Two of the other shows on the island are Son Amar and Casino Palladium, both very different and breathtaking, acts that you will only ever see once in your life. At Son Amar during a particular performance one of the fully-grown Bengal tigers escaped. Usually the tigers are in a cage where they are made to disappear and appear again. When the illusion is finished the illusionist opens the cage and strokes the tigers. This time the tiger ventured outside the cage and had the illusionist, who is also his trainer, pinned down on the floor. The front row of seats is very close to the stage but the audience were not sure if this was part of the show or not. To get the Bengal tiger under control handlers came on coaxing the animal away from the trainer so that he could take control of the situation. This was not in the script but concealed very well with the audience unaware of the dangerous situation.

As part of our job we had to sell these shows to the holidaymakers, but we did get treated very well. We were shown back stage and given VIP treatment. Son Amar was good but my favourite was the Casino Palladium, more variety and not so much dancing. I was looked after by the public relations team very well at both venues but especially the Palladium. I took my girlfriend to the Palladium show as it was in Magalluf near to where we were staying and she was very well treated all night. The PR girls showed us to our seats for a reason, which came apparent when she was picked from the audience to go on stage with the clown driving a car. This was totally unexpected, as I had no indication that this had been pre-arranged. I was just as shocked as she was but her performance was funny. I had seen the show before so knew what she was about to do. When she had finished her act she came back to the table, downed a glass of champagne and gave me a glare.

My favourite act was the wall of death where motorbikes drive around inside a metal cage performing amazing feats of skill. I had seen this on TV but never live. I had a chance to see the cage for real standing by it. It looks much bigger on stage with the lights creating an illusion. The roar of the bike's engine noise sets your heart racing as they ride around the stage. In the cylindrical cage the riders go round and around, sometimes two at the same time, how they do not get disorientated I find incredible, the concentration must be mind-blowing. I must have seen the show twenty times, never witnessing any accidents.

I also went to the casino itself a few times and had success winning about £130 in one go on the roulette wheel. This was after the show when my girl-friend came with me to have a little flutter; she must have been a good omen. I can see now how people become addicted especially if you win. Having this extra cash meant we could stay there longer, having more fun, having a go at all the games.

At Portals Nous there is a very expensive marina, I have always had a fascination with boats and liked to relax there and rub shoulders with the rich and famous. Prices for the many different exotic boats go up to millions of pounds – how the other half live! I saw a cruiser, painted all black with gold trim, tinted windows, speedboat shape, the works. One of the crew was working on the deck so I asked him who the boat belonged to, he just said an English busi-nessman not giving any names. I had to go away still wondering who was rich enough to afford a small cruise ship. If I worked all my life I could not afford that boat.

Another good show is watching the dolphins and seals at a small sea world in Portals Nous. You can get close enough to touch them as they come up to say I love you, one of them being called Stevie Wonder. As you know they are always popular with the public and like to show off whenever possible. The park itself is not big but good enough for a day out and to experience something different.

One of the main attractions on the island of Mallorca is situated in Palma the capital. This is the cathedral which is hundreds of years old and has much his-tory behind it. It is a landmark for all visitors to see. Every picture you see of Mallorca nearly always shows the cathedral in it. This is also known as the unfinished cathedral as the architect who built it died before its completion, so there is one brick missing somewhere and nobody yet has found its where-abouts.

Some of the lads including me decided to spend a night in Palma. We wanted somewhere to go that was different to the norm, we had never been in Palma for a night out why not give it a go. We started walking around not taking long to get lost or losing our direction through the maze of streets. We just happened to stumble across a brothel and because it was late at night and raining, we de-cided to stay and have a drink but nothing else. We had to work the following day so whatever we did had to be quick. The working girls were very attractive and full of conversation but just as things were hotting up we had to leave. At least we were kept dry preventing cold or flu. I don't know why but sailors always find brothels, not that I have been into many but my mates have. Some of the characters are comical with the men bent as a roundabout. While we were sheltering from the rain indoors we had to watch the dancers moving around. They had a stage with a couple of poles (Russians were not bad either – joke) erected. Every sort of sexuality would be strutting their stuff trying to attract attention using the poles as a weapon. One very loose guy stuck out (excuse the pun)as he was cross-dressed wearing a thong getting himself excited. My only advice is if you do go make sure you are in a large group of lads for maximum fun and do not stay for too long.

My next repping duty was in Lanzarote. Before I went there my name preceded me and I had a reputation to protect. Disco Dave had come about through years of hard graft working and playing, always doing a good job. When out socialising the number one priority was fun and lots of it. I made lots of friends along the way bumping into them from time to time. I was based in Puerto Del Carmen, the capital of the island, the best place for nightlife. I had to look after two complexes literally next to each other. To get back and forward to work we had a company car, which was very handy, as I do not drive. An arrangement was made so that I would get a lift from one of the girls who lived below me.

I also made good friends with staff at a nightclub and in various bars where the reps had discount on food and drink. I was there over Christmas and New Year, so lots of parties. The nightclub was never that busy but the staff were very sociable people. I made good friends with all of them, being a frequent visitor. If I was off work they would pick me up in their jeep and take me places, normally other bars or restaurants. I was invited to their staff functions so was never at a loose end over the festive season. At the same time there was the works parties. It was tiring work but someone had to be seen to fly the flag. I was always at work on time during this strenuous period while others were falling by the wayside.

All the way along the main street in Puerto Del Carmen Christmas decorations were up. A stage was set up for bands and a firework display organized. The display was actually very good and the street was mobbed with people. The stage would be busy if it did not collapse with three or four bands playing into the early hours. The bands were not famous outside the Canaries but were musically talented. This became an old-fashioned street party.

Also as part of the Christmas theme we did a pantomime for the kids. *Cinderella* was our choice and I had a few parts to play. One was as a Teletubby. The costumes where so old that they were torn and also built for short people or so it seemed, as I am over six foot. When going on stage I could not turn round as the costume had no back, the front being held together with pins. The costumes had been used so many times that they were in need of a seamstress. I was also a cheerleader without the pompoms and had a cameo roll to play. The audience were our holidaymakers who got to know us during the working week so every time their rep came on the kids especially would cheer loudly.

In a second show, we had to perform a few short sketches during an interval while the main characters had a rest, so we did the Levi Jeans laundrette advert. I had to wear white underwear but covered the bottom of my pants with brown colouring for effect. The curtains opened and I walked out to music and sat down. I took my clothes off including the jeans and put them in the washing machine leaving only my Kelvin Klein boxers on. Then three lovely girls came on stage taking it in turn to tease me but they would all run off pretending that I smelt. Once they had finished I would pose for a bit then bend down taking my clothes out of the washing machine showing my brown bottom. There was always a chuckle from the crowd, especially from the kids who really did think that I had made a mess.

The comedian was very good. He used to be on TV, although before my time, and did an impression of E.T. playing the guitar, the best impression I have seen to date, as you were not expecting what happened next. The comedian went behind a counter starting a smoke machine, pretty normal so far until the front of the counter dropped down and there was E.T. The model was made from papier mâché looking like the real thing but with the comedian's arms coming through two holes in the false front blending in well with the playing and singing space creature.

A female singer also performing had been on the short list to be a Spice Girl but got pipped to the post by Victoria. She was blonde and had a cracking figure and voice. For a small restaurant with a stage and a capacity crowd of three hundred people the quality of performance was breathtaking as I have seen acts on much bigger stages not half as good or funny. This show was always a talking point the next day, the audience loved it, a lasting impression of their holiday.

There were also quite a few drag acts taking place in the resort of Puerto Del Carmen, with one being really funny – a bit like Lily Savage but funnier. She, he or it did an impression of Dave Bowie and Space Odyssey where she was suspended in mid air pretending to be in a capsule fiddling with knobs; very effective. I had been to Lanzarote before, many years ago, so knew a bit about the island and its night time activities, but the drag shows can be a very good source of entertainment.

For our Christmas outing a large group of us went out to see such an act, we had a few beers and were very jolly. One of the guys, not me thank goodness, was being picked on by the drag queen and invited him up on stage to be tied to a chair. Then he, she or it ended up putting squirty stuff down the guy's trousers and then bouncing up and down on his knee before setting some chest hair on fire. It was a very good evening with many adult sketches, not for the faint-hearted or kids.

I got drenched once when on the island of Lanzarote we had the worst storm for some time. The flooding was so bad that the drains were not able to cope with the sheer amount of water falling from the black sky. I was on a coach transfer taking people to their apartments or hotels when the heavens opened and the main street was awash with running water, like a river. The drain covers were being lifted up and in some cases being taken by the current down the street. The coach could not wait for the rain to stop as it had a deadline to meet passengers somewhere else, so we had to carry on with our transfer. The walks to the hotel receptions were only short but you got very wet in a matter of seconds. After a few journeys doing this I was soaked along with the customers. I had never seen so much rainfall in such a short period of time.

When being a Holiday Representative you have to deal with situations that are out of your control. Staying at my apartments was a particular holidaymaker who had booked a four-day holiday for himself and his boyfriend. They had lost most of a day due to the flight being delayed because of bad weather. He was seeking compensation for the delay and wanted to argue with me. I explained to him the situation and said that if you read the brochure it does say that weather is an act of God and no compensation is given. When you get back to the UK take it up with your insurance company. Then came the old line "do you know who I am?" He showed me his Labour Member of Parliament card and had a tantrum. I hate MPs at the best of times and I thought to myself, if you're an MP why come on a four-day holiday and stay in 3-star accommodation. He was obviously up to no good as he had booked a cheap holiday with his boyfriend when he was earning a good wage. He was probably after a dirty weekend, not telling his boyfriend back home what his intentions were. He was a real arsehole and deserved to be stabbed in the back, excuse the pun.

I had a nightmare situation once when a holidaymaker locked himself in the toilet, not a problem so I thought, I would get the spare key. No key could be produced and I found out that the guy was claustrophobic so time became a real issue. His wife was talking to him trying to calm him down. I tried to find a crow bar or something that was lying around to smash the door down. I managed to find a large rock outside the complex so tried to bash the lock with it but nothing was happening. I then tried with my foot but this did not budge the door. By now I was starting to panic as he had been inside the toilet for twenty minutes. By this time everyone had heard the noise so I fetched some big lads from their rooms to give me a hand knocking the door down. I was also concerned about the noise that I was making as this would make the guy more agitated. The guys came and by sheer strength it worked, the door broke to find the guy inside sweating, shaking and shouting. When he finally saw daylight he came out after blood, mine. Evasive action was the best way to deal with this situation so I made myself scarce as I was going to get abuse, maybe a punch. Whilst family and acquaintances were calming him down I was planning how to cope with meeting him again. I was fortunate that the acquaintances were strong lads able to restrain him. I came back later to find him much calmer and not so hostile.

Generally in Lanzarote there are quite a few cockroaches that find their way indoors. The apartments that I was looking after were no exception. I was on duty and had the duty mobile for twenty-four hours when I received a call from a holidaymaker in the early hours of the morning. He said that his apartment was being overrun by cockroaches, could I find him somewhere else to stay. I got there as soon as possible expecting to find maybe one or two cockroaches. The couple were outside, packed ready to move. They were definitely not going to spend another night in the room. They told me what had happened and to have a look in the bathroom. There were hundreds of cockroaches running around, a nest must have burst open under the bath. I did not expect to see so many of them. I was actually quite shocked myself and felt that something had to be done. Luckily I had been speaking to my colleagues and I had remembered in the conversation about some spare rooms that were available in a hotel up the road. I arranged alternative accommodation until the problem had been cured. The apartment had to be fumigated and left for a couple of days and checked before people were allowed back in. The people who this happened to were in my apartments, so my responsibility. This meant that I could check to see if the problem was being rectified and cockroaches gone before any one else moved in.

After this, back to Mallorca and the east coast to do a week's induction course at a resort called Cala D'or. We had a really good time and everyone gelled together perfectly. As soon as I arrived I knew someone from last time when on the island. This group was different to the rest because when we went out we all went out in a group staying together for the duration. No one left the group, everybody compatible with each other. It was one big holiday camp. We again went to all the excursions and shows during the day and partying at night. One of the public relations girls at Son Amar, Aunty Sue, travels around all the hotels and is a real character and always has fun wherever she goes; not bad for an old girl. She becomes everybody's friend. When at Son Amar she kept us amused for hours. When she was eating with us she had butter with everything going through six sachets with her chicken and chips.

We had parties in our rooms before and after going out into town and it was a shame when we all had to be split up when sent to our different resorts. I was sent to a place called Calas De Mallorca, which was a very small resort but a superb beach for tanning. I was in one of the bigger hotels that Airtours own along the east coast. I was to be a Customer Services Representative again. I would be sharing with a couple, the bloke I knew before when based in Magalluf. Our room was directly above a pub with a huge balcony so that you could sunbathe. In the flat we had a spare bedroom, so if any friends or relatives came to stay it would not be a problem. In the resort we were a small team of about twenty-five people altogether, tending to be really close friends. One of the girls who was in charge had a boyfriend and he owned a bar, which was always packed, as there was not much competition from other owners all the reps got drinks at a discounted price.

The best part of the resort was the beach, a little sun-trap. I had a fantastic tan looking a healthy dark gold colour. I was having lots of time off due to the fact that I had changed jobs to a transfer rep, this is where you take people from the airport to the hotel and vice versa. My hours of work were mainly at night with three days off, all in all a good arrangement as I had more time to work on my tan. I did help out with guiding excursions as sometimes they were short of manpower. The beach itself was surrounded on three sides by rock, with the sea the other. The sea was warm and clear enough to snorkel in.

The only trouble with this coast was that all the excursions were a long way by coach. For example the Pirates show was a two-hour journey there and the same back. To keep the holidaymakers amused on the long journey we had a quiz for them and told a few clean jokes as there were kids present. On the way back you could guarantee that someone would be sick. I will never forget one bloke who filled up about two bags full of sick; the trouble was I had no more bags so we had to stop the coach until he felt better. I hoped and prayed that his stomach was empty. This does not go down well with the other passengers so your people skills come into action diffusing the situation that is not of your making.

The only time that I have felt bad myself was when taking a coach full of families to the airport and a young lad about seven years old sitting directly behind me was sick more than once. He suffered from travel sickness and sat near the front for easy access to the door and me. He was getting whiter, complaining to his mother of feeling unwell; his mother told him to give her prior warning if he was going to be sick. There was no warning just a noise and up it came covering himself. This happened a number of times turning him into a smelly sick bag. He had now started a chain reaction and another three children followed suit. It got so bad we had to stop the coach on the side of the road for the young lad to change his clothes, as he was covered in diced carrots. I felt sorry for the lad, as we had to find his case in the boot amongst all the others, which was not quick. In the meantime he was stripped off with a pile of steaming smelly clothes beside him awaiting his fresh outfit.

The coach drivers being Spanish have a very short fuse and do not have much patience before they get annoyed. Most of the reps can speak enough Spanish to know what they are saying. You do not want to get in a situation where there is a confrontation between a driver and holidaymaker. I nearly had that once coming back from a show called Son Amar and quite a few people were drunk at the back of the coach. A holidaymaker came up to me and aggressively said could the air conditioning be turned on. It was on but most of the people had turned their individual air conditioning off and fallen asleep, so I turned them back on. This all happened as we were nearing our resort. He could have told me sooner giving me a chance to rectify the situation before he became uncomfortable. When we reached our last drop-off point, guess who was left? Correct, and the holidaymaker would not leave the coach because of the discomfort caused by the lack of air conditioning and people being sick. He insisted that he should get money back for the discomfort caused by the coach being very hot and stuffy. His wife was there as well so she joined in. By now the coach driver wanted to go to his next rendezvous and because of the time wasted by the argument another coach had arrived. The time was 3am and the coach had to be somewhere else. Eventually after twenty minutes of discussing the problem the coach driver started to lose his rag and brought his mate into the argument. I persuaded him to leave by telling the holidaymaker that he could stay on the coach but it was going back to the airport. Both the coach drivers just nodded and started the engines. The guy's wife managed to talk some sense into him as by now he was ready to have a fight with someone, not caring who it was. If a fight had ensued the guy would certainly have come out second best as he was carrying a walking stick to support his bad leg. The bus drivers were two in number and a lot younger. I give him a note saying what happened but he was not a happy man and was going to complain to the hotel rep in the morning about the incident.

The Spanish drivers on the roads are amazing. I was taking a coach load of people to their hotels when on a main road, yes, a main road, a car stopped in front of us for no apparent reason. There was no indication or warning just slowing down before stopping. The driver got out and started to clean his windscreen. The coach could not get past as the car had stopped right in the middle of a two-lane main road/motorway, one lane up, one lane down. The coach driver began tooting his horn but the bloke cleaning his car windscreen carried on. In the end there was a heated argument between the two drivers with the bloke in the car driving off shaking his fist. Our coach driver stayed very close behind because the bloke in the car was deliberately slowing down annoying the coach driver who gave him a nudge forward every so often.

I did not mind being a transfer rep as this gave me more chance to sunbathe. I had the best tan ever because the beach is set in a cove so the sun gets concentrated and you bake, have I mentioned that before? Sorry, not really! The beach was a meeting place for the entertainers who were mostly Scandinavian and were very agile practising gymnastics and acrobatics; great to watch, as I did not want to damage my dark golden tan by joining in. The Scandinavian entertainers were a very talented bunch, each speaking three or four languages. They looked after themselves as they were very fit especially the females who had tremendous well-toned bodies, bodies to die for.

The water was clear enough for snorkelling and diving. This made the sea very inviting, which helped in promoting the tan. To this very day I have the outline of the Speedo swimming trunks to prove it. I always have some colour having been on the beach for many a month, my skin will never be white again.

During this time we had a four-day coach strike over the whole of the island of Mallorca. This affected everybody who was involved with tourism, the companies and holidaymakers. The stupid thing was that the coach drivers doing this action would make the relationship between rep and driver very awkward and bitter. During the strike all the transfer reps would be at the airport on a rota system working twelve hours on, twelve hours off, staying in a hotel near to the airport. The hotel had holidaymakers staying there so as soon as we got back it was straight to our rooms not getting involved in any conversations. The last thing you wanted was abuse and an angry mob.

We would use taxis as transport as no other vehicle was available. The taxis made a small fortune. At the hotels taxis would be flagged down so they could charge whatever they wanted knowing that the price would be met. We got the holidaymakers to the airport early to avoid people being stranded. At the hotels we had a system where the early flights went first, giving everybody a fair chance to catch their flight back home. This system came unstuck as people were not bothered what taxi they occupied, getting into the first one they could see.

Once at the airport it was chaos, also there were delays because of an air traffic control strike so the airport was full of people not going anywhere. The reps would try and assist the holidaymakers as much as possible but information was limited as not many planes were moving. The coach drivers were making everybody angry and tensions were running high. They would block entrances to the airport, if any cars did go through they were spat at and kicked. Sometimes violence broke out and cars had to find alternative routes. We had cases of hired cars having their tyres slashed, reps being set upon and harmed by some coach drivers. The police were around but did not interfere much as they were all Spanish and looked after their own. To give the reps more cars and transport options we had designated drivers in unmarked cars to drive to and from the airport all day.

Inside the airport itself we were giving out vouchers for meals and drinks doing everything in our power to help, but we were under frequent abuse from the holidaymakers. Every rep was threatened at least once with violent behaviour, including being threatened by teenage girls and women. The thing was that we were only passing on information that we had been told. In fact the people stranded at the airport knew more about the plane situation than us, they were constantly on their phones to family and friends who were looking at ceefax and teletext.

The first time I was threatened was when asked to go over to a building and tell a long queue of people that they had to go back over to the main terminal. The building they were going into had beds in it and a snack area, changing facilities and comfortable surroundings, which they could see because the lights were on. At the last minute the airport authorities decided to change their plans and not open the building. The passengers had to be told so the company sent two people across, a girl and myself. You can imagine the passengers' reaction. Because I was the first person from Airtours they saw I got the brunt of their anger and was surrounded by furious people. I feared the worst, all I could do was stand my ground and try to reason with them, I could not run or hide.

The second time was going into the departure lounges surrounded by people and giving them the bad news that their flights had been cancelled. I spent the next long hours again getting abuse, but this time constantly. The flights were being delayed by as much as forty hours. The biggest problem was where to put all the holidaymakers gathering in the airport terminal. The strike was that well publicised it was all over the papers and on the news. The airport was running out of food and supplies so we had to make various trips to the supermarkets hampered all the time by the coach drivers. These trips were like a military operation. We had to travel in an unmarked car and these always had to be two people in constant communication with Airtours airport controllers. I can honestly say that was the worst and most threatening time of my life.

The strike was going to end any time soon as the drivers had come to a compromise with the government, getting a good deal. We had finished our shift and decided to go out in town as we needed to let off steam. We found a bar with an ex-rep as the landlord and not many holidaymakers. He looked after us all night giving us free food and drink at times, he understood our need for compassion. I will never forget seeing the first coach for four days through a glass window sitting in a pub. The strike was over, so we had a small celebration that night but we knew that the fun was just beginning.

After the strike was over there would be a backlog of passengers and it took another 3–4 weeks for the system to get back to normality. As far as the reps where concerned the drivers got no favours from us, as they were tolerated but never forgiven. They were the highest paid workers on the island before the strike and got another 17% pay rise. They had asked for 25%. I was disgusted and had no respect for them, with many other reps feeling the same way. Some of the reps resigned because of the trauma they had been through, others had counselling, some had shattered nerves.

Strikes are a common occurrence at Palma airport, because Palma airport is one of the busiest in the world. A strike has a major impact, that is why every year strikes follow one after the other. One strike involved the cleaners; their behaviour was again brainless because they made such a mess. Toilet rolls were strewn everywhere, plant pots were turned upside down, and slogans were written on walls amongst other vandalism. When the strike was over they had to clean up their own mess. The point they were trying to make backfired on them as getting another cleaner would not be a problem.

Another incident, which is far beyond a rep's control, is flight delays. We cannot do a thing about it but take the flack. With flight delays you have to be diplomatic and try not to worry the passengers. For example can you imagine saying to a passenger you have been delayed six hours. That would cause outrage. If you said 2–3 hours the impact is less. You want to avoid an angry mob or rumours starting that are not accurate. If you get an angry mob one person is always the ringleader, he is very dangerous having a great effect on the others. The best option would be to shoot him but that is against the law. After all that I needed a holiday myself with hopefully no hassle.

Towards the end of the season quite a few transfer reps were leaving due to the fact that the strikes had caused a knock-on effect of flight delays and there was continuous hassle from the holidaymakers who wanted to get home. Transfer reps would spend more time at the airport than anyone else coming into contact with passengers every second of the day. This was a very stressful time and many of the staff could not cope with any more abuse. I was asked to move to a place just up the road called S'Illot, a very small resort that I had never been to. I was one of the older staff members and had experience in dealing with the irate customers so was put into a small team. I knew some of them from last time on the island. I was sharing an apartment with a girl whose housework kept the place very clean and tidy. On the coach journey to and from the airport we had a good view of the planes coming into land because we had to go under the flight path and cross the end of the runway, sometimes if we were lucky a plane would take off or land. You could see the underneath of the planes very clearly as they were so low. This moment of light relief was always good as it took the mind off a possible wait at the airport.

At the end of the season I went on a golfing holiday to Portugal for a hassle and abuse-free rest. The flight was originally delayed by six hours. This had no effect on me, just meant more time sitting down. I felt really sorry for the duty staff as customers were verbally attacking them, which was like me three months ago. The good thing on the staff's side was that the police spoke English, which did make a difference as tempers were hotting up. I just sat watching and ear wigging the staff taking all the bullshit people think of under stress. The best was to come when they cancelled the flight, and then we had to fly to Spain then transfer onto a coach taking us to Portugal.

At Gatwick airport when this was announced in the departure lounge passengers were going daft and I felt relief for the staff as police turned up ready for action, handguns visible. All you can do is go along with it and be patient. I kept quiet about my job. When we finally flew people where so unhappy that they moaned all the way about everything and anything. We were then met by a rep at the airport who would take us to our hotels by coach. I knew her and had worked with her in a different resort, a very pleasant young girl. The coach journey was long but I was comfortable snuggling up to a friend who I had met on the journey. We stopped a few times to stretch our legs, by now no complaining as everyone was nearing their final destination. When my girlfriend and I parted we swapped numbers but I never saw her again. We finally arrived at our destination fifteen hours later. I was on a golfing holiday and worth the wait as I played some great golf. So as you can see there is no point in getting stressed about a situation out of your control.

My next season was in Gran Canaria part of the Canary Islands. This name came about because Christopher Columbus discovered the Islands and found many wild dogs running around. The Latin for dog is Canari so hence the name Gran Canaria. I was on a week's induction course and as soon as I landed I got recognised straight away as Disco Dave, so my name again preceded me. We all stayed in the same hotel and went out every night to bond together. We stayed in one of the main resorts called Playa D'Ingles. We used to go to the same pub every night because we had reps' discount cards that allowed us to purchase cheap drink. One night I walked into the pub and I was invited up to perform a karaoke number by Tom Jones "It's Not Unusual". The DJ and the other reps were so impressed I sang every night from then on and I was announced when entering the pub as Disco Dave. It's quite scary when people actually say that you can sing because with the confidence that gives you it makes you sing more songs. The booze helps as well to loosen the vocal cords.

I was dancing nearly all night so the DJ got me to do a solo dance to "Night Fever", I could have killed him as I was surrounded by people. So I tried to dance, started off well, impressing some of the chicks, but the record never seemed to stop. I started to wilt in the heat after an encore performance. I enjoy dancing, never turning down a request to have a go, especially when relaxed and under the influence. Disco Dave had risen from the ashes once more in front of his adoring public.

We went all over the island of Gran Canaria and saw all the touristy spots as well as a brilliant show called Gatsby's. I thought that the shows I had seen in Mallorca would never be beaten or equalled but this was up with the best. The treatment we received was excellent and each table had its own singing and performing waiter or waitress. They never stopped entertaining all night and we had a laugh leaving a tip at the end, which for reps to do is unheard of. They had a special table for the reps and two people got up from our table to go on stage and be embarrassed.

A good day out was the Jeep Safari. For this we had to wear old gear as it was going to be really dusty and dirty. Our driver was fun and made driving along dirt tracks with a sheer drop one side look a piece of cake. He was throwing the jeep around like a rag on the dirt tracks, creating a dust cloud along the side of the mountains. Every now and then we passed a few cars that had not been so lucky and were lying in precarious positions half way down the mountain. If we passed any cyclists on route the driver would reach out of the jeep and have a chat to them or take a video of their feet. He only did this on the main road, as the tracks were a different story. I did not fancy being stuck in a jeep half way down a mountain, as the region was so wild and rocky.

On our way down to flat land we saw a herd of mountain goats being shepherded back up the mountain to their ranch so we stopped the jeeps and got off for a rest, marvelling at the athleticism of the goats going up steep paths where we could not go. You would always know where the goats were as they all had bells around their necks. Our guides got out of the jeeps to show us an edible fruit that grew in the wild. The fruit was green in colour, no surprise there, but when cut open an eye catching deep rich red colour was revealed. The fruit was protected by a thorn bush giving a message of not edible, but there is a knack to getting the fruit out. The fruit is covered in tiny sharp needles, which if you get into your skin are very painful, but you can overcome this. You need to break off a large needle from the stem of the plant scraping the tiny needles off the outer skin of the fruit. Then cut around the top off the skin, a bit like cutting open the top of an egg before squeezing out the fruit. When the fruit comes out be very careful, if the red die gets onto your clothes it will never be removed. When you have finished eating, your mouth, tongue and hands are a very bright red bloody colour.

One of our trips that we had to sell was a day out at a camel farm with lunch provided. The first stage was a ride on a camel, I had done this before so knew what was awaiting us. We had a talk and the guide gave us tips about camels. Tell your customers not to wear perfume and to wear long trousers such as jeans. We would be going along a man-made route in a long line of camels each attached by a rope controlled by a man with a stick. Camels do get very close to you but wear muzzles so they cannot bite. One of the girls must have been wearing perfume as a camel was getting very affectionate towards her. This was funny as she talked and screamed at the camel, as if the camel could understand her words of wisdom. When we stopped to get off she leapt out of her seat like a young salmon swimming to a point of safety, leaving the camels in her wake.

A baby camel had been born very recently and it was on display in a stable. It looked like a baby horse, as its hump was not yet showing. Also in the stable were other young camels, with their humps prominent and they were steady on their feet. This experience was new to me and once more opened my eyes to the wonders of nature.

On the last night of our induction course we all went out and had a curry and then onto an Irish pub which we had not visited before. We were originally going to stay for one drink before moving on but plans changed. They had a band playing live music. At the interval the landlord Paddy, honestly that was his name, came round and was after singers so the others volunteered me. The thing was there were no words to follow so the song was live. I knew the song, "American Pie", fairly well. The words that I did not know I would make up as I had done this many a time before, so much so that it had become my party piece. My mates back home are always telling me that I make up words to songs. I always say if the words make sense stick them in, how many people listen to the words in songs anyway? Once I had started, the others joined in and enjoyed singing with a live band backing them. One of the girls had a good voice but needed a bit of courage and confidence as she does enjoy singing but gets embarrassed. Once the ice was broken a few more of our party got up to sing and we stayed in there for a long time.

I also had another name before I left, Captain Beaver. This came about when we were in a coffee bar in Las Palmas the capital of Gran Canaria. We were just chatting and the subject of beavers came around, how and why I cannot remember or could it be that in our group we had two stunning female specimens. Being a military man I was given the honour of being called captain.

Being a captain I had to have a few girls and a couple volunteered, so now they needed a name. We came up with the Beaverettes.

We all went out into town and Captain Beaver and the Beaverettes had a late night with a group of lads. One particular lad was intrigued with the Beaverettes and wanted to see their beaver. The captain had to be consulted first and the answer was no because beavers are a protected species. Also every morning there was a beaver inspection by the captain and I did not want to see perfect beavers damaged, they had been well looked after with no blemishes. The lad was disappointed but funny with it and we had such a good laugh because the lad was offering anything to see the works of art on display. The other two lads who were his friends were also pulling his leg and could see the funny side, taking the joke in the right spirit with only his ego being damaged.

Chapter 9

HOLIDAYS

In 1978 I went to see the Seven Wonders of the World on a school trip starting off at Split in the then Yugoslavia on the SS *Uganda*. The ship was built in 1952 and was converted to a school ship at a cost of around 2.7 million pounds carrying well over 1,000 passengers. The port was huge full of large oil tankers; our ship was not big compared to those. The places we were going to visit would be Egypt, Venice, Greece, Italy, Rhodes, Turkey and Pompeii.

We set off on our voyage visiting the Pyramids and Sphinx. The pyramids of Giza are situated eight miles south west of the centre of Cairo and are three in number – The Great Pyramid of Giza, Pyramid of Chefren and Pyramid of Mycerinus. The Great Pyramid of Giza was built around 2690 BC and is the most gigantic piece of architecture in the world. It was originally 481 feet high but earthquakes and vandalism in past ages have reduced it by 31 feet to 450 feet, still tall enough not to be missed and very imposing. It can be climbed from the outside under guidance as steps have been created, inside active people can make their way through passages to the burial chamber (Kings Chamber). The Pyramid of Chefren was built around 2650 BC by the Pharaoh Chefren. Smaller than the Great Pyramid it is built on higher ground so appears even larger than its neighbour and has a vertical height of 447 feet. The Pyramid of Mycerinus, smallest in the group, was built in 2600 BC by Chefren's successor Menkeure (in Greek Mycerinus). It cannot be climbed or entered by tourists as it is still sealed.

The Sphinx is the largest piece of sculpture ever to be carved by human hand. Its Arabic name is Father of Terror having a lion's body and human head. It is 66 feet high and 240 feet long. I had not realised the size of these monuments or knew much history about the stones but it must have taken various craftsmen many years of sweat and tears to complete the task. When you see them for real it is difficult to imagine how they were actually built, no hydraulics or modern machinery just shear blood and guts. The Egyptians must have had engineers far advanced in building knowledge as the construction of some building structures is still unexplained. They must have been the first to invent scaffolding or a building frame that you could sit or stand to work on. The Pyramids all point to the same position in the sky and are spaced out into calculated areas. The stones themselves are huge blocks that can be seen because of the winds and sand eroding away the outer layers. This poses other questions that have not been answered, for example how did the stones get transported from A to B across the sea and how did they get the stones onto the ships?

As you can see the old get older.

We also spent some time in Cairo on the way to the pyramids visiting a museum, which has a superb collection of Egyptian antiquity giving us an idea of this ancient country. Excavations have produced exhibits continually bringing to light signs of the old Egyptian civilisation. The most popular exhibits are the collection of mummies and the exquisite and perfectly preserved gold from the tomb of Tutankhamen. Inside the tomb the air is cool but once outside the heat was tremendous. The heat at times was overpowering as it made you thirsty, which meant finding clean drinking water. For this we had to walk around the town and buy bottled water. The town was not like in the UK where everyday needs are catered for.

The one thing that I found hard to come to terms with was the poverty that I had seen and being hassled by children all the time for shoe shine or just begging for loose change. I was only fourteen years old myself, first time abroad on my own so I was impressionable with the different ways of life and cultures. I saw dead dogs that had starved to death lying in the gutter and animals being tied up with wire, to me this was a big culture shock and I did not realise that poverty on such a scale could happen in the world today.

After a hard day's work sightseeing it was back on the boat and homework. I have always hated homework and given the circumstances we were under very reluctant to do any, but I did my best to do the tasks but there were too many distractions on the ship to fully give one hundred per cent concentration. This was my first time on a so-called cruise ship and I intended to make the most of it. In the evenings they had discos for us and various games. But my real fascination was the Mediterranean. The sea is almost tide-less but what tide there is circles in an anti-clockwise direction. By evaporation the water becomes more saline, therefore increasing in density. There are also sunken wrecks and cities, which are being preserved by saline in the water. The fish that are present are a real variety such as sardines, hake, ray, mullet, shellfish and mackerel. So the food onboard due to the vast amount of fish was fish. I'm positive that the ship had a secret net being pulled under the boat catching breakfast, dinner and tea.

The Corinth Canal is a major shipping lane in the Mediterranean but so tiny, I was expecting something bigger. I had heard about the canal expecting something like the Suez Canal but nothing like it, just big enough to fit a large tanker through but not a super tanker. The journey time this canal saves is a vast amount, which in today's society means money and going through the canal can save so much time and millions of pounds for large companies. Nothing has changed for hundreds of years which is astounding when you think what machines are capable off. The canal could easily be widened giving access to more trade.

Everywhere you go there are amphitheatres, the acoustics from these horseshoe shaped arenas are beyond belief considering they are outdoors and made of concrete or stone. From the back seats and high up you can hear everything that is being said on stage creating a fantastic atmosphere. You are still able to create a picture in your mind of the splendour of these vast arenas being full all those years ago. There are also many palaces around which again in their day took some knowledge of building. Although most are ruins now you still get an idea of the magnitude of the task in hand.

Greece is situated at the far end of the Balkans and the southern end of the Dinaric Alps, being the furthest south and east of all countries in the Eastern Mediterranean. The country consists of one large peninsula and many islands. Greece was the home of at least three great civilisations: the Aegeans, Athenians and Byzantines and these had a profound and lasting effect on the whole of the Mediterranean area and subsequently on the Western world. Although the early ages of Greek development (the Cycladic, Minoan, Helladic and Mycenean civilisations) and the later period of decomposition up to the Roman conquest are important, it is the classical period (500–33 BC) which is most notable.

Facing up to the Persian threat, Greece united and the Persian wars did much to enhance the prestige of Athens. Under Pericles' democratic rule the civilisation reached its highest point, art and literature flourished, particularly as regards drama, which is still in evidence today as many plays are done in keeping with the old traditions. Athens and the port of Piraeus became the centre of trade and communications, with goods from all over the world transported there.

The Acropolis was built in the 5th century BC. The end of this period resulted from the climax of an old antagonism between the two super powers at Sparta and Athens, and other Greek city-states. Philip the second of Macedonia imposed his rule over the divided Greeks, and later his son Alexander The Great was recognised as leader in campaigns against the Persians and Egyptians.

After the death of Alexander The Great in 323 BC the Greek empire broke up into small kingdoms under his generals. The Romans first made their appearance in the 3rd century BC and by 27 BC Greece was incorporated into their empire. Three centuries of stability and peace were enjoyed allowing people to express themselves showing what skill they had in their arts, crafts, design and buildings, until the division of 395 AD when the country fell to the Byzantine Empire. Eventually the Ottoman Turks conquered Byzantium in the 15th century.

Next we visited an island called Crete and Heraklion its main city, to see the palace of Knossos. The palace itself is massive and some sections are still preserved. The sections that are standing give a good indication of the architecture and how skilful the builders were in erecting such intricate structures. The actual artwork must have taken years to complete but such was the skill of these people that it has lasted for centuries, allowing us to marvel at its splendour thousands of years down the road.

Italy and Naples came next. Did you know that the Italy is an incredible country because it extends 1200km from north to south and has a coastline of 8500km? It is bounded in the north by the Alpine range and has borders with France, Switzerland, Austria and Yugoslavia and is surrounded by four inner seas – the Ligurian, Tyrrhenian, Ionian and Adriatic. Italy is one of the cradles of European culture and civilisation. There is evidence of various settlements in the region as long ago as 2000 BC, but Rome wasn't founded until 753 BC. The Etruscans in the north were the first to develop a large area but were weakened by several wars. The capital Veii was captured by Romans in 396 BC. Following Romulus, six kings ruled Rome, but in 510 BC it became a republic hopefully stopping all the bloodshed. Despite many setbacks the empire grew under the rule of the Triumvirate, which was formed in 60 BC. However in 48 BC Julius Ceasar was elected emperor for life and took sole command until four years later Brutus murdered him. The Roman Empire spread far and wide with the conquering of the Carthaginian and Grecian Empires, but eventually began to decline and was overthrown by the Goths in 476 AD.

Turkey is an amazing country with 97% being in Asia (the Anatolian Plateau) and 3% in Europe (the hill country of Thrace). This supports a population of over forty million people. The European and Asian parts of the country are separated by the Dardanelles, the Sea of Marmara and the Bosphorus, while as a whole it borders with Greece, Syria, Iraq, Iran, Russia, the Black Sea, the Aegean Sea and the Mediterranean. The coastline of its four seas is over 7000km long. Settlements date back to 6500 BC with the oldest Neolithic town being Catal Hoyuk, however the first settlement at Troy wasn't until 3000 BC. The Hittites established the most ancient historical civilisation in Asia Minor between 1750–1200 BC until they were defeated by the "sea peoples" which resulted in the destruction of Homeric Troy.

In 1301 the Ottoman principality was established and in 1453 Constantinople, the Byzantine capital was captured and renamed Istanbul. The Ottoman Empire did not go into decline until the 18th–19th centuries having very much established itself, even to this day the foundations of a civilisation still surviving.

Having sided with the Germans in the First World War Turkey was occupied by the allies and partitioned among the victors in 1918. Turkey was to become a puppet state with a Black Sea coastline only. Mustafa Kemal however led a national revival, which led to the withdrawal of Britain, France, Italy and Greece. Because of The Treaty of Lusanne signed in 1923 this meant that the allies were obliged to recognise the sovereignty of a Turkish state. Between 1923 and 1938 Mustafa Kemal transformed oriental Turkey into a western nation; among his changes were the transfer of the capital from Istanbul to Ankara; the abolition of the fez and encouragement of Western dress; the abandonment of Arabic in favour of a national Turkish language. Kemal died in 1938 and in World War II Turkey remained neutral. The Turkish Republic of today is a nationalist democratic and secular state although 99% of the population is Moslem.

While I was there I went to see an old town called Ephesus situated about 50 miles by road south of Izmir. In 334 BC. Alexander The Great gained control of Ephesus but after his death another new city was built in the valley further west. Ephesus later came under Roman rule and became the most important port of the Roman province of Asia. In the early days of Christianity St Paul came to Ephesus, where he spent three years, founding the first Christian community. St John also came to Ephesus and is said to have written his gospel here. According to tradition Ephesus was the last home of the Virgin Mary. The Goths destroyed Ephesus in 262 AD and the city never regained its former importance. Eventually the site was silted up and marshes formed, malaria finally drove the inhabitants to settle on the slopes of the surrounding hills.

Pompeii, everybody has heard about it, but do you know where it is or why it is so famous? It used to be the ancient city of Campania, Italy, lying 1.5 miles from the sea at the south-east foot of mount Vesuvius. It was made a Roman colony in 80 BC and became a small flourishing town and seaport, also a pleasure resort of wealthy Romans. Then it became wrecked by an earthquake in 63 AD, and was hastily rebuilt though much remained in ruins. Then it was overwhelmed by a great eruption of Vesuvius on 24th August 79 AD. Thousands of small pieces of pumice stone covered the town to a depth of 8–10 feet followed by a fall of ash. Sulphurous flames suffocated about two thousand people. In 1748 discovery of some statues led to an exploration of the site. They found Roman temples, theatres, gladiator barracks and at the east end of the city an amphitheatre. The more interesting remains are private houses, which illustrate the life of all classes.

As you can see, plenty of information to take in and digest giving a good insight to the history of the world where most people were poor and had to fend for themselves but still manage to live and produce such works of art with their bare hands. I think this is incredible.

Back now to modern times and less taxing on the brain, another place I have visited is Paris, France. I had always wanted to go there and see the fashion and some of the various attractions that it has to offer. I went with a friend and stayed for a week. The French revolution was a major piece of history and the revolutionaries got around the city by using the sewers. We visited the sewers which are big and like a city beneath a city. There was a slight smell but not overpowering because machines were used to clean and keep the sewers flushing properly. The tunnels stretch from the Turgot gallery to the Eiffel tower along the river Seine. We needed to flush our throats after this so we found a watering hole.

In Paris Jazz music is quite popular and we found a pub with live jazz music. The music was very good and relaxing. We stayed in there and used to use that pub as our local or to meet up if we wanted to go our separate ways. One thing I found about the French in Paris is that they have different prices in restaurants or coffee shops. For example you get charged differently when you sit outside. If you are a tourist and being English you get charged more, even the time of day morning, afternoon, evenings and after midnight has an influence on the price. By the end of the week I was not happy with this so I started to speak French and the difference in price was incredible, everything was literally half price or less. After all, what favours have the French ever done for the British?

One of the places that was good value for money was the Hard Rock Café which had a menu so a standard price and a good portion of food. They also had a large glass coloured window with Elvis and John Lennon on as well as the usual memorabilia decoration. This stop was a tactical manoeuvre forced on me. We had gone into a real French bar beforehand for a traditional coffee to practice our French lingo. While in there a French bloke was clocking us in a sexual way. I was not too concerned initially because there were two of us, both straight. We left that bar moving on to the next. Next bar this guy followed us, trying to catch our attention. He was getting closer and closer until within speaking range. I went into the Hard Rock Café partly to avoid a poofter who was after my body. I even told the bouncers outside not to let him in because if he came near me I would not be responsible for my actions. I would probably stick something so far up his arse he would never shit again out of the same hole.

Paris is definitely full of surprises with its own unique style of doing things. In one bar they had a miniature train going around at head height, which was something different and a good gimmick. The track was so low that if I stretched my hands above my head I would have touched it. That is the one and only time that I have seen that in a bar.

Paris is known for its fashion and some of the shops just oozed class and money. Money that is an obscene amount, which I will never have in my lifetime unless I win the lottery. When browsing in some shops there was no touching of clothes allowed, that is how much fashion means to the people as the look is everything. I am practical anyway so for me to spend £200 on a polo shirt I would relate that to something else, such as two or three nights out with the lads on a weekend after watching or playing sport in the afternoon.

The parks were very neat and tidy with French people playing boules; this is where you have to get nearest the jack with silver coloured balls, the balls being slightly bigger than a cricket ball and heavier. It is like us playing golf on our weekend off, it is that popular with the peasants. I have played this on holiday a few times when on the sandy beach as you need soft ground not concrete.

You would come across bronze and gold monuments of famous people all adding to the Paris scene. These monuments were imposing and could not be missed as they were not hidden from view but out in the open. This gave the area a bit of prestige and sparkle as they glistened in the sunlight.

We travelled on the underground frequently which is very similar to London, all signposted which told you where to go and different coloured routes told you the line to take. We did get lost ourselves on more than one occasion negotiating our way to various destinations somewhere in Paris. But that was part of the fun; we never knew where we would end up next. One thing I did find scary was crossing the road as the pedestrians were there to be aimed at, not avoided.

We did the sightseeing items as well including the Sacre Coeur church in Pigalle, the red light area. Not my cup of tea but we had to see it as it was steeped in history. It does look impressive and stands out in a crowd. Inside it seemed very cold, damp and dark, not a good place to spend the night if you are scared of ghosts.

The Eiffel Tower is a must when in Paris and to stand at the bottom and look up is quite something, you get a feeling of intimidation and feel inadequate. You can go all the way to the top which is what we did and can see most of Paris, there is a lift which takes you part of the way but the rest you have to walk. Due to the fact that the structure is like a Meccano set, you can always see the ground, which can be bad if you get vertigo. I can remember seeing a James Bond film where he jumped off the tower and parachuted to safety; people have been known to do this but without a parachute or safety net, a very safe way to commit suicide.

New York, the Big Apple. This was probably one of my best holidays ever. I went with a mate from the Navy so we had enough money on us to have a good time as we had just come back from sea with money burning a hole in our pockets. On the plane we were sitting next to a girl who was a really good laugh and joined us in a few light refreshments. It was only a five-hour trip over to New York so we had to drink fast. Anyway we found out that this girl had a friend and both of them designed clothes for a pop group in Britain called Ziggy Ziggy Sputnik. They had just appeared on a music programme called *Top Of The Pops* and had a major selling recorded single in Britain. So we had something in common to talk about and were invited to their shop in Manhattan.

We all had a bit to drink and my bag was in front of my mate who felt a bit sick as we were descending, I had never seen him sick before and knew that he could take vast quantities of booze, he had a cuddly frame with a large larder. He was also a nervous flyer and produced what was in the larder all over my bag and himself but not over me, phew. As you can imagine there was quite a mess. The plane stopped and I was dreading getting out of our seats having to walk through the narrow isle between the seats inside of the plane. When we got up to leave I carried the zipped-up bag, which had been zipped up all the way through the flight, which was lucky as no sick penetrated the inside. If it had I would have cried, never drinking again that day because the smell was making me feel sick. I managed to get my bag covered in sick off the plane and into the airport, all the time head down walking fast. I was heading for somewhere that had running water and towels. In the toilets I washed the smelly crusty-topped mess off the bag while my mate cleaned himself up. We came out of the toilets new men on the outside but stomachs could still erupt with no warning. We got to the carousel managing to take our cases off without incident. It was a relief to get outside to the welcomed fresh air and relative calm. We then got a taxi to our hotel where we took our stained clothes off and into bed, not together I might add as we were both straight. When we woke up and back to the world of the living we realised that the taxi driver had overcharged us by about twenty dollars, a perfect start to our unwinding and tranquil rest. Our holiday was to start off in New York for five days, Washington D.C. for one week finishing at Los Angeles for five days with the accommodation booked for the first night in each place. After that we had to find our own rooms.

We had arrived and did not unpack, as it was only a short stay. We managed to find accommodation at 44th Street so began our tour of New York. As we were walking we noticed all sorts of things going on like horse and carts, street people playing instruments and break-dancing, body-popping, mime and other such crazes, all these people very talented and busking for money. New York also has a subway and to get around it is very convenient though dangerous but we never had any trouble. I think that this can be said about any underground system, if you go on your own late at night and it is quiet you are bound to attract the wrong sort of attention, especially being a tourist.

We went to Chinatown where I bought a pair of Chinese slippers really cheaply and were so comfortable you could wear them anywhere, even in the sea. There are many Chinatowns around the world, most of them in China! This one in America was bigger and better than most, as you would expect. The most striking feature was that you could have been in China, hardly any other nationalities other than Chinese present. Every now and then firecrackers going off and a few dragons appearing breathing fire from their costumes.

Central Park is huge and busy with lots of activities taking place. We listened to a band playing in a small amphitheatre and at the same time there was a cycling race going on around the park, always something to look at or do. Large picnic areas, people playing sports, rollerblading and that is only the tip of what happens. Very pretty and exciting during the day but night time a whole different ball game, a place to stay well clear of if you want to see tomorrow.

We had to go and see the World Trade centres, which sadly no longer exist but was a real landmark then. The elevator that took us up to the top was very quick and we were up there in no time. The view from the top was breathtaking and could see all the way around Manhattan. These Trade Centres made the skyline very different from anywhere else on the globe and was in every picture of New York that I came across. Can you imagine being a window cleaner, at least it would be an all year round job.

I never thought this picture would be one of a kind. The traffic is so small it gives you some idea of the height of the building, also the bridges giving the impression of an island. Saving the best till last, the view. You can literally see the whole of New York from up here.

Around Manhattan all you can see is bridges connecting other areas and the Statue of Liberty cannot be missed, as it is one of the landmarks of American history, a gift from a different country.

Next stop, Statue of Liberty. To get to this we had to get a boat across the bay to Liberty Island to see the statue. I didn't know quite what to expect but I was a bit disappointed. I thought it would be bigger and you could go all the way to the top of the cone held high up by the arm. The statue itself does give you a sore neck when looking up as it is vertically challenging when standing close. The lift was broken so we had to queue and gradually climb the stairs with the other thousand people waiting for the view and to see what was at the top of the crown. When we eventually got there you looked through a little window across the bay to Manhattan and the World Trade Centres, that was it. You got a better view from the outside looking across to Manhattan.

After this we decided to head back into town using the underground and find the shop that the girls owned. The last time we had seen them was on the plane and not feeling or looking well. To find addresses is quite easy because all the roads are in a grid starting at 1, so if they are at 35 and 20 that's 35 streets up and 20 across. We found the shop and it was shut but they would be back soon so we decided to go for a beer and wait for them. When they came back after lunch we went in and had a look around the shop. It was a leather shop with a difference, everything from whips to thongs. A girl was trying on a dress with large slits all the way up both sides and she had a good physique. As they were busy with clients we met them for a drink afterwards and had a good chat about the nightlife in the area. This time we were very controlled with our drinking and made a better impression with the ladies. One of the girls gave us her card to get into a nightclub called the Limelight Club. Apparently Grace Jones frequented the place from time to time, the girls told us where it was giving us good directions.

My mate was not into clubbing so I went on my own, and to find the place was a nightmare. Outside in the darkened streets there were no neon lights or anything-bright saying Limelight Club. This would have helped immensely as I was not sure what I was looking for. In England the clubs have bouncers outside for one thing and have obvious flashing lights. I had been positive that I had the correct address but could not believe what was standing there. I had passed a church a few times but thought nothing of it until I asked someone and he pointed to the same church that I had been puzzled with. There was nobody outside, it looked deserted, I knocked on the little sliding hatch and a head appeared then disappeared and the old wooden door creaked open. I went in and showed my card and I must have put on a slight accent, the guys on the door said where are you from, I just said out of town, they said from Chicago, I said yes and in I went. Inside it was an old church converted into three discos with a stage in one for various acts. The roof was really high as well allowing permanent balconies to be built. The windows were coloured glass as in churches. I enjoyed it, as it was free to get in and totally different to the clubs back in the UK, more of a party atmosphere and not as hostile. I stayed there for a while dancing and having a few drinks before walking home afterwards and somehow found my way back to my own comfortable bed. The place we had found to stay was near to 42nd street and most of the evening all you could hear were police sirens up and down the road. So we had seen a lot of New York and it is very similar to the city portrayed on TV.

Next up was the capital of America, Washington DC (District of Columbia). This was part of a package deal, the first night in a hotel followed by a bed and breakfast for the remainder of our stay. The B&B was clean and tidy and the landlady a sweet, generous and kind coloured mama. She had an Alsatian dog that was not very well but a real softie. The dog could not get up because it had lost the use of its back legs so it had to crawl everywhere. I had to chuckle as the mama was a stereo type of what you would expect adding "boy" to the end of sentences. I did not realise how much there was to do and see in Washington D.C.

We started off touring the bars finding out information about the city. We managed to find a bar near to our bed and breakfast, our local. We got on with the local punters very well, especially the girls as they loved the English accent. One particular girl we adopted and she spent a lot of time with us taking us around the city. The bar tenders were amazed as to how much we could drink and we would often order a pitcher or half pitcher with one pint glass each. The Americans are not used to this, one American guy called us "amazing" because of our Olympic drinking habits.

We were out one night for a quiet beer and bumped into a couple of American Marines, so we got chatting and told them we were in the British Navy on Submarines on holiday. So they invited us to see a display done by the 8th & 1st Marine Corps, which they participated in. We accepted thinking nothing was going to happen, but it did. We had a phone call on the morning of the display and we were going to be picked up and taken to the barracks where they would meet us and take us in. At the time we had made good friends with a girl from our local pub who had been showing us around so she went as well, being invited by two typical English gents. She was excited because apparently this display often has senators there and sometimes the President himself attends. There is only a limited amount of public allowed to see the display. We got ourselves smartened up and waited for the taxi, a limousine came with a chauffeur and we could not believe our eyes, our girlfriend was speechless, we got into the back and found a note saying "help yourself to beer or a drink". As we were pulling up there was quite a queue of people outside the barracks but we drove straight past and to the front where we were met by the two lads dressed in ceremonial uniform looking very smart and impressive. So we met them shaking hands, it was like having our own guard of honour as people looked on probably thinking we were from the American congress. Once inside they took us into the NCO's (Non Commissioned Officers) mess and gave us a drink, everything was on them all night. They then showed us to our seats before starting the display.

First there was a military band as a preliminary to the display. For years the British have always been the best at military ceremonies but this was I thought on a par or better! There was not one obvious mistake. One of their sequences was a silent drill containing a hundred different moves, sounds easy but not when you have to make patterns and shapes in a set routine all from memory. The marines also got inspected but with a difference, a sergeant would march along the front of the soldiers and every so often stop. Holding out an out-stretched arm, a rifle would then be thrown into his hand, he would then inspect it before throwing it back to the soldier without looking. Also with the rifles they would spin them around their fingers and do other spectacular tricks. The whole display lasted for about two hours, I can honestly say that after the display I had never seen, nor will never ever see, anything better than that in my entire life. I was astonished how professional it was, the experience living up to far beyond my expectations. Afterwards we went back to the NCO's mess and had a buffet meal and congratulated the lads on such a wonderful display. Discussing the display I told the lads that we were overwhelmed by the entire spectacle, not able to detect one mistake. They said that mistakes were made but to an un-trained eye not apparent. Our girlfriend talked about this whole experience from start to finish for weeks afterwards, she had only dreamed about seeing some-thing like this. I have never seen those lads since which is a shame because I would like to thank them personally for giving us such a brilliant evening, but I am the world's worst for keeping in touch.

Another place we went to see was the Arlington Cemetery. Nestled in the beautiful, wooded hills of Arlington on 617 acres is the final resting place for many of America's patriots from foot soldiers to Presidents, from the well known to the unknown kept in immaculate condition, every inch of ground being used to create such a spectacle. Bright white stones set in a grid pattern and a carpet of well-manicured green grass. Also there is the house of Robert E. Lee where he signed the surrender to the Union in the American Civil War. There is so much to see here, for example the Tomb of the Unknown soldier, this is a tomb to commemorate all those soldiers of many wars past and present who have died fighting for their country. The tomb is guarded by soldiers and while we were there we watched the changing of the guard.

Another place that is a must for the tourist is the Vietnam memorial, where along a black marble wall are the names of men and women who lost their lives in Vietnam. Thousands of names but a tribute to those who fought for what they considered to be a worthy cause. When you stand looking at the wall you feel a sense of why, it is never a warm place with always a slight chill in the air, a very silent place. There is nothing grand to look at but it will always be in American minds.

Washington D.C. is divided up into four quarters with a large white domed building being the centre of the city. Like in New York the streets criss-cross forming a grid. Near to the centre of Washington D.C. is Capitol Hill where there is a large park. The park gives you a good view of the city from where you can see many famous buildings. One of these is The Washington Monument (which looks like a tall knitting needle) standing erect overlooking a large man-made pond. From the top of this you get a fabulous panoramic view of the city. An awesome view of the White House greets you, in fact you can wave to the President and he could wave back if he was at home. There was a programme called *Fame* on television following the training of performing arts students. We managed to find the particular building and could imagine ourselves having a wonderful time at the college, being on stage and having our name in lights.

Speaking of which I went to a soul concert to see a legend. Freddie Jackson was performing so I decided to go along as I like coloured music especially, jazz funk, soul and Reggie. I went on my own as my mate was not well. I set off early so as to find the venue, the venue being miles away, the other side of town to where we were staying. It was a hot day so I had a walk through the park and arrived in the main town containing most of the shops and theatres. I found the venue early as I had given myself plenty of time so I went into a bar next door to rest my weary legs. Also having a few beers were some of the stagehands so I got talking to them to pass the time, some of them being from England. When I went into the theatre I was the only white man there. I was not bothered but did stand out. I have no attitude towards West Indians as I have worked with them and found them to be fun loving people. I had a great time dancing and getting into the rhythm, the concert went on for a couple of hours playing many of his catchy numbers.

Getting back took me ages, I decided to walk thinking that it was not all that far but it was, probably about 6–7 miles. Doing that at night without a compass is not recommended. I had a few stops on the way to have something to eat and drink, I was getting well lost, asking people for directions. I found a police car when the sun was starting to come up so I flagged down the car and we had a chat about who I was and what I was doing out at this time. I must have said the right things because the policeman identified me as a stranded tourist and took me home. When I got back mama was up making black coffee and mud pie.

Other tourist attractions are the Lincoln Memorial, which is a large statue where Lincoln is sitting on a throne made of concrete, not moving a muscle – he's been there for so long he has got stiff. There is a Roman style building surrounding him. Probably to keep the pigeon excrement off him. As with everything in America the statue is big, wow.

Now came our longest flight across to the west coast and Los Angeles, this took seven hours flying with one stop. When we finally arrived at L.A. airport we were so glad to get off the plane and stretch our legs. We were then picked up by a courtesy bus which was very pleasant indeed and taken to a hotel, we arrived late and decided to try out the pool before it shut. Connecting the indoor and outdoor pools was a small canal which you could swim through. The outdoor pool was warm considering that outside was dark and it was the winter season. There was steam coming off the water so this kept us amused for hours. We had been joined by a few other people by now so a bit of a party ensued enjoying the relaxing facilities.

The following day we managed to find a motel to stay in where we decided to stay for the duration of our holiday, the rooms were good and for the price we paid an excellent choice. We also had an outdoor pool and snack bar. Now it was time to do some exploring, we hopped on a bus and went downtown passing the Hard Rock Café with Elvis Presley's car on the roof, he must have been drunk at the time. We also passed a place called tar pits where natural tar is bubbling from the ground in a small pond. This is not man-made but a freak of nature, for effect large plastic mammals are scattered around for imitation. This took me aback, as I never expected to see tar coming up from the ground in a pond full of water.

We ended up at Sunset Boulevard and had a good shop around, we saw where the big names in Hollywood have prints of their hands and feet on the public footpath and could see the Hollywood sign on the hill. The good thing about sightseeing in America is that it is cheap and you get your money's worth.

We then went on a tour around Hollywood. The complex covers many areas and does not look much from the outside. Our first adventure was going into a spaceship and seeing a mock battle, a bit like Buck Rodgers in the 20th century, the set had been used in a film but I cannot remember what, but the acting and sound effects were very clever. As the tour bus drives slowly through the planet a spaceship appears guarded by people in space costumes. They appear unaware that an attack is imminent. The lighting then reveals their attackers hiding behind rocks waiting for the signal to go in. The battle commences, laser fire, explosions and small fires. The actors doing a fine job in creating an action-packed mock battle.

We went across a collapsing bridge, which did actually collapse. You could feel yourself tipping as the various struts gave way under your vehicle. The bridge when approached looked very real, made of wood. All the effects were achieved by hydraulics but it was a scary experience, and you did feel as though you were tipping over the side.

A flood was our next disaster as a mass of water cascaded down and almost washed us away. The noise was loud and you could imagine yourself being in a disaster movie. The guide on the coach was excellent as he shouted, "Quick look to your left, everybody, brace yourself." A wall of water was upon us cascading down through a small narrow street in a small town, we were far enough away so no injuries, the water had lost its power and momentum by the time it reached us. I can imagine kids absolutely loving it large; I was having a most lovely time never mind the kids.

Then came the *Jaws* experience, the music getting louder as you approach the sea, you see a fin in the distance, looking ominous, then it disappears and your heart starts to race, where is the shark? All of a sudden it appears by your legs and what a magnificent beast, one thing you do notice is the eye looking at you putting your face in its memory for next time should you go swimming late at night in the dark. Every picture tells a story, look below and see for yourself, but not too low as it might bite you.

Your number's up, big boy.

Whilst we were there we saw them filming *Jaws 4* with the boat and a back-drop to make the scene look authentic. I can remember seeing that film looking out for that particular scene, I spotted the scene straight away. The piece of action where the coloured chap is standing at the very front of the boat. They used this backdrop a number of times.

We came across a burning house that was used for many scenes. This from the front looked a terrifying experience as real flames were coming out of all the windows. But when we went around the back we saw how this effect was created, with flame throwers and gas fires, simple but effective. One thing that did puzzle me was that the house itself seemed to be made of wood and wood burns in fire.

The best bit for me was seeing how they made some special effects in the film *E.T.* For example in the film they show you some young lads on bikes flying over the rooftops of houses. The bikes are stationary on a moving platform with a bright blue background, a film can then be shot against the blue background and special effects added later.

The same sort of thing happened in space scenes, the astronauts are on wires with a projected background. Again, clever lighting and sound create the effect and as the spacecraft door opens it reveals two astronauts. They make their way into space moving in slow motion being held up by thin but strong wires and a pulley mechanism. Normally you can see if someone is being held in this position but no sign of wires or sudden movement visible, all the actions very smooth and well disguised. They then had a big screen showing you the finished product that would be going out to people's TVs all over the world.

When making *Flash Gordon* they showed the scene of the rocket in the air travelling through space before landing, recreating the picture in the movie for us to see. The rocket always had something strange about it when watching the programme on TV. This was revealed, the answer being a firework sparkler in the back of the rocket used for propulsion, something you can buy in the shops.

It was then time to walk around outside in the Californian sun not knowing what could be outside waiting for us. When we were walking around we saw *Night Rider's* car Kit, you could actually sit inside and talk to the computer pretend to be driving it, good for any age.

A good film is *Back To The Future* where they use a clock on top of a building, which Doc eventually slides down on a wire. We saw the film set where the picture was made and could recognise the building made from wood and not brick. The clock is the focal point of this scene looking very real but this too is made cheaply. In the film Doc is on a very blustery and rainy ledge doing a great balancing act trying not to fall off. Here is a puzzling question for you – how did the rain materialise? Was a helicopter used with a large watering can or was it actually raining? All very deceiving to the eye as everything is made to look real, the material used is wood or polystyrene not concrete or brick.

Universal Studios is a day well spent and lots to see and do. When going through on the tour bus we saw a helicopter crashing onto a street that looked very real, lots of flames and large explosions. The helicopter started off in the sky in a large hangar, so not exactly in the sky but a clever illusion. Sound effects had you on the edge of your seat. Helicopter loses control starting to wobble, the pilots have no chance to regain the initiative before the helicopter takes control of their fate. Once all hope is lost it is only a matter of time before it nosedives into the ground at speed, the pilot's fate is sealed as flames engulf them. Don't be alarmed as Hollywood thinks of everything. The pilots are robots.

As we get further along the track we hear loud noises from the wild. Sounds like gorillas or apes. Turning the corner we are stopped by a large King Kong whose face and body was dwarfing our tiny bus. He was very close and could smell its breath as it was quickly upon us almost touching the bus. Everybody on the bus was quiet through shock and fear, knowing there was no escape from the King. All of these special effects are in a large hangar, which makes it more incredible.

They have a section especially for stunt men, this was a must on my books. Stunts like people falling off balconies in the cowboy films and such like. During the stunt shows some incredible inch-perfect timing was demonstrated. They had a guy standing in the middle of the arena talking to the audience, all of a sudden the whole front of the building behind him collapsed, the guy did not move a muscle but the impressive thing was that if he had been out by inches he would have had a headache. Near to the top of the building was a hole, just big enough for a person to fit through so the precision had to be spot on. This to me was clever bordering on stupid but he did survive to collect his large paycheck.

They had a mock fight scene in a saloon involving cowboys and Indians. People were being thrown through glass windows made of sugar and falling off balconies and rooftops onto a cushioned area. This was awesome to watch as you had the impression of a real fight. Chaos seemed to be the order of the day. Nobody paying much attention as to where and how they might fall. When they did fall they were still acting through the air and falling from high enough to break a bone or two. Professional stunt men would not do anything without the job being well organised and protecting themselves against injury. To the human eye it looks the opposite. There was so much to see in such a short time. I could have easily gone again to the show realising how good at their job and talented these guys and girls have to be.

Another attraction in L.A. are the beaches, especially Venice beach. We had heard about the beach being full of life and plenty to do. There was volleyball and various bands playing as well as women of your dreams getting a tan on every part of their body. So we set off early to spend the day there. We got on buses missing a few connections, asking all the time where Venice beach was, nobody seemed to know and told us to get bus number? After spending about five hours looking we still could not find it. We ended up lost, our final drop off point being just in front of some sand dunes. What we did not know was that on the other side was a beach, probably Venice Beach but there was nobody around and we could not hear any noise coming from that direction. So we made our way back to a bar to console ourselves. It turned out that where we had got dropped off there was a large bank of sand to our left and the beach was behind there. So to this very day I have never been on or seen Venice Beach. It was back to our Motel and a dip in the pool. Not quite the same but who cares. We found out later that Venice Beach is full of big strong puffed-up nancy boys who might not take no for an answer. Maybe we did ourselves a favour in the end.

At the snack bar of the motel we perched and clipped ourselves onto the bar as we had just got out of bed and were going to have a quiet afternoon eating and slowly drinking some cool cocktails chatting up the barmaid. As people came to the bar we would chat to them. One particular person was an American airline pilot flying for Delta Airlines. We got on well with each other and had a few drinks together, getting to know more about each other's life. He was very interested in submarines and we were fascinated by flying. He told us all about how to take off and land a plane, we were fascinated listening to every word he was saying. Like when a plane lands it can only be doing forty miles per hour, a fact I found mind blowing.

One evening he and a few friends invited us out into L.A. for a meal. He would arrange for a taxi to pick the three of us up, so no one had to drive, and take us to a very posh restaurant, which he had been to before. When we arrived at this restaurant it looked like something from a Hollywood film. Dark inside with lighted candles on tables but very glitzy and showbiz style, all the staff dressed in smart evening attire. The customers flashing money around as though they were playing monopoly, the ladies flashing jewellery around, mostly gold. So we sat around our table and had a tasty meal with all the trimmings and some expensive claret wine. Looking around the restaurant it was very classy, even the food was not bad but the presentation excellent. When the bill came I knew that it was not going to be cheap, we did not mind paying as we had money to burn but our host insisted he would pay for us all; we all thanked him for many days afterwards, as the bill must have been over £400 for six of us. I suppose he could put that down as expenses or claim it back somehow. Our time in America had been excellent and could not wait until our next visit. We were not looking ahead with any relish to the eleven-hour straight flight back to the UK via Greenland. America had been relaxing and a laugh, one place that stood out with us both was Florida.

We arrived at Tampa, Florida on a baking hot day looking forward to meeting some old acquaintances. We had made good friends with the residents whilst on the football exchange trip the previous year, so were kindly met at the airport by a friend who had invited us to stay for as long as we liked. On the news we had heard of an American space shuttle, *Discovery*, that was having difficulties being launched, it had been in the papers back home for months. They had been having tests to try and find out what the problem was ending up in exploding rockets but with no solution. Until this was overcome the launch could not take place. The actual space shuttle was on the launch pad waiting to take off, so we went to NASA to investigate.

We saw many models of rockets and a museum telling the history of the American space age. The spacecraft gets assembled in a large tall building before being wheeled out along a straight track onto the launch pad; the track goes all the way from the assembly building to the launch site itself. The base supporting the spacecraft must be sturdy, robust and large because it has to support the spacecraft during this manoeuvre. Once the craft is in position the final piece of the jigsaw is the lift-off, all systems and operations are taken over by mission control once the countdown starts.

If you want to see the launch you must be a safe distance away. The launch was timed for lift-off on the following day, but the launch was again cancelled as a further fault was found. If the shuttle had taken off lives could have been lost and the reputation of NASA dented even more. I loved to watch films about space and always had questions to ask, given the opportunity, wondered how, why, what and where. But when you talk about space you talk about infinity. NASA was good as it answered questions and put things into perspective. For example how far planets are away and how long it would take man to reach them.

After all that excitement we had to let off a bit of steam so we went to a theme park called Baseball and Broadwalk. This was about a fifty-minute drive from Tampa. In America most of the rides are big and fast, this park was no exception. My mate had a go on a few rides and came off looking decidedly unwell. He invited me to have a go but no chance. The thing that interested me the most was the baseball and the shows. I have never understood baseball but always thought that hitting the ball cannot be that hard as I played cricket back home, but it is a totally different way of hitting the ball. I had a go in the nets setting the speed not particularly fast but medium; I probably hit one out of twenty pitches from a machine. I could not believe how hard it was, the more you try to whack the ball the more frustrated you get and end up pulling a muscle. I then watched, as the professionals practised, making it look so easy, but they have been coached and play every day.

The shows were spectacular involving horses, rope tricks, dancing and singing routines from the 60s. The horses being very tame allowing the riders to have confidence in their own ability whilst performing their act. My favourite bit of the Wild West Show was when the rider was jumping in and out of the saddle with the horse galloping at a steady pace, not slow. All done by professionals who must have practised for many hours to put on such an entertaining show.

The 60's show we went to see was *Grease* and we were not disappointed, I only wish that I were that talented. Superb singers and dancers, costumes spot on and a high-energy performance. The only way to describe the entertainment would be to say that it links the thrills of a classic amusement park with the excitement of America's national pastime.

We were having a drink in one of the many watering holes when the barman poured us a drink in a really smart glass. We were so impressed we decided to keep it, putting it with the other twelve we had collected. We did not make it obvious, or so we thought, until walking out one smashed alerting the bar staff, we had to give the very decorative glasses back, all fifteen of them. A real shame because the glasses had some great colourful patterns on and would look impressive if the guests came round to our digs. Looking back on it now we were lucky not to be arrested and thrown off the complex or you could say nothing ventured nothing gained.

Having had an introduction to baseball I wanted to see a top-class game in action, so a girlfriend of mine took me to see the Cincinnati Reds play a league game. The atmosphere is electric, even if you don't quite understand the rules it is worth going for the experience. I was asking my girlfriend so many questions she was glad when the game was over. I almost had a baseball as well, if the players hit the ball into the crowd the crowd can keep it, the ball was hit and landed very close to me but not near enough to catch, I was waiting for another chance to collect a souvenir but it never came. An innings can be over quickly sometimes, hitting the ball seemed to me to be more luck than judgement as not many batsmen connected with the ball but the crowd cheered every shot anyway.

Softball is similar to baseball but the ball is slightly bigger and not as hard. During a barbecue we had a game and I was given one of those big gloves, I could not get on with them as I was so used to catching with both hands. Also I found that it was impossible to close your hand around the ball if you did catch it. All the Americans have a glove to practise with starting at an early age. Softball is a more social sport with many small leagues all over the country teaching kids the basics of baseball. Another good point about the sport is that it is not expensive to start and can involve all the family during a day out.

Next stop one of my favourites – Disney World, stupendous for adults and kids. I can remember as a kid seeing lots of Disney cartoons and films. Real classics made for family viewing. Have you noticed today how many films have violence and swearing in, far too many.

One of the attractions was sailing around the Mississippi on a paddle steamer listening to some jolly old foot-stomping music, or watching a game of poker in the saloon. The actors and actresses on board were in character with the period and would talk to you in a deep south American accent. The paddle steamer itself went around a lake very slowly giving you time to digest all the happenings around you.

How about going under the water with Captain Nemo on his very own submarine, not a real one as it has windows so you can see all the fish. The sub has a small crew of about three people, a driver, co pilot and one sailor. The sub is on a track following a path under the sea. You see mermaids, sunken wrecks and divers with funny shaped air tanks collecting shells.

Or you can just walk around meeting Goofy, Pluto, Donald Duck and all the others. There are so many of your heroes walking around – which one do you go to first? I had a smile on my face all day and loved to see the kids chasing after Mickey Mouse having their photographs taken with him.

There are also parades during the day and evening. These last for about half an hour and are very colourful with lots of floats going past. The evening parade is the best as all the floats and people are lit up with fairy lights, it is a bit like a carnival with a procession of characters and stars of your favourite cartoons. All of this accompanied by Disney music that you cannot help singing along to.

You could also get a train around the complex taking you to Goof's barbershop and other attractions such as roller coaster rides. The complex covers a vast amount of ground containing lots of different areas. We spent a whole day there and never got bored once. This was definitely the "wonderful world of Disney". After being hot and sweaty running around it was time for a water park.

We found Adventure Island. Water parks are not just water parks unless you are in America. Here they are all frightening, fast and exhilarating. I went on the Kamikaze and at the top had to be held by two lifeguards, as the drop was almost vertical. They said don't look down and keep your legs and arms crossed. I did this through sheer fear and seemed to reach the speed of sound. When I hit the bottom I was eating my trunks and checked myself over for any breaks. I enjoyed it that much I did it another four times.

Another one was the slide, I went down picking up speed as I went and could see myself flying over the edge so I had to sit up and slow myself down on one corner otherwise I was heading for a crash landing, there was no other way of saving myself as I was rocking from side to side, getting higher and higher up the walls of the half moon shape slide. All the rides were very similar in that you could reach incredible speeds.

Another ride where my life was in danger was in the tubes or tunnels. The tubes are shaped for maximum speed. One section has a couple of humps where the bottom section drops from beneath you. I actually hit the top of the tube whilst going over a hump and came out the other end like a hot vindaloo curry, fast. Again a wonderful experience and plenty rides to squeeze those cheeks. The weather was hot and sunny so by the end of the day we were tingling a bit, not paying much attention to avoiding sunburn.

Not too far away was Seaworld; this is definitely the number one in the world as far as aquariums and sea creatures go. We headed for the Shark Encounter first and before we went into the tank we had a short film of a weak and bleeding shark being eaten by his mates. This took about sixty seconds, and then we saw the real things.

In the crocodile pen I saw this massive and I mean massive croc. Its head alone must have been 6ft and was the biggest one there. It was not moving apart from opening one eye just to see who was around, no human beings. I have seen crocs before but this one was dwarfing all the others probably too fat to move. I would hate to pay his keep.

The seals performed a gangster version of *Romeo and Juliet* dressed in costume, wearing little waistcoats and trousers, playing their parts very well and had the audience in their flippers. The show starts off with a little Al Capone getting out of a black car holding a gun, if anyone moves they are dead. The seal walks across the stage calling over his buddies and so it goes on as they dive into the water keeping their distance from the cops.

Then to the dolphin show, the handlers and dolphins seemed to enjoy it as much as each other. The dolphins were flipping, twisting, catching fish, jumping over bars and all that carry on. They were even doing synchronised swimming. Shamu the Killer whale and family were next. This was the first time that a killer whale had been born in captivity and survived, so they were keen to show off their new addition. The best bit for me was when the diver made a circle with his arms and Shamu came up from beneath, managing to lift the diver up high into the air by appearing between his arms. The diver doing that for the first time must have been a bit brave or stupid to let a Killer Whale stick his nose in his face at speed. They were also surfing on the whale's back, cleaning his teeth and putting their heads in the whale's mouth. Not good job prospects. In a smaller pen was a small white whale that looked like Moby Dick but not doing any tricks apart from eating, this was apparently the only white whale in captivity. Other smaller creatures were a three-legged turtle; one had been lost before he was captured, conga eels, stingrays to name but a few. However the best attractions for me were the shows without a doubt.

Another park was the Epcot centre; this contained a real mixture of things. One of the main landmarks is a large golf ball with a roller coaster inside. Some of my friends had a go but not me, I have never been into those kind of fairground rides, apparently inside it is really dark so you don't know what is coming up, it could be your dinner. Far too dangerous and scary for me. There is a monorail to take you around the complex as it is vast. We went into a 3-D show; it was a weird experience as we were given glasses to wear for the full effect. In the film were Michael Jackson and a small fairy; it appeared as if the fairy was actually in the room flying around and not on the screen, at one stage she seemed to be within touching distance.

A good illusion was the trip down the Grand Canyon by helicopter. Nobody has ever followed the Grand Canyon to the very end by boat; many have died trying, as it is a challenge no one has achieved. By helicopter it is a lot easier and you don't get wet. You stand in a circular room with a large screen all around, the whole auditorium is a screen giving you a panoramic view of the whole canyon rock by rock. The film is then played and the sense of reality is brilliant as you end up ducking and diving, you don't want to crash.

A funny thing happened to me that day, as I was paying to get into an attraction the lady on the counter asked me if I was a film star, I had on a T-shirt with a picture of myself on the front and Universal Studios underneath. The lady mentioned some film and called her friend over. I just agreed as I had never heard of the film before. She asked me to sign an autograph for her and her son, so I did but signed my own name and who knows it might be famous one day. I did not have the heart to tell her that I was only a holidaymaker.

After all this excitement we needed a few days on the beach to recover so we had a lazy time and chilled out. Clearwater beach is one of the best as the sand and sea are like the brochures, we did some snorkelling and bird watching. We watched a couple of American guys throwing a Frisbee around and were very good, it must take a lot of practice as we tried some tricks but none of them came off. On the beach most of the people have a good physique and slim figures. I was getting a beer belly and my mate already had one so we did stand out a bit. We were waiting to be harpooned.

Once the batteries recharged it was off to a medieval fair in Sarasota. Some of the usual events that were present were jousting, sword fighting, juggling, minstrels (not chocolate), jesters and sword swallowing. The actors seemed to put their heart and soul into the events, as if they were living in those times. The jousting was terrifying as the riders were galloping full speed into each other with long poles and not holding back, so it seemed. The mock sword fights were not for the faint-hearted either, as the swords were real and heavy. The first aid station was busy on that day as every time we passed it an actor was being treated.

The tavern had an oldie worldie atmosphere with wenches serving the ale, dressed up in costume. Drinking was from wooden goblets and you ate with your fingers. Most of the food was things you could eat with your hands such as chicken pieces torn off the carcass.

The chess match was interesting; if the pieces came into conflict with each other a small fight would take place on a proper chessboard. Whoever won the duel would stay on the board giving a definite advantage to your side. If you have never played chess before let me explain. One of the pieces is called a Queen so a girl dressed as a Queen would be playing. Every character was in authentic costume down to the last detail. The orders to move were given by the king. It really did come across that you were in a medieval town where knights were knights and wenches were wenches.

One night we had a surprise, we were to be taken to a game called Pelota. I had not heard of this before so did not know what to expect. We got there and collected a programme. There was betting on various games played by a number of players and if your player won the game you collected your winnings, the same as in horse racing. We sat down and the court was similar to a squash court but much longer and wider and with four walls, the fourth one being transparent so the audience could watch the players fight it out. The ball itself is the most lethal of any sport, it's three quarters the size of a baseball, harder than a golf ball and has clocked speeds exceeding 150mph. The ball is made from hand-wound Brazilian rubber with two goatskin covers, and after about fifteen minutes of play the ball must be replaced because of the battering it takes during games.

When betting at the back of the programme it tells you of all the combinations that are possible and is very exciting to watch your player in action. The transparent side provides the best action as the players climb the toughened perspex to get the ball. When climbing to retrieve the ball the players reach some amazing heights. Sometimes the players to get more length on the ball will throw themselves to the ground causing the basket or cesta to gain more speed.

This is the only time I have ever seen this sport played and loved every minute of it. I could not stop talking about it for days and what a way to end my trip to Tampa. We had been there for quite a while and what I had seen would stick with me forever.

On one occasion I had a phone call from a friend to see what I was doing for the next two weeks as a work friend had dropped out of their original party to go on holiday. I said a simple yes and my place was booked. This was my fourth holiday that year; work was no problem as I was only part-time in a Leisure Centre. We were off to Ibiza and San Antonio, the party capital; it was going to be a lad's party. It started at the airport, while we were waiting for our plane we had to make some ground rules. In one of the bars we were making up a points scoring system, starting at 1–10 with bonus points on the way. For example a kiss being one point and going all the way having the full Monty 10 points. We must have been quite loud as when the final chart was complete a stranger from another table looked across at us and she just smiled. She knew the score as she was on the same flight as us. This was not good as our plans had been uncovered already. We had to find a way to limit the damage so we bought her a drink, only time would tell if this gesture was going to come up trumps.

The first couple of days we were settling in and relaxing by the pool doing our own thing until the rep got us to go on a pub games night. We had not been to the welcome meeting so we were not aware of this outing. We did this as it was a good chance to get some points on the board, we played games with string and balloons amongst other things as this was an 18–30's night out. You can imagine what the other games were. This was an evening for groundwork

On the way back on the coach one of our party was sick and a large black bag put in front of his face so he could not miss, he was sick more than once and did not score a single point. Getting of the coach he could hardly stand but doing a good impression of a break-dancer clinging onto the black bag. One of us took him back to the apartment while me and a mate carried on drinking and socializing. We did not stay out much longer but had our eyes set on a couple of girls, hoping to set up a rendezvous for a later date. When we arrived back we had scored no points and went straight to bed avoiding the ants around the bottom of his bed in our room.

In the morning what a sight for sore eyes, besides us all looking like a bag of spanners or Liz Taylor without any make-up on. The guy who had gone to bed early never recovered from that party. He was in such a bad way that for the rest of the holiday he only had two pints and that was it; his stomach's capability had been altered, churning inside like a washing machine not stopping to unload. I went into the lad's room to see if they fancied a cuppa, one of the guys still in bed the other lying on the edge of the bed not looking comfortable. I went around the bed to have a further look at the guy to see if he was still with the living. I came across a sheet in the corner of the room all crumpled up; in the middle were diced carrots and peas. By the side of the bed was the same with some on the pillow and sheets. Also he had a wet patch around the seat of his bottom making him our first casualty of the trip.

After that night if we went anywhere the sheer smell of alcohol and he would feel bad. Towards the end of the week he did try and have a pint but failed miserably as he had lost the will power to even sniff. Meanwhile we went to a large nightclub called Manumission, this was one of the biggest in the world containing four nightclubs in one. There was also a swimming pool in the middle of the club and podium dancers dotted around. Two of my mates left early and two of us stayed. The club was open until 9am so we decided to dance all night. There were so many people there the atmosphere just took us along. Bottles of water were expensive as they were handing out energy tablets (Es) to keep people going but we did not have any as we do eat sweets containing vast amounts of sugar which gave us high energy levels anyway. We lasted till 9am not a problem. When we arrived back the other lads had only been in the room for three hours as we had given them the wrong key so they slept on the sun beds by the pool.

We went out every night and one quiet night we had a few slammers with a difference, we had to wear a crash helmet and stand against a wall with a cork background, scary but true. We then knocked back the slammer keeping the contents in our mouth; our head was then bashed against the wall and swayed from side to side giving a washing machine on fast-spin effect, after that we could swallow the slammer which by now had soaked into our skin.

Part of being on a lad's holiday must be the wet T-shirt so we went to a club, which was full of water. The venue was basically a swimming pool covered over and a raised stage for the DJ in case he got his equipment wet. We certainly got wet along with everyone else. As we were dancing jets of water were shooting out filling the pool, keeping us cool. We had also met many people and always had drinking buddies, but the four of us got on so well we made our own fun much of the time. As the party went on and things started to slow down I noticed the colour of the water, very dirty and probably full of pond life coming up to the level of our waists. This was never a problem as sometimes when you have to go nature takes over. The water was starting to get a little warm around the edges.

The booze cruise was fun as we had jugs of vodka and orange to throw down our necks. This was again organised by the 18–30's rep. We also had a good swim in the sea diving for champagne, the deal being if you collected the bottle you could drink it, any time, any place and anywhere but had to be drunk before getting to the beach and the self-service buffet lunch and barbecue. In the sand pit we had some more entertaining moments. A few bands were playing during our meal with the lead singer of one looking like the lead singer from Status Quo; I had to have a second look just to be sure.

We entered the sand pit and games involving eggs and everyday sexual positions, especially 46 and 69. Two teams had to pass eggs by mouth along a line to the end, one team of lads and girlfriends split their egg with the contents going on the sand. One bloke picked it up from the sand with his mouth and carried on passing the egg in a liquid state, the crowd gave him a big round of applause as one person eventually took the egg off him to carry on the game. I was very glad that I did not enter this joviality as by now I would have passed on more than an egg – diced carrots spring to mind.

One of the reps had to go into the gung (horrible liquid) tank, the gung being full of nasty liquids and smelling of rotting food, you could tell that she was not enjoying this by the daggers look on her face and her choice of words. We enjoyed it as the person's character changed instantly.

On the last night we went with some others to a small fair with a bucking bronco enticing us to have a go. I did not have a go as I wanted to go home free of injury but some of the others were brave. No injuries so far until one of our party fell off and hit his ankle. At the time he did not say anything as he could still walk and no obvious marks, he had a few beers so was relaxed and enjoying himself not thinking of his foot. As the evening went on his ankle got gradually worse, we thought he was being a wimp so had no sympathy for him. We had gone out with some friends we had met during our stay so we were all in the party mood not paying much attention to detail. In the morning he could hardly walk, his foot was twice the size turning many different colours. We were going back that day so we again gave his constant whining no attention. In the airport at Ibiza we told him to act natural and show no pain as he might not fly back to Britain should he start whinging. On the plane he was in serious pain having to take his shoe and sock off. To cut a long story short at the airport we had to put him on a trolley and wheel him through customs with nothing to declare as by now he could not walk at all on his ankle. On the way back we did feel some sympathy was due and made him laugh his socks off!

Once in the car back in the UK heading home our journey was not over yet. We had to take him into the emergency unit at Reading hospital to drop him off, this was at 5am so no rest for the wicked. A tired nurse appeared and he was kept in overnight, it turned out he had a fracture of the anklebone. The cure for this is rest, keeping off the injured foot as much as possible. He had done the opposite. He was in pain after all, being mates we knew he was not comfortable so were trying to keep up his morale day and night. This was best done by a debriefing of the holiday and announcing the winner of our girlie chart. It was a four-way tie with no points each.

The first time I went to Corfu was with a friend from the Navy, we stayed for two weeks in Moratika, a small place near to Corfu town. This is going back to 1984 when the cars on the roads were minimal so hiring a scooter or motor-bike was safe. We hired scooters for the week and mine only had to be changed once whereas my mate's had to be changed nearly every day. On a couple of occasions we had to push the bike back to the shop.

We got on the bikes early ish in the morning and went to find a beach that was fairly quiet and not full of kids. We stayed there for the day and went back when our bodies were looking good. This was our routine for our duration in Corfu. It must have worked; we both came back with a very good tan. My mate pulled this bird with the biggest pair of melons I had seen for a while, especially when she went topless. When she turned over I got slapped in the face.

We were soaking up the sun when we saw some jet skis, by this time we were getting bored so we decided to have a go. Off we went into the distance doing figure of eights and playing about when we had a slight collision, not a great impact but a slight bump where our jet skis touched. When we got back in the Jet Ski people on the beach had noticed our collision and were trying to get us to pay for damages. We said no chance, as we could not see any damage and they could still be used. We went back to our friend and thought nothing of the incident, just carrying on as normal. A few days later we had a note through our door saying "you owe us money", but there was no way we were going to pay the money as we only had five days left.

Our apartment was at the bottom of a long road, which was the main street for nightlife. We had gone on a pub-crawl and made it to the end where a large nightclub was situated. We entered the club pretty well oiled and when it was time to go I went to the toilet and it was as if someone had shot me. I could only stagger and made it to the toilet eventually. In the toilet I was in trouble as being sick my eyes were flowing like a waterfall and my nose full of snot. I had to empty the pan a fair few times to stop it getting blocked. I must have been in there for some time as when I appeared again there were less people, or so it seemed in the club. Walking back to my seat was still unsteady. Coming out of the nightclub I just wanted to go to bed and made my way home but in the wrong direction. My mate had left after he was convinced I was sober enough to walk home. I only lived twenty minutes down the road but walked for an eternity or so it seemed, going the wrong way was not a bonus. I met on the way some stray dogs which made me turn round and go in the correct direction as there was quite a few of them and they seemed hungry and up to no good. This was very fortunate as I would have ended up walking off the end of the island. I arrived back at home in the early hours of the morning fairly sober. I had just completed a three-hour walk around the houses of Corfu, people run marathons in a quicker time. My excuse is not always walking in a straight line and finding many obstacles in the way trying to trip me up, obstacles like trees and dust. I hit the pillow and went straight to sleep probably snoring like a trooper.

Chapter 10

FRIENDS

My uncle and I went to Newbury Races and the Hennessey Gold Cup meeting, which is the top meeting on the calendar. I won a couple of races including the Hennessey and we had a good day. At the event was royalty in the shape of the Queen Mum, a figure you see but never expect to meet. We were just walking around minding our own business when my uncle noticed people gathering around us. By now a few policemen keeping the public away from whom we did not know, but it seemed like us. We carried on walking and plain-clothes policemen appeared but not bothering with the two of us. We thought this very strange until my uncle looked round and said to me the Queen Mum is behind us. I did not believe him so carried on walking paying no attention to this unlikely story. My uncle looked around a second time saying the same thing. I said "bollocks" in a very loud voice and turned around, the Queen Mum was literally about five steps behind us, I could not believe how close she was. I am not exaggerating when I say five steps either, and that is the honest truth. So we stepped out of the way to let her through and she gave me a look of "I am not amused" before carrying on her walk. I invited her around for tea to say sorry but she never replied!

Our dog Prince was amazing, he was a Heinz 57 variety but so soft and gentle he would lick you to death rather than bite. He used to jump up from a standing start as high as me and I am just over 6ft, not only did he do this once but time after time. Once he had something in his mouth he would not let go and you could lift him up into the air, swing him round and still he would not let go, his teeth and jaw were very strong. He was mainly jet black with comical markings. He had amazing tan coloured eyebrows that stood out on his face.

The insurance man came once and Mum and I were in the house alone. Mum invited the insurance man in to discuss a few points; he was not usually scared of dogs. The guy only came as far as just inside the front door as he could hear this barking and banging. The banging came from the dog running and jumping at the glass-panelled door. Looking at the door all you could see was this black mass of dog, looking like a round beach ball silhouetted against the glass. The insurance man was rooted to the spot with fear, telling my mum not to let the dog out. I suppose with all that noise anyone would be scared.

Prince used to have a habit of catching and playing with animals in the garden, one of his favourite being hedgehogs, which is unusual for a dog as hedgehogs have sharp uninviting spikes all over their body. Despite the pain he would manage to turn them over and kill them with his bare claws. He also ate bees and wasps, which pleased my mum, as she hated them. For a small dog he could eat for Ethiopia, twice. He was always hungry and liked everything. We always gave him the left-over chicken meat and his plate was overflowing thinking that he would make his meal last as there was so much of it. We put the bowl down and I timed him knowing that he would waste no time in eating some of the bowl. He ate the whole lot, licking the bowl clean; he had eaten the whole lot in 2 minutes 57 seconds, probably a world record. They do say that owners are like their dogs and this is true as I am a fast eater. Prince then went outside to have a rest after all that hard work, letting his food go down. The trouble was that his food came up a bit later. The bowl of chicken that he had demolished was produced unchewed and no different from what was in his bowl. I felt so sorry for him as he gave me those cute dog eyes and was shaking whilst being sick.

He was a very fit dog giving us hours of pleasure, when he was tired he would rubberneck especially in the front room by the fire. If he was lying down and just dropping off he used to try and stay awake as long as possible, his eyes would slowly shut and head droop. Once asleep if anything moved he would soon wake up, not missing a trick. The funniest thing is that my dad's favourite chair is by the fire and if Dad was in it he would get a shock. Prince always would lie down the same way with his bottom facing dad's chair. If he farted he would without fail wag his tail causing a waft of polluted air into my dad's face. My dad was always quick to smell the danger as the gas had a violent wrenching odour. He reacted by moving swiftly to another chair well away from Prince's bottom.

He also used to get so close to the fire that his fur was red hot and almost burning, if the sun was out he would sunbathe, which is a bit daft as his coat is black. When Dad was doing the fire he had some gloves to protect his hands, every so often one would go missing, as Prince would hide it in a rubbish tip at the top of the garden. When Mum was hanging out the washing he used to try and jump into the basket, as he hated to be cold. He would actually sunbathe in the hottest part of the garden but being black he never changed colour.

In the kitchen was a large electrical lead coming off a storage heater. One morning the heater was not working so Dad checked to see the problem. The problem was the lead had been chewed through and the dog had that cheeky look on his face. He was lucky to be alive as the voltage from the lead if on would have killed him. He would have been a barbecued dog. He had chosen to chew the wire when the timer on the heater was in the off position.

I went with some friends to a place called Western Park in Mallorca; this is a park containing Western themes and displays by various animals and birds. The best display in my mind has to be the diving display and the human fireball.

A guy sets himself alight and is actually on fire as he flies through the air diving into the pool below. Also a guy dives from a high board being 100ft in the air with stacks of danger involved, as the board is not very wide. Also you can sunbathe and go on a few water rides.

A man's best friend

Four of us had a picture taken in fancy dress, the two girls dressed as saloon wenches and myself and friend a cavalry officer and Red Indian. I had to put on warpaint for the effect over my body, which took ages to come off. By the time I had finished in the loo the sink was a rainbow colour.

Whilst I was working on the cruise ships sailing around the Canaries we went to the disco on board. We would do this most nights as we had nothing else to do but sleep. One of my friends had left her camera on the table, they had all gone off to get drinks and have a dance or something so I took a photograph of myself. At the time I thought nothing about it as we were always having a laugh together. One morning I went out of my room to start my duty and stuck to the door was a photocopied picture of a person in a photograph, because it was early and I was still half asleep I thought it was my room mate, so I get to the purser's desk and people kept on saying "good picture". Then I noticed a large coloured picture of me on the desk opposite. The penny then began to drop and for the next month I was the talk of the ship with my photograph being every-where, even the Captain commented on the good looking fellow in the picture.

My friend was the nurse on board and they always say that nurses love to have fun, I should have guessed really.

I have a few true friends who have helped me or been concerned when events have taken place in my life, not always for the best. If there has been a place for me going on holiday with them they have kept the opportunity open up until the last minute, or if I have been in a job where it has not been to my liking they have made a journey to see me or have kept in touch cheering me up. True friends will do things for you beyond the call of duty.

While I was moving house we borrowed a van to transport all the equipment back and forth to my new home. A friend helped me move and between us we spent a whole day moving all the items – fridges, cookers, settees for example. Heavy work but saved us money and time. My friend got the van free and he knew of someone who had brand new furnishings for a first-time buyer to start off their new home. I was buying the flat from my friend's girlfriend who had kept it in good condition so I could cut out the middleman making things much more straightforward and cheaper. I was able to collect from a friend's friend a settee, armchairs, cooker, microwave, cabinets. I could have had a fridge, brand new bed and other items but would have felt guilty taking any more. I could take what I wanted for £100 in total. So this was a fantastic start, all down to friends. I have not seen him for ages and would like to catch up with him again as we used to have the same hunger for sport and winning when working together in the leisure industry.

If I have ever wanted money a particular friend has always been willing to lend me the money and pay him back later. He trusts me and I trust him. I have never taken him up on this offer and never would, as I would never borrow money from anybody, in particular a friend, as it is the easiest way to lose one. I have been working overseas for the past four years and whenever I go away my friends always take me out the evening before I go away usually involving a curry. A particular friend and his wife usually arrange the details with the others leaving me just to turn up and have a good time socialising.

Having drinks with friends is always a good evening especially when you get a lock in (after hours drinking). I was with two other mates and a girlfriend who we knew socially and she had a reputation as a drinker. We were asked to stay behind for a couple of social drinks, which we did on a number of occasions. As the evening went on, more beer was drunk and stories told of days gone by. I had not noticed putting my hand on the girl's thigh and not taken it off as I carried on talking, it was very comfortable where it was. By this time we were all drunk and slowly losing the plot. The landlord finally threw us out and sent us home in the small hours. The following day I saw the girlfriend and she had woken up with a large handprint on her thigh, which would not go away. I later bumped into the lads and told them about the handprint, they were not surprised as I had my hand on her thigh for over an hour. I did not realise that amount of time had passed. The handprint was still visible four days later. I said it was the hand of god but did not score. We were quite safe staying until late, as the landlady was a magistrate.

Another time with the rugby club lads we had an all-night party, this was when my mate got well and truly drunk as he was drinking some real nasty mixtures. Because we went into the pub at night and left when the sun came up in the morning we had a special club called Dave's Daylight Club, Dave being the landlord. Part of the initiation was a kangaroo court. Let me explain, this is when a person has various charges against him, he can appoint a friend in his defence to try and persuade the court that he is not guilty. The court is made up of a judge, usually the landlord, VIPs, this could be one of the rugby captains, and a few carefully chosen men. Every so often the court would go into recess and drinks served at the bar. My mate had a total of fourteen charges for all his misbehaving. He was acquitted of four charges leaving him to drink ten concoctions of the court's choice, I felt sorry for him, as he did not have a strong defence. His defence being one person who was a bit of a turncoat, not trying very hard to put up a defence for the lad in the dock. He had drinks with egg in them, tomato juice with Tabasco source and other nasty liquids. After he left that morning he was not seen drinking alcohol for months afterwards as even the smell would send him to the nearest toilet. I fortunately never was given the privilege of joining such a well-known club, just being in the audience.

The friend who I went with to Corfu invited me down to stay at his place for a few days and nights before going on holiday. He lived alongside Lake Windermere in an old cottage with his parents. In the lake he had made his own diving platform involving a large rock. This was in the summer so we went to the lake and had a swim most days giving ourselves an early morning bath. The water was not too bad once moving around but quite a few mosquito-type flies hovering above the water. Night time was good as we had parties by the lake, sometimes going skinny-dipping. My mate had lived there for quite a while so he knew most of the youth in the village. We even had a bonfire going to keep away all the flying insects and dry us off after swimming naked, sometimes one of the lads would bring his guitar and we would have a campfire sing song.

Whilst I was working for Leisure Company we had our Christmas party in one of our hotels that we were involved with. We also stayed overnight and travelled back in the morning, I did not have too far to go as the hotel was in London and I lived in Newbury. The theme for the party was James Bond and we all dressed up for the occasion, some of the costumes were hand-made and others hired, as everyone was dressed up for the occasion. Most of the girls looked very sexy. After the meal we had a proper casino arranged. Fun, music and song was had by all but the best was to come. We found the keys to the leisure centre so we went in after the party had finished. In the centre was a large swimming pool, sauna, jacuzzi and steam room, this was really relaxing with everyone meeting up in the large jacuzzi. One of the lads had a great thought – let's get naked. He took off his pants holding them in the air, so a call of "pants off" to the rest of us was a worthy shout and we obliged without hesitation, also displaying our pants. This had almost shocked the girls for a split second but not for long as we were all gym instructors and it was nothing new to see fit bodies of all shapes and sizes. Some of the girls, half of them being topless anyway declined the offer to go completely naked. This was a slight disappointment as it was a good way to bond for future reference. The steam room was getting steamy and a good way to tone up as I caught a friend up to no good sweating like a bear in a sauna. The company were very successful in the leisure industry and staff parties were always a good way to relax and let your hair down, as everyone was out to have a good time.

Playing sport against friends is always good because we are all sports mad people and hate to lose. When working at a local leisure centre the boss and myself got on really well and were keen to make each other suffer if losing a game of sport. We used to play quite a bit of squash with me coming out on top more often than not. So coming off the court the staff used to say who won and I would say "me". My friend used to hate this as he would be reminded of the fact every day until he beat me. At the end of the day it was all a good bit of friendly banter.

Similar story with another friend who, I have to say, is a very good cricketer as he played cricket for England and could really not stand losing. Working together at a sports centre we decided to have a five-sport competition to see who was the best, once and for all. We had decided upon five sports where we had the same ability. The sports were penalties at five-a-side football, basketball throwing from the free throw line, badminton, and short tennis and if the score was still even snooker in the evening. I did not need this as I won the badminton to go 3–1 up and win the match. My friend for a whole year was after revenge, his girlfriend at the time often used to comment how grumpy he was, even now he is often reminded of the thrashing he took by me. On the other hand I hate losing and over the years have calmed down but still play to win.

My temper when playing golf as a junior was always volatile, on a knife-edge. I used to throw my clubs around and give myself a good talking to. One time I whacked my club so hard on the ground that the club head disappeared into the mud and it was a struggle to pull it out. I have also thrown clubs away, but never lost any, hit my golf bag hard with a club, but never broken any shafts. I have even walked back into the clubhouse after only completing some of the round I have been so disgusted with my play. I did this once after only playing two holes. If I had no chance of winning I also lose my rag, getting grumpy.

Without friends there is something missing in your life, the good thing about friends is that there is no commitment and no pressure to do things. Special friend are different as they are only a phone call away and do not mind coming to your assistance if needed. I am privileged to have friends like this and have needed them from time to time, which is reciprocated from me to them.

This is the end of some tales of a normal person's life who has enjoyed himself whenever the occasion has arisen. I do hope you have had a laugh reading this book and don't take life too seriously but work hard and play hard to get more out of your time in this world.